Her Spirit Moon

Kate O'Neill

Her Spirit Moon

Copyright © 2014 by Kate O'Neill

All rights reserved. No part of this book may be reproduced or transmitted in any form or by any means without written permission of the author.

ISBN 978-0-9853600-1-6

Library of Congress Control Number: 2014956650

This book is a work of fiction. Names, characters, places and incidents are products of the author's imagination and/or used as fiction. Any similarities to actual events or persons living or dead is coincidental.

Published by Thistlewood Publishing; DuBois, PA 15801

Visit our website at www.thistlewoodpublishing.com

First Edition 2014

Cover illustration by: Zeno Sanchez-Ramos

Cover graphic artist: Me'ven Zabat

Edited by: Linda Berardelli and Melissa Demarast

Chapter One

Abo

Abo trudged from the reek of steaming dung to clear his head in the winter air. An errant gust of wind caught a wave in the river dousing him in icy spray. He gasped and raised his chin.

On the opposite bank a girl rode a brown mare, her legs covered in hide. Two wayward horses gathered in front of her, the warmth from their bodies steaming in the dwindling light. Scanning the far side, she let out three whoops and directed her mount in a tight spin.

Abo's eyes followed her. He slipped his hand from his pocket and held an arm high. Across the waterway she laughed, took the reins in one hand and waved. Abo beamed and watched her guide the horses away.

Over dinner at the table of Dietrich Gottschalk, Abo laid down his fork, "Sir, what do you know of the people living north on the river's edge?"

"Hm, little. The people are the Potawatomi," the lean man studied his blond-haired boarder. "I've read the village chief's called Mettawa. They're all to be removed, sent farther west. It's there in the Weekly Democrat." Dietrich gestured to the mantel above the hearth, "They've reprinted terms of the Indian Removal Bill passed earlier, spring of 1830."

Abo stood and swept up the news pages, his blue eyes scanned the words as his brother smiled. "If it's about a woman, invite her to Sunday dinner. It's only suitable we meet her," Dietrich commented and looked to his wife.

Fair Abo had a square head and broad cheeks. He shied from the bellowing, flies and stench of the slaughterhouse, rambling the riverside where seagulls swooped for discarded bread crusts while his brother passed work breaks with the other men eating the apples, cheese and biscuits that Elke Gottschalk provided.

Working to accrue knowledge of the native community, Abo questioned the Lutheran Minister, Schoenhofen on Sunday after church service, "Minister, what knowledge've you of the people across the river?"

"The native ones? Best you speak with the Jesuit missionary. I've had no opportunity to minister to them." Abo sighed, nodded and gave a small bow.

Dietrich pulled him aside to share what another white-haired elder knew. The senior man gazed into Abo's eyes, "They're a people wedded to the earth, more so than us. The young often burn with hatred for the loss of lands; their women bare their dislike less openly. I've heard Chief Mettawa's a gracious host, offering a woman to warm the bed of a passing trapper, but that's an old tale from happier years. They may've all left the village by now." Abo's lips tightened and he dipped his head.

In the frigid winter of 1833, on days favoring travel and if Dietrich had no pressing chore, Abo ventured to the far side of the river after Sunday service. By his regular appearance, the ferryman and Jesuit missionary came to hail him. News of the girl or her community made his returning steps light.

The village lay a distance away. Travel by foot might take half the day and Abo worried the menfolk might object to his sudden arrival. He considered the girl might be married or bound to someone, but hope drove his desire.

As spring blossomed Abo grew dispirited and glum, embarrassed by the intensity of his devotion and the amount of time dedicated to pursuing the dark-haired girl.

In May, the U.S. Land Office opened an agency in the flat above Church's Market on Lake Street. Offered for sale were lands acquired through a treaty with the natives.

The brothers visited after work on a Saturday afternoon. The map posted to the wall bore the names of buyers who had purchased land plots. Surnames scrawled across the acreage sites. When at last Gerolf caught the eye of the office clerk he asked, "Are there no smaller allotments? Most parcels I see are six acres and more."

"A moment, please." The man wound past others who stood studying the document. "Yes, there's one. It's here." The assistant took a pencil and marked the location.

"How large is it?" Abo asked while the man defined the boundaries.

"It's a fine property. There's an old cabin made by John Bean for the Indian agent of earlier days. They say he laid the stone floor with cinder mortar. It's solid, sits in a meadow and already has a well. I believe it's slightly over two acres."

The brothers looked at each other and Abo inquired, "What's the cost?"

"They're asking $1.20 an acre and half that for the cabin."

Abo shook his pocket and faced his brother, "I've got Mexican silvers, how many do you have?"

Gerolf pulled out his the coins, grabbed his brother's arm and hustled to the line of men waiting for the sales clerk's attention.

Grandmother

In 1816, our chiefs allowed the white man's government to claim the land. Men in soldier's uniforms brought out quills and ink and every member at the gathering made their mark on the sheaf of papers.

The Treaty of St Louis, the white man called it. Those grounds stretched from the southernmost point of Lake Mishigami to the setting sun for an ample distance. Some years later, the man called Archibald Clybourne paid Mexican oros to the same authority for a land portion bordering the river.

The floodplain lowlands were swampy when the first long horned cattle waded into the mud and swam to the east bank of the Chegagou River. The herd pastured and dwindled by winter's middle, satisfying the appetites of soldiers and their families at Fort Dearborn.

On our side of the swamp river, horses ran loose and cows wandered and drank from the water. A day's walk north of Clybourne's slaughterhouse a hundred people from five families sang and hunted, fished, raised vegetables and cared for livestock. We built porches on our lodges and covered our buildings with birch bark. The village lay among the cover of trees along the banks of the Plain River.

Every year the clans tapped the sugar maples. Sipped from a bucket or simmered thick, the sap gave us a product for trade. Its nourishment sustained our people during the hardest days of the season, when the ground lay soft and receptive but plants had not yet budded. The flow followed a succession of warm sunny days and freezing nights, and lasted over a moon's length. The trees were a gift to mankind from the Great Spirit. That year the trees stood untapped.

By May's middle in 1834, the ground had thawed. With few seeds, we scanned the compost piles for spontaneous growth. A handful of us Bodéwadmi remained in the village. Too old and infirm to travel, the old man and I chose to breathe our last days on the grounds we had always known. Two wide-hipped, widowed sisters stayed to care for their aged blind father. With them, the dark-haired girl I called Redheart remained to care for me, her grandmother.

The tribe left us a basket of wild rice, dried cranberries, a sack of dried corn and strings of dried brown potatoes and apples. Horses had pulled the sleds they packed with belongings and the villagers had led the cows and goats away.

From time to time a tribal member called, bringing fresh meat, pemmican or dried fish. Without visitors and their gifts, the widows pounded corn kernels to crumbs, added water and combined the paste with wild onion. If we were lucky, Redheart found shaggy mane mushrooms that added flavor to our meals. We cleaned our teeth and brewed tea with sassafras twigs.

Redheart laid the snares carefully, the way her younger brothers had shown her, masking her scent by working her hands with earth and dragging the sinew through mud. Forest animals, thin from winter sleep and aching for a meal foraged to fill their empty bellies. If Redheart was blessed to catch an unwary squirrel or rabbit, the flesh was lean and tough.

The widows combed the once occupied homes, running their hands over the dusty surfaces. Their sense of touch confirmed what their eyes saw and what they could not believe: no food lay there. No amount of wishing produced what they longed for.

In our sleep we savored coffee, honey and chocolate given by the Indian agent. We ate potatoes, drank milk and smelled turkey fat dripping into the fire, but woke with gnawing bellies to sip tea in the chilly morning air.

A dream prompted Redheart to recall hiding a clutch of coins her father had given her. Mentioning the silvers to the sisters, they shrugged and tightened their blankets around their shoulders. She had buried the gift beneath the floor in the home where we had lived. Attacked by a band of drunken militiamen, they burned our house to cinders and rubble. Those who were able ran and hid in the trees.

Redheart set her traps and tried to recall the limits of the former dwelling. I knew the previous place well, and she urged me to remember it. My memory shifted continuously. She shook her head at me, chose a side and began digging. Finding a piece of clothing and a thimble gave her hope. The widows watched and agreed, "Her spirit's cracked and dried with no food for its nourishment."

I heard her gasp and bellow her discovery. From inside the cabin, I shouted praises. Clawing away the dirt, she pulled the pouch from the packed earth. The sisters drew closer. Redheart wiped her face with dirty hands, leaving streaks. She skipped, grinning and waving the sack, the coins jingling inside.

At my doorway, I saw taut smiles of hope spread over the widow's faces. That evening, we planned where she would go and what she would buy. We agreed on a cut of meat from the white man's slaughterhouse.

Abo

The dark-haired girl appeared in late May of 1834. Alone but for the wolf dog, she bought a large smoked ham and swung it over one shoulder. Abo saw her leaving by chance. A worker flung a door wide. He dropped the cleaver, held his breath and rushed out to the female figure.

Directing the dog away in her own language, Abo hailed her in his birth tongue, arms gesticulating in the air. She turned to look at him over one shoulder.

She wore buckskin breeches under a dark cloth dress that fell past her knees. A corset made of hide tethered her breasts and deerskin boots laced her ankles. Her eyes were deep gray. A thin strip of leather secured her brown hair.

Her gaze wandered to the group that stood with the brother, watching. Waiting, the wolf dog at one side, her eyebrows rose. Abo finished speaking and offered his hand. The canine growled and he swiftly withdrew. She spoke to the creature, and lowered the load to one hip. Leaving the animal, she advanced, extending her own hand.

Abo swallowed it with his large paw. A child? No. The wide mouth and cheekbones of her face held the freshness of youth. He glimpsed her exposed wrist, so slender.

She scanned his face, shoulders and hair. The sides of her mouth turned into a faint smile. He grinned, brought her hand to his lips, and kissed it. Behind him, the men crowded to see at the open door. The girl stood with wide eyes welling with tears, which flowed in sudden streams.

With a husky voice for so small a woman, she explained, "My family hungers. I must return with the pork." Overwhelmed that she had spoken, and in English, Abo's mind raced. She had a family then. His heart sank while embarrassment reddened his face.

Drawing her hand from his, she turned away.

Abo stepped forward. The animal growled, the fur at its shoulders standing on end, its eyes steady. He paused, recalling his weekly trips across the river, met her eyes and sharply bid the young woman, "Come back again, return to me."

She glanced back at him and smiled lightly. Abo raised his palm. The girl nodded and returned the greeting. The animal trotted after her, its tail up.

Abo returned to the building. The supervisor began shouting mild insults. When the men ignored him, he pushed them back indoors with threats of deducted wages. Abo moved alongside them. They shuffled in and resumed where they had left off.

Abo recollected her face and the size of her hand while he performed the daily butchering tasks. He still did not know her name. Why hadn't he asked? Her eyes swam in tears and his heart tightened for her, but what had moved her? He had kissed her. Remembering the smoky scent of her skin, he licked his lips, searching for some evidence left of her.

Grandmother

The widows shaved thin strips of ham for me and their father with few teeth. We savored the salty, smoked meat around the night fire, giving thanks to the pig who gave its flesh for our vacant bellies. Over the next several days, when the meat, fat and thick rind became memories, the sisters stewed the bone then cracked it open and we sucked out the marrow. When it was gone, the women tasted the fire's stones for any remnants left behind.

The apple trees around the village bloomed with small pink flowers and the scent wafted through the empty lodges. Seedlings grew taller in old gardens and we pulled the weeds from around them, coaxing them from the soil. Daily the younger ones ate cress, fungi and rose hips and as twilight covered the village, we rested and drifted to sleep, our heartbeats sounding in our bodies.

Despite the warming days, we grew thinner. The sisters who were once wide in the hips developed sunken cheeks and their dresses hung loosely from their shoulders. My girl Redheart no longer endured her monthly cycles. The widows passed more of the day lying beside their father, sipping tea sweetened with the maple water they managed to collect.

The old blind man died in the night. In the morning, the widows painted his torso with designs in red clay. They carried the body to the place of the dead, some distance from the village. The sisters whispered later they set the elder on a burial platform above the earth and sang the death songs. Returning, they ate raw mushrooms and dandelion greens from along the way. The girl stoked the fire to simmer a broth of pulverized acorns, partial corn kernels and wild onions.

Redheart offered me her food, but I felt the tug of the Great Spirit and wished only to hear her sing. When she finished my favorite song, we cleaned ourselves, darkness fell and we lay down. The wolf dog returned and settled by the door.

In the morning, my worn body lay still and cool. The sisters helped Redheart wash and dress the faded flesh. At the grounds of the dead, they repeated the songs. Redheart folded my other clothing, securing it in a bundle with a stained, beaded belt and laid it beneath the head. The women picked flowers and set them in the shallow of the sunken abdomen.

I watched her the next afternoon casting and retrieving a worn fishing net from the riverbank. Fish launched themselves into the air and splashed back into the depths. When her efforts were fruitless, she discarded her clothes and waded into the cold water, rubbing sand on her flesh until her teeth chattered, her lips turned blue and her skin shone pink and clean. She chewed the watercress and watched the shallows for prey. Lying naked in the sun, I saw her meager thighs and how her once round breasts spread flat against the wall of her chest. She sighed, allowing the warmth to soothe her, while the smell of grass drifted into her sleep.

Redheart woke to the clucks and purrs of turkeys. Opening her eyes, she glimpsed them threading through the high grass near the riverbank, close to her outstretched arm. She took several breaths and sprang on the closest bird, forcing its head around quickly, bracing the body on the ground between her knees. The creature squealed and kicked wildly. The others panicked, fleeing in all directions. Gradually, the bird grew silent in her grip. A sob choked her and she coughed, her tears running. She blew a prayer into her palms and raised them to the air, then dressed and headed back to the lodge.

The faces of the widows changed when they saw her. Redheart sat and yanked feathers from the carcass. The older woman assisted, discarding bits into the wind. Plumes in the low fire created smoke and a putrid stench, but they persisted until the pale body held only small pinfeathers. Torching the remaining bits Redheart gave the bird to the sister with the knife. She placed it on a low table and made an incision near the tail. Poking a finger into the flesh, she pulled out the innards and threw them on the fire, which hissed and smoked profusely. She drew out the lungs, kidneys, liver and heart dropping them in a bowl.

The bird's eyes stared up from the wooden table and she began to sing. Holding the heavy blade shoulder height, the sister brought it down through the bones of the neck in a swift clunk. The head flew. My girl retrieved it, rinsed it and tossed it gently in the fire, which threatened to go out under the wet remains.

Washing the hen, the sister dressed it with currant and chokeberry leaves from the border of the abandoned garden. With more logs for the fire, they added water to the iron crock, and set the vessel over the flames.

Evening approached as they watched the turkey sink deeper into the pot. The older sister served spoonfuls of wild rice with dried currants and rose hips. With something to occupy the emptiness inside, they spoke. My girl told them, "On the far side of the Chegagou River a young man with golden hair took my hand and asked me to return."

They nodded with solemn faces. The younger sister conceded, "You may belong with the pale ones. Your father's one of them."

Redheart swallowed her last kernel of rice, "Surely you should come with me. This man'll need those who cook, wash and cultivate a garden."

Neither widow met her eyes. The dog smelled the cooking food and loped through the trees. Inspecting the edges of the fire, he swallowed the organs the girl spilled into her palm, and settled along the backs of the stools, facing the darkness that began to enclose them.

Food provided energy to prepare for leaving. Redheart gathered soapwort that grew in patches under brush. Discarding the stems, she kept the rhizomes. The women washed their clothing and blankets in the river, working fabric against stone, rubbing soiled areas with sand and plant roots before spreading them flat on warm rocks to dry. Naked, they washed their bodies and hair, scrubbed their feet and cleaned beneath their nails.

Returning to the village with laundry smelling of fresh wind, they pondered leaving. Walking in the direction of the setting sun, by nightfall the widows would arrive at the settlement of a family that had once lived among the clan. The dog would provide security.

In the morning, they loaded the toboggan. No one hurried. Their irritation swelled when they noticed the garden's beans would ripen soon. They would leave the beans for others passing and scavenging animals. While the women hugged, their tears fell. They looked to their new directions and set a fresh pace.

Chapter Two

Redheart

The brown dress felt stiff from having dried flat in the sun. Walking alone without family or a home, Redheart wept for her grandmother, the widowed sisters and her animal companion. More resolute, she strode eastward to the Chegagou River.

The sun began to descend. The scent of the river preceded the water flow and she caught a whiff of the slaughterhouse. Taking the ferry to the east bank, the smell of feces, fear and rotting litter grew stronger. Approaching, the wind brought the sounds of bellowing animals and she wondered who could work in such a place. Redheart stood and rethought her options, waiting for courage or another opportunity to present itself. She might still meet up with the widows, though it would be hard. Leaning back against a cottonwood tree, she closed her eyes.

Abo

Abo saw her there, back to the tree, eyes shut with one knee bent up, her foot against the trunk, open palms steady on the rough bark behind her. Could it be her? He signaled to his brother to wait, while his mind flew to the stink his clothing emitted and as he trod closer, her eyelids lifted.

Smiling widely, Abo offered the girl his hand, "I've not yet learned your name." Still leaning against the cottonwood trunk, the girl extended her palm. She scanned the dung-covered breaches, his eyes and head. Pausing at the width of his shoulders, her lips loosened into a smile that gradually lit her face. Withdrawing, she turned away. Lightly touching her shoulder Abo asked, "What's your name?"

She turned back to him, "My grandmother called me Redheart . . . though my father named me under the full moon, in the way of our people, after his own mother, Corabell."

"Corabell." Abo said her name, feeling the way the word moved in his mouth. "Come with us to dinner," and he offered her an arm, but she shook her head no and pressed back against the tree.

Looking at him squarely she told him, "The elders in the village've passed on. The widows hope to join the clan. They took the wolf dog to pull the sled and're bound for lands west of the Great River. You once asked me to return and I have."

His pale eyebrows rose high. Abo took off his hat, ran a hand over his wet hair and took a step closer, smiling. "Have you a wife?" Corabell asked her eyes fixed on him. His gaze fell to his mire covered pant legs and he stepped back as the brother laid a hand on his shoulder.

Abo turned to Gerolf frowning, swallowed and faced the young woman, "No, I've no wife. Otherwise, I'd not have asked you to return." Looking down into her gray eyes and attentive face he saw the information pleased her. The tension in her form and features eased and he offered her an arm, "It'd please me if you'd stay with the family where my brother and I board." She nodded with a tight smile. Gerolf bowed grandly at his brother's side when introduced.

They walked down a beaten trail to the home of the Gottschalk family, drawing the eyes of other filth-covered workers. The men stared, unabashed.

"My brother and I've purchased an old cabin on a plot of acreage just north of here." Abo told her. You'll like the floor; it's made of stone and cinder mortar."

Dietrich greeted the visitor and ushered her into the home. "Abo's spoken of you often since he first gazed upon you. May I've your name?"

"Corabell Labue."

Corabell watched Abo step away from the back door, "Frau Gottschalk doesn't allow us in the house in such a foul state."

Naked at the well, Gerolf pumped water and prodded his brother, "Where're her people? Why's she come?"

Abo crouched under the water flow. Shutting his eyes and rinsing soap from his neck and armpits, he told his brother, "I asked her to come back. Her people've gone west to other lands." Excitement and cold well water animated his body; a smile broke over his face as his mind ran. While he washed his ankles and feet, he noticed his erection. Glancing around to the house, Abo directed his white buttocks in the direction of the windows and took over pumping from his snickering brother.

Elke

Frozen at the sight of the native in her doorway, Elke's gaze defrosted slowly while she scanned the young woman from head to toe. Gray eyes the shape of almonds; her face was wide. At Abo's side, she appeared child-size, though her carriage suggested mature femininity. A deep blue shawl draped over her shoulders. Elke stood with a hand pressed across her bosom, her eyes riveted to the guest.

Having been pounding pork cutlets for wiener schnitzel when the young people appeared at the door, Elke drew an extra seat to the table for Corabell, who volunteered, "May I help?" Dietrich gestured with a hand that the girl sit and she complied.

Elke pushed the basket of potatoes across the table, "I'd be grateful if you'd cut the eyes from these and then wash them. The basin's here." Elke waved to the side counter. Dietrich passed the window and spied the young men at the pump, nude and frothy with soap. He drew the curtain closed, plunging the interior into half-darkness and left the room.

At the table, the native girl sat and removed the outgrowths from the tubers. "Cut them into large chunks, please," Elke directed while opening the curtain to let in the last of the sunlight. She saw the brothers, their naked bodies a familiar sight for the time of day. With the young woman present, things would have to change.

Under Elke's guidance, she trimmed the red-veined leaves and scrubbed the burgundy roots, frowning when their liquid colored her palms. "Smaller chunks for those, we want them to cook with the potatoes," Elke told her. She dropped the hunks into the kettle as instructed. The water quickly turned the pale potatoes pink.

"What are those?" I've never seen such vegetables before."

"Last year's beets." Elke smiled, took the iron skillet and knelt by the fire positioning it on the grate above the embers. "From our home country." The bacon grease bubbled and sputtered. Elke lowered a flattened, crumb-coated piece of pork onto the sizzling surface.

"Your plants grow well in our soil." Corabell commented flatly, as she watched.

Elke stiffened and met her eyes. She wondered whether she saw disappointment there and responded, "Yes, they do." The smell wafted around the kitchen, mingling with the scent of sweet cake. Setting the cooked meat on the table, Elke motioned Corabell out the back door to wash for dinner.

Abo carried two buckets brimming with water. His heavy boots thumped on the creaking back porch. Gerolf followed with two more buckets for drinking, bathing and morning coffee.

Elke washed her hands and Abo poured a scant ladle of brown soap into Corabell's upturned palm. The girl felt the slick, rosemary-scented liquid and told him, "I've walked a long way. I'm covered with grass seeds and dirt from the journey."

Abo's eyebrows rose. "Shall I pump water at the well for you?"

"Thank you, but does this family use a privy?" Abo pointed to a wooden structure beyond the garden, the path to it strewn with straw.

Elke scanned herself in the mirror, secured a few gray hairs into her bun, then took the broom and swept the stairs. Returning from the outhouse, Corabell poured herself a bowl of water. She bent over the basin, rinsed her face and washed her hands with soap. Elke turned to the guest, "I must ask, where's your family?"

Corabell swallowed, "My mother lies in the place for the dead, up the river in the village where she lived with her husband."

Elke tightened her lips, nodded, and patted the girl's shoulder, beckoning her to follow. When she opened the small scorching door, a fiery current of air escaped from the oven set in back of the stone fireplace. Using a long paddle, Elke lifted a round tin from the hot, clay surface. She set three cakes one by one, on the windowsill slab of rock. Their aroma warmed the air and soon the men stood gazing at the sweetbread, thick with eggs and leavened with pearl ash and buttermilk.

After several minutes of silence at the table, Abo spoke of his plan to move into the old cabin on the lane. Gerolf watched his brother. Dietrich asked, "The cabin's been uninhabited for years, is there much work to be done? And when do you think you'll move?" He looked over his fork at the blond youth across the table, who shrugged while finishing a mouthful.

"It could use a good cleaning, surely. As yet Sir, there's still no plan."

Dietrich turned to the darker brother, "I presume you've no plan as well?" Gerolf met his eyes and nodded. "Well, you need to alert your parents in the homeland about the property you've acquired. I'm sure they'll be pleased." Dietrich drank before he raised a hand and waved it lightly, "But I can't allow the young woman to live in the cottage alone with you, if that's what you're planning. She'll remain here in the Gottschalk home, if she lacks for lodging." Dietrich turned to Corabell. "And you Miss Labue, what of your family?"

Corabell set her fork on the plate, "American soldiers assisted my kinfolk and Chief Mettawa in crossing the Des Plaines River when they moved to lands farther west. Most everyone went but two very old people. They'd asked to have their bones rest with the family in the sacred space for the dead. I stayed to care for my grandmother." Tears brimmed the girl's eyes and she paused. She swallowed, "Two widowed sisters remained in the village as well." Dietrich nodded.

In time, Dietrich directed his words to the older brother. "Abo, you must inform your parents about, well perhaps, your forthcoming marriage." The last word fell on the table. Dietrich paused and waited for some expression from the blond boarder. Gerolf looked over at his brother and then at the girl who concentrated on her dinner. Abo met the older man's eyes and the men looked to Corabell.

The abrupt break in dialog caused her to lift her gaze. Corabell glanced at Abo, the fork idle in hand. She scanned his shoulder's width and symmetrical features. Smiling, she said simply, "Yes." Abo beamed.

Dietrich continued with his concerns. "It's customary," he explained, "to ask the father of the bride for her hand in marriage. Where does your father live?"

Corabell set her fork and knife against the sides of the china plate, "Sir, I've not seen my father since I was small. A trapper and trader of furs, he gave me the name Corabell for his French mother, though his own name was Louis Labue."

Dietrich inquired, "Were you the only child of this French father?"

"Yes," she nodded and paused before continuing. "Well, my mother bore only one baby from her first husband. That was me. A kind deed, our village chief gave my mother to the French trapper Labue, to be his wife. She was very young, then. They traveled gathering pelts before Labue wished to return to his own lands beyond the sea. He left my mother with her people. By that time, she had borne a daughter, given the name Corabell. My mother wed again. She left the village to live with those of her new husband, farther up the river, leaving me under the care of her mother, my grandmother . . . who I cared for not long ago. But my mother bore more children, my brothers, who visited when hunting."

Dietrich sat silently. Corabell picked up her utensils and continued eating. Elke asked, "What's the procedure when one desires to wed, but is without parentage?"

Dietrich cleared his throat, "Hm. We'll have to consult the minister on Sunday." Corabell met the older man's eye and nodded her agreement.

After dinner, Corabell insisted on washing. She explained to Elke, "Washing's a task of the younger women in the home, and done out of respect for those with more years." The mature woman gazed at the girl, nodded and began putting away food.

Later Elke took a tooth stick, worked the end into a mass of frayed edges and gently rubbed it over her teeth. She stood in the doorway and picked the pins from her bun. Finished washing, the girl asked to bathe at the pump. She had walked a long way, and explained, "We sleep better, free from the dirt of the day."

Elke shook her head, "No. Women don't bathe in darkness. Bring a bucket and towel. I'll show you to your room."

Chapter Three

Corabell

Corabell woke as roosters crowed and the first hint of dawn turned the sky hues of pink. She walked barefoot to the pump with a towel, bucket and river shell filled with liquid soap.

No one in the house stirred. She tossed her dress and bodice onto a patch of grass and pumped. When the water rose at last, she filled the bucket and bolted under the cascade of water, wetting her head and face. Lathering her limbs and neck, she worked soap behind her ears before pouring to rinse. Pumping once more, she filled the bucket for the house, donned her frock and leather bodice, and headed to the hearth to start the fire.

Corabell found Elke's tinderbox on the mantel above the hearth. A few downward strikes of the steel edge against the flat flint sent sparks into the tinder, creating smoke. Blowing to make the tinder blaze orange, she held a char cloth to the embers, which flashed into flame. She held a candlewick to the blaze.

Ash from the previous night went into the bin. With bits of straw from the floor, pieces of kindling and sturdier branches, Corabell made an orderly pile. After applying the flame and blowing, a small fire glowed. Filling the kettle, she set it on the cooking grate and sought out her comb. Elke emerged as Corabell worked the comb through her wet hair.

"I'm off to milk the cow," Elke whispered. "When I return, I'll make coffee."

Corabell carried out the wash water from the previous night, set it on the porch and resumed combing. The younger brother wandered through to the porch where he threw water on his face, returned and fell into a chair. Shortly after, Elke poured milk into a saucepan to heat, retrieved the pot and bag of milled coffee, "Corabell, do you like coffee? I buy it pulverized from the market in town, such a convenience."

"Yes, thank you," Corabell combed the hair back from her brow, and secured the tress with a leather strap. Separating the tail in three sections, she began to braid. With eyes on her hair to avoid tangling the ends, Corabell asked, "Frau Gottschalk, what morning chores would you have me do?"

Elke smiled, cut the corn cake and served Gerolf a wedge. "The chickens can be let out and given fresh water and corn shards. I didn't check for eggs, I'd appreciate that."

"I'll feed them and look for eggs," Corabell reached the end of the braid and looked up. Gerolf watched from the table and Abo gazed at her from the doorway. Her cheeks flushed and she scanned the table for the lace she needed.

Elke pulled a blue ribbon from her sewing basket, wound it around the braid base and tied it in a bow. Corabell's eyes filled with tears she blinked away. As she vanished out the door, Elke called, "Wear the wooden shoes at the bottom!"

Corabell reappeared while Elke poured steaming water through the bag of milled coffee. The scent met the air and Corabell set the basket of eggs at the base of the hearth. Bacon slices sizzled on the iron skillet. Elke asked the blond brother, "Ready to shave? The water's hot."

Dietrich entered the kitchen fully dressed. Elke poured him the first cup of coffee adding scalding milk. His wiry hair stood away from his scalp. He sat bent forward at the table, leaning on long slender forearms, his boots emanating an odor of damp leather.

Elke broke eggs into the sizzling bacon grease, depositing the shells beside her. Her cheeks grew pink from the heat. She spooned eggs onto the platter aside the bacon and dunked the hot pan directly into the washbasin where it hissed. The water from last night's washbasin, the bucket from Corabell's room and Abo's shaving bowl contributed several inches of murky water to the bottom.

Dietrich growled at the table, "Mein Frau, there're no oats this morgen. Would you have your man sit all day in the stinking outhouse?"

Elke turned and disappeared, resurfacing with a large vessel tilted upon the curve of her hip. "Would anyone else like plums?" The brothers declined but Corabell nodded and passed a bowl. From platters on the table, they served themselves, passing items when requested. Elke poured mugs of coffee.

Her brothers had brought home the last coffee Corabell drank, though they also carried chocolate and spirits. The young men got so drunk it took days of nursing to make them right again. Chief Mettawa declared liquor poisonous after that, allowing only the elders to dispense the poisonous fluid though it did not stop the men from trading for it on their own.

Corabell rose and hurried out onto the straw strewn path. As she neared it, the outhouse odor met the surrounding air. She noted how all pit toilets smelled the same.

Gerolf stood shaving on the porch when Corabell returned and left the wooden shoes below the bottom step. Her coffee had cooled and Abo had finished eating. He sat with a mug in hand and asked Elke, "Frau Gottschalk what're the day's duties?

"Wash the dishes, sweep the floors, work the garden, prepare dinner and consider a wedding dress." Elke smiled and her eyes looked to Corabell.

Elke hesitated, a hand found her chest and she sought Corabell's face, asking, "What do you think of wearing an American dress? Would that suit you? Perhaps there's something else you'd prefer?"

Corabell dipped her head, "I've only the frock I wear, and my buckskin breeches, nothing more. I'd be grateful if I might borrow something, or perhaps I could sew something myself."

Elke gave her a nod and told Abo, "Your bride'll need a pair of shoes, though boots might be more practical. Unless you think she ought to marry in her Indian garb." Behind the chair, Gerolf stood and tapped Abo on the shoulder.

"Bruder. Come, the day's light. We must leave."

Abo stood. Corabell's eyes followed him, her face tight, eyes large. He settled a hand on her shoulder, then bent and kissed her cheek. She brought her head against his, feeling the smooth shaved cheek on her exposed flesh. Abo withdrew, turning away from Dietrich.

Corabell saw the senior man's stubble-covered face clench. He loudly bade the blond brother, "NO. Wait. Sit! Sit at the table next to the girl." He rose and stood too closely in front of them as Gerolf waited, watching at the back door threshold. Dietrich exhaled loudly. "You must wait three weeks after the bans are announced in church, before you may marry. Until then, there'll be no bundling, no canoodling or other blatant displays under my roof."

He paused, his eyes on Corabell. "Neither will I play the role of constable. These're the rules, and if you don't abide them, you may board elsewhere." Corabell's head drooped. Dietrich waved his arm at Abo, "You may leave."

The blond one clumped wordlessly across the wooden floor and out the back door, and the younger brother followed. Corabell remained sitting. Dietrich glanced at the departing men before he spoke. "I must tell you, I've been entrusted to care for the Bachmeier brothers by the minister and parish. Their journey took months of labor and sacrifice. I won't allow anyone to lead them astray. So before there's another word about marriage, I need to know some important facts." Dietrich spat out questions quickly. "How old're you? Have you ever married? Are you a maiden, or have you lain with a man? What do you want with Abo Bachmeier?"

Slowly lifting her head to him, Corabell answered steadily, "I'm seventeen years old, have only lain with my young brothers while trying to get them to sleep . . . I've never had a husband, though my mother wanted me to marry a man of the neighboring clan . . . But my village and the others on the river left. I could join them or seek Abo, who'd asked me to return to him."

Dietrich stood silently before asking again, "Hm, but why Abo?"

Corabell met his face in silence and glanced at Elke, who stood motionless in the doorway. Shrugging she answered, "He asked for me. I thought much about him, especially the width of his shoulders and golden hair." Her gray eyes fell to the hands loose in her lap, "I chose to find him rather than take the road to my clan, with the widows." Dietrich began to pace in front of her.

Elke entered and picked dishes up from the table, "Would you like to shave now?" Dietrich nodded, dismissing Corabell with a tip of the head and a curt rumble in the throat.

Elke

Before her spouse strode to work, he summoned her, "Mein Frau, see if you can find something for the girl to wear on Sunday, perhaps an old dress from one of our girls. With the hair pulled up and something less plain, she may look less like the Indian." He took her face, kissed her forehead and left.

The girl stepped into the lane of beans. The bushes lay near the soil and Corabell picked the largest weeds as she went, turning the roots skyward to dry in the sun. Directing her down the row, Elke called out, "Cut the thickest asparagus from the plants at the end!" In May, Elke planted vegetables at weekly intervals to provide a continual supply of ripening produce.

Later, they sat on the porch with their legs dangling and drank water. Corabell commented, "I saw the herbs. My grandmother had certain ones she used for good health . . . Can't remember a single name . . . but I can water the seedlings if you like."

Elke rose, "Please. Let me find the watering can." She wandered into the house, her voice trailing, ". . . the pitcher's so heavy when it's full."

Corabell watered, repeatedly filling the cumbersome can, sprinkling the ridges of new growth. At Elke's request, she washed the young mustard greens and returned to the house carrying a fresh water pail and vegetable basket.

Elke appeared her arm laden with fabric. Noting the bundle, Corabell wiped her hands. Elke explained, "It's been many years since my girls wore these. I saved them for the material, thinking they'd have some use. I've three grown daughters and several grandchildren who'll soon be women, as well." She smoothed the top garment. "Maybe you can find something here that suits you. With some alterations we may have a wedding dress." Elke thrust the mound into Corabell's arms. "Go now. Come back wearing something different."

Corabell's eyes met the floor, "I'm afraid I own nothing like the undergarment you wear."

With one hand pressed to her bosom Elke countered, "That may be, though the bodice you wear above your dress is a corset, of sorts."

Corabell

With the heap of material in her arms, she stepped into the small dark bedroom and lowered her nose to take in the smell of the fabric. Detecting no hint of the prior wearer, Corabell shifted through the garments while dried rose petals hit the floor. She left the door open for the light it provided.

Underneath the top dress lay a dark finely woven linen apron, and two pale cotton shifts. Corabell pulled off her clothes and slid into the dress she liked best, blue cotton with narrow brown vertical stripes. With the frock buttoned, the shoulders nearly fit, the bosom bloused a bit, the waist fell loosely around her and the fabric pooled at her feet. She sighed, hiked the length up and went to show Elke.

Elke tilted her head, and then swiftly set to tugging the waist, shoulders and folding up the excess material from the floor. "If we cut several inches from the length, and add some stitching here, I think you could wear it. You might try your corset on top. It'd secure the extra material at the middle, though it may cause the bosom to pucker. Alright, try another." She waved Corabell away.

A different person had worn the next dress. The shoulders fit, as did the bust. The waist hung loosely and the hem needed pinning up. Deep terracotta, the fabric bore a small flower pattern in a deeper hue. Elke smiled, "My youngest daughter wore that when she was twelve or thirteen." The fact caused Corabell to scowl.

Corabell tried on the last dress and told herself firmly this was a fortunate event. The plum colored garment with large hyacinth flowers resembled a costume. Pale purple contrasted with her caramel skin and deep brown hair, and her gray eyes shone. Elke reckoned it was a bit too large and a tad too long, but some alterations would amend both. Corabell confided, "My body used to be more ample. The days in the village made us thin. Even my grandmother was lighter when we wrapped her in the end." Elke gave her a nod but no words.

The women heard boots on the porch. Abo and Gerolf filled the doorway with scrubbed faces and bloodied clothes. Abo, standing mute on the threshold spied Corabell in purple hyacinths. His eyes moved slowly over her. Gerolf grinned and pounded his brother's shoulder. Dietrich followed the two. Entering his home he dismissed the butchers, demanding, "Go! Go out. Clean yourselves at once." He smiled at the female boarder and spoke with his wife in German. Corabell gathered the dress up and went to change into her customary brown linen frock.

Gerolf and Abo brought sausage home in a wooden box. With no available bread, Elke asked Corabell to dig up several wintering potatoes, and handed her a basket. She set out the back door. Hearing the pump in the distance, Corabell glanced up and saw the two naked men working themselves paler with soap lather. Corabell paused absorbing the sight of white buttocks and thighs, and chests with hair that grew in lower regions as well. She turned quickly and sank down close to the old plants, their leaves brown and dry.

Shaking the stalks to loosen the soil, she ran her hands through the earth, searching for round forms. Finding a potato, she inspected it for worms and rot. Not daring to move further or attract attention, she stayed and felt for potatoes, knees in the straw. When the rush of water quit, Corabell swatted the dirt from her dress, returning to the house with the basket on her hip. Elke's gaze lingered over Corabell, who nodded and slapped several straws from her skirt. The kettle on the fire began to boil. Elke asked Corabell to chop the vegetables into manageable chunks and left to milk the cow.

Dietrich and Gerolf lingered about the kitchen, eyeing the browning sausage in the skillet. Elke clumped up the stairs, found Gerolf idle and handed him plates.

He set them at the table, arranging forks by their sides. She brought the salad and snap beans to the table. When her back turned, Gerolf stuck his fork in the bowl, bringing a mouthful to his lips. Dietrich shot the younger brother a disapproving glare as the young man settled into a rickety chair, cleared his throat and began a German evening hymn.

Gerolf sang with vigor, and complete lack of self-consciousness, substituting words he had forgotten, tapping his boot on the floorboards and fork on the water pitcher. Corabell sat at the hearth, alternately pouring milk into the potatoes and smashing them. She shifted the kettle back into the fireplace to warm thoroughly. The heat at her face made her cheeks flush and her brow sweaty.

The second time Gerolf began the hymn Elke joined him, her soprano notes mingling with the deeper voice. Dietrich descended into the cellar, returning with an earthenware drum. He filled Gerolf's cup and sat at the head of the table, nodding in time to the song. When Gerolf finished the last verse, Dietrich raised the pewter pint in a toast.

The mashed potatoes formed white peaks as they puffed up from the bottom of the pot, threatening to burn. Corabell swung the container away from the direct heat. Scents of potatoes and sausage mingled, forming dinner smells that escaped through the open windows.

Dinner sat cooling on the table and they waited for Abo. Dietrich fumbled with the empty stein while Elke sampled Gerolf's cider. Boots on the porch planks made their eyes shift to the open doorway. Abo stood holding flowers, his face light. He offered the blooms to Corabell. She closed her eyes and lowered her nose to the pink blossoms of bee balm and white glade mallow.

Dietrich sighed heavily and drummed the stein on the table surface, "Where've you been? We've waited for you and hunger dearly. Be seated and I'll say grace."

Gerolf poured his brother hard cider and they bowed their heads in German prayer. Corabell followed the gesture, with no appreciation of Dietrich's foreign words.

As the group passed dishes, Gerolf offered Corabell cider, handing her his cup when she raised her shoulders in a shrug. Tasting the apple's sweetness, she drank her water, and gave Gerolf the empty vessel, thanking him. With food on their plates, the five ate with little conversation.

Elke

On Saturday afternoon, Elke set the pots and kettle to boil for the weekly bath. In the summer, the slaughterhouse butchers bathed daily at the pump. Corabell made a habit of bathing before the household woke, lighting the fire and putting the kettle on for coffee.

Dietrich announced to the boarders, "We'll need a privacy barrier to conceal the pump. Mother's been yearning for a trellis to grow string beans. Why not erect a framework using tree branches bound with rope? As the legumes grow, they'll cover the dry branches with green vines." Abo met his eyes and gave a nod in reply.

Corabell wore the purple hyacinth dress to church, her leather bodice on top. Elke arranged her two long braids in a wide bun that spread from ear to ear, low on the back of her head. The dress was long and covered her feet and Dietrich made no comment when Corabell wore her native boots.

Corabell

Gazing at herself in the porch mirror, Corabell noted her fancy hairstyle and made a final trip to the outhouse before waiting on the steps of the front porch. Abo joined her wearing a gray coat, dark trousers and a white linen shirt with a gray scarf at the neck.

Abo stood several stairs beneath her on the trodden grass with his straw hat in hand and appeared her height. She ventured to the edge of the porch and he suggested, "We should go into town and purchase a pair of boots for you."

Lifting her dress hem, Corabell displayed her footwear. A thick line of blue beads ran along the edge of her foot. "These were made for me by a man of my village."

Dietrich appeared with a dark felt hat in hand. He caught sight of Corabell's uncovered head and scowled addressing his wife, "Mein Frau, the girl's not yet dressed. Der hut!" With both hands he beckoned to his head, and secured his own broad brimmed, round crowned hat. Elke emerged moments later, clad in a navy dress that appeared more functional than glamorous. She wore a russet colored bonnet; silk flowers of the same shade lined the upturned brim. In her hand, she carried a modest straw hat. Lined in dark silk with a wide black ribbon around the crown, she placed it carefully on the girl's head.

Corabell made no comment when Elke fastened the ribbon securely under her jaw. The woman of the house took the arm of her spouse while Corabell fell in between the arms of the brothers. They set off on the trodden path to church.

Constructed with long timbers, the church had a tall pitched roof and a large fireplace along the left side. The walls inside were finished with plaster and white wash, the floor wooden. A white cross against a blue background filled the round stained-glass window in the space above the heavy front doors. The east and west walls held three high rectangular windows with clear glass. The altar stood plain and wooden. Behind it, a large cross hung from the northern wall. Rows of unadorned pews lined both sides. Between them, an open aisle allowed access to the altar.

The windows tilted open to catch any breeze. Dietrich led the way to the pew, to the left of the main aisle. The organist to the right of the altar began to play. Gerolf handed a songbook to his brother. Flipping to the page, Abo nudged Corabell gently, and whispered, "Corabell? "Do you read the English language?" Her gray eyes met his and she managed the smallest head shake of negation.

Corabell watched a woman in a black dress and hat with a sizeable veil approach the pew where Gerolf sprawled across the empty space. She moved in smiling, young girls trailing behind. Nodding to Dietrich and Elke, she held the hand of her smallest daughter who pressed her lips together tightly, the edges of her mouth turning down at the corners.

The organist began the hymn in earnest, hitting the keys with dramatic gestures and the congregation stood to sing. Corabell looked up at Abo, who pointed to the German words within the musical bars. She made a gesture with an open hand, shaking her head. He replied with a tip of his head and sang.

The minister chanted the German service and the congregation responded in like tones. Sitting close to Abo, Corabell felt his chest reverberate with the response notes. The chant lulled her. She dared to shut her eyes, lowering her chin so the brim of her hat obscured her vision.

Abo shifted and elbowed Corabell gently. She woke and pulled herself straight. The youngest children in the pew in front had seemingly turned to stone and sat propped up against one another. From the Jesuits Mettawa had allowed to abide in the village, Corabell learned the body and blood of the Savior Jesus Christ were symbolized in the wafer and wine. With the younger children, she watched from the safety of the pew.

People filed out through the open doors, while the minister shook hands and wished everyone a blessed day. When Dietrich got the opportunity to speak, he pressed Corabell and Abo forward, gesturing while he spoke in difficult foreign sounds. Corabell watched the community fall quiet, listening to Dietrich's German words.

The women of the parish scrutinized her, lingering on the shape of her eyes and tone of her skin. They noted her dress and bonnet and the unfamiliar leather bodice. Abo saw the swell of attention, covertly found her hand and clutched it. Several women spotted the gesture and feigned outrage while Dietrich continued to elaborate.

With a final flourish of an arm, he ended his words. The pastor pulled Corabell closer, gazed into her face and raised a palm for her hand. He reached for Abo, taking his hand as well. Lifting their hands to the silent congregation, the minister announced, "I announce to you this day, Abo Bachmeier and Miss Corabell Labue intend to marry. The second ban shall appear in next week's announcements, prior to service." Lowering his arms, he set his palms on their heads, blessing them in the foreign tongue.

Chapter Four

Abo

On Sundays, the Gottschalk family gathered for dinner after church service. Abo took Corabell's hand and the two walked in silence before he inquired again, "Corabell, you've not learned to read and write in English?"

She dropped his hand and looked up at him. "I don't need the white man's ways. I've my own... My mother spoke this English, and my grandmother as well, but we also spoke our native tongue."

They walked for some time in silence before Abo told her, "Reading and writing, Corabell. I wish to teach you the English way." He retook her hand and she gazed up at him with little expression as he continued, "We'll need to sign a document when we're wed. If you've no knowledge of writing, then you'll make an X, like the chiefs of your people, but if you allow me to teach you, you'll inscribe the letters of your name with pen and ink." He waited. Corabell tilted her head, smiled and nodded.

"In my village when two are wed, the man enters the woman's lodge. Shedding his old clothes, he stands naked before her and the woman dresses him in garments made by her own hand. Then the woman visits the home of the man and receives new clothing from his family, and they are sealed." Abo smiled at Corabell speaking softly of nudity.

Dietrich withheld comment when Abo held Corabell's hand, and walked the distance home meandering behind the more composed members of the household. Gerolf accompanied Elke and Dietrich as they discussed the welfare of Widow Eva and her three girls.

Corabell

Elke Gottschalk insisted her grandchildren read to her while they prepared dinner. Nola, the eldest of Widow Eva's girls, read from the Democrat. The dark haired girl perched on the top step of the back porch while Elke sat below pulling feathers from a chicken that would become dinner.

Projecting her voice as Elke required, so she could hear and continue her tasks, the girl recounted, "In May of 1834, eighteen land deals were concluded."

Elke, squinting with the sun in her face, looked up at the girl, who continued to read and asked, "Nola? How many?"

"Eighteen." Elke stood, the chicken in hand and set her other hand on her hip, as her granddaughter continued, "the figure for June 1834: twenty-three lots were purchased."

"Who's buying all the land?" Elke wondered and sat back down, adjusting herself so the sunlight no longer blinded her and she could see Nola's face.

The girl carried on. "The square mile bounded by Madison, State, Roosevelt and Halsted Streets sold October 4, 1833 at an average cost of $60 per acre, a substantial increase from 1830, when an acre of land sold for an average of $1.25. Oma, do you really want to hear the business section?" The girl looked over her shoulder at her grandmother.

Elke responded, "I surely do, please continue. Corabell dear, this's Freda my middle daughter." Freda gave Corabell a wide smile with a dip of her head. She brought over a basket of green beans and began snapping the ends off. The women sat surrounded in various colored feathers as the tortoise-shell cat stalked a suspicious twirling piece of white down.

Corabell stood in the threshold of the back door watching Nola as she spoke the printed words on the paper, revealing the sums paid for sections of earth. She swallowed her fear that soon the white man would claim, section and sell away her village. Why else would soldiers have escorted her community to other lands? She shuddered and headed to the outhouse, touching Nola on the shoulder lightly, "Are you skilled at writing as well?" The girl nodded, her finger holding her place.

On returning, Eva's youngest daughter Romy ran to Corabell and fell in with her stride. She gazed up at Corabell squinting, "Miss Corabell? Mama says we need an adult in charge." The girl grasped her swinging hand and continued on to the porch steps before she asked, "Can you come make biscuits with us?" Corabell nodded. Uta stood by the countertop where she had gathered flour, salt and lard. The younger sister called out to her as they passed Nola on the steps, "Uta! Corabell's going to help, we can start."

"Mama always thinks we'll make a mess, but we make better biscuits than she does." Uta confided softly when they were within hearing distance. Pale aprons covered Sunday dresses, and their bonnets hung from the front door pegs.

Abo returned from the pump with two buckets of water, set them on the porch and threw a towel over them. Gerolf followed his brother speaking in

German. Striding in, Abo stood in front of the girls, "Corabell, Gerolf and I're going to assess the cabin's well. If it fails to function, we'll have to deepen it. It's been ages since it was built, before 1804 I think. Neither of us has seen it. We'll go now, Dietrich has no objection." Abo scanned for the elder's presence and brought a hand to her waist. He bent and set his cheek against hers and lingered there with his eyes shut.

Uta and Romy stood watching at the tableside. Corabell's eyes riveted to the doorway and she stepped away, a tight smile on her face.

"We'll return soon. If the well's bad, it'll delay our move." Noticing the two staring young girls, Abo bowed quickly, and tipped his hat, "Girls."

Corabell struggled with wearing the white woman's dress. The bountiful skirts tipped the chairs at the table and the color continued to alarm her. Her belly tightened when she thought of the impending requirement to read and write the English language and she chided herself for holding her tongue and not speaking on behalf of the displaced clans when the young girl read off land sales.

Soon scents of chicken and biscuits filled the interior and heat from the hearth permeated the space. Dinner lay prepared on the table and Abo and Gerolf had not yet returned. When Elke suggested they dine outside to take in the breeze, Corabell helped Eva carry the table onto the porch, and the young girls assembled the seats again.

"Emily and Henry are here!" Romy shouted. A young blond woman arrived carrying a casserole of finely sliced onions and potatoes baked in heavy cream. She entered the house swiftly, sought Corabell out and offered her hand at once while introducing herself, "Hello! You must be Corabell. Abo's spoken of you and your village for some time. I'm so pleased you're finally here with us." Corabell took her hand and smiled faintly. "Sorry, I'm Emily, the youngest of the Gottschalks. My spouse's Henry O'Shay; he's seeing to the carriage."

Her taller, darker headed sister smiled as she approached carrying a bowl of trimmed green beans on one hip. She gave Corabell a small head shake as her younger sister continued talking, "This's Freda, she's the middle daughter. I don't know whether you noticed Willa, she's the eldest sister with four little ones."

Corabell followed the sisters outdoors where Dietrich dallied with a knife in hand, ready to cut the large roasting hen. He paused, set the knife on the table and gestured to the group, "Come, let's say grace before I cut the meat." He bowed his head, paused and spoke briefly in German.

Abo and Gerolf appeared and took seats at the table. The older man turned to Abo and inquired, "What's the news of the well?"

"It's filling. The water lacks any odor. But the cabin roof needs repair. There's an area where water's seeped through. It needs a thorough cleaning, to rid the space of spiders, leaves and animal debris. We could do the work, perhaps, in the night of the next full moon. Surely, there'll be enough light."

"Hm," Dietrich muttered, wiped the remnants of sauce from his plate and looked up, "I know Abo plans to marry the girl and live in the old cabin, but you son, have you any plans of your own?" His gaze settled on Gerolf who served himself another spoonful of potatoes.

Abo filled the silence with an assurance, "You're welcome to live in the cabin with me and Corabell."

Gerolf's eyes wandered across the table and fell on the dark-haired widow, before he answered, "Sir, I've no plan ready to reveal, though I'd happily give up the slaughterhouse. The butcher's pay's good, but the work wears a man. If I could choose again, I'd pick the carpenter's craft."

Dietrich shook his head. Henry commented, "There's ample need for carpenters. Shall I mention you to my father? He used to farm, you know, but began working construction when my mother bore only daughters."

"Yes, please do," Gerolf nodded with a smile.

Chapter Five

Corabell

On the summer solstice, Saturday June 21st 1834, the strawberry moon shone whole and bright. Corabell quickly washed the dinner dishes. She gathered rags, a vial of brown soap, a broom and bucket, a bundle of dried rosemary and asked Elke's permission to borrow the tinderbox.

Ready, she waited outside for the brothers. Abo and Gerolf secured the tools from the barn. Still bright, the sun had not descended behind the trees along the river's edge. Abo took the broom from Corabell and hoisted the leather tool bag across one shoulder. Corabell swung the bucket of cleaning supplies as she walked. The linen bag stuffed with roof shakes hung across Gerolf's chest, larger wood pieces perched on his shoulder. The day had been fresh and cool and dragonflies swung over the grass, whirring in the evening air.

They followed Gerolf, passing a lane marked with a stake where cottonwoods edged the banks of a seasonal stream. Across a field of low prairie grass, they saw a stone chimney on the western side of a cabin. Just south of the lodge, a stand of small trees stood in a row. "Ahead, there," Corabell pointed to the cabin, "Are they trees or tall weeds?" Apart from the cottonwoods farther west flanking the lower land, they were the only vegetation of substantial height.

"We were told the house was built for the Indian agent. He must've brought them and planted them at once. Surely they're apple, though I'm not sure they're still alive," Abo replied.

They followed the animal trail Gerolf had taken with its folded, trodden grass and arrived at the cabin door as his tune merged with the night. Abo let the sack of tools down alongside the broom and scooped Corabell up in his arms. She hung onto his neck and lowered the latch on the door, flinging it open. The smell of mouse urine and wood ash struck them. She wriggled from his arms to investigate the dim interior, while Gerolf blew into the scant flames in the hearth. Opening the windows, Corabell hoped to catch the breeze.

The floor was a combination of mortar and river rock. With the passage of time, a layer of organic debris had filled the depressions. Using her hands, Corabell cleared away the ash that littered the sides of the fireplace. Gerolf moved aside her, adding thicker branches to burn. Above, Abo's feet treaded across the pitched roof. The axe pounded the wooden shakes. The blade and head came through the rotten lumber on the next blow. With a warning call, Abo dropped the softened slats into the interior. Corabell gathered the refuse and fed it to the growing flames. As the light grew, Gerolf stepped outside and Corabell saw the interior more clearly. Abo called to Gerolf and he climbed up to his brother.

The walls facing north, east and south contained a window each. Though the cabin was small, the sharply slanted roof stretched high above the floor. The notched log ends sat squarely into one another without nails. Exposed rafters held ropes, hooks and gear the previous owner had stored out of the way. On the west wall beside the fireplace, a ladder rose to a sleeping platform. A roughly hewn table stood in the corner.

Corabell took the rungs of the ladder to the loft where she swept webs from the walls and rafters. Finding a pisspot, she brought it with her when she began sweeping the floor. She carried out a mound of leaves from one corner, and a creature scuttled across her toes. Considering the pisspot again she set it on the old table, noting a second household item.

Throwing damp debris out the door, Corabell recalled the ceremonies of village couples. Clan members provided needed household items: a tinderbox, kettle, blanket and chickens. She ached for her grandmother. Summoning the chant of the widows, she sang. Her voice in the air sailed through the windows and over the soil, her people had called home. Sadness in the tune connected her to the village. The widows would be content for her. They would say she was where she belonged.

"Abo! Which way is the well?" Corabell gazed upward as Abo appeared and pointed north, and then scrambled down to join her. The rising moon filled the night with a cool glow. Corabell walked soundlessly and soon spied the low rock wall. She wondered how long the walk would take and how many trips she would make every day. Abo's feet lumbered to catch up with her. She did not startle when he laid his hand on her back.

"Wait for me, you walk too fast."

Corabell slowed as Abo's hand found her waist. At the well, she pushed him back lightly speaking softly, "Abo wait. We're never alone." She stepped away to undo the leather laces and slipped her corset off, loosening her brown dress.

Corabell closed her eyes at his touch and his breath warmed her neck. She kissed him without reserve, opening her mouth to the invasion of his tongue. His hands found her buttocks and followed the heat of her body, his cheek brushing against her covered breast. When she found the hem of his shirt, Corabell lifted it over his head.

Abo's hands on her thighs made her aware of her heightened breath, and she pressed herself against him so firmly no air separated them. Abo fumbled to unbutton the fly of his trousers and when he did, Corabell ran her hands over the sides of his thighs, feeling the strength of his erection and the solidity of his muscles. Baffled by the largeness of his body, she wondered briefly if the act would work. His hands found her thighs, and she let fear go as his fingers explored her regions. They sunk into the cool grass. Abo held her while he moved into her. Corabell moaned and he pushed inside until she held him entirely within her. Then he plunged into her warmth and wetness.

With Abo's waning erection, Corabell felt the width and length of his penis and with it, the soreness of her flesh. Abo fell aside her speechless. Her hands explored herself for some evidence of strain.

Corabell remained where she lay, then giggled and stood. With her legs wide, she looked up to the moon and down at the man who watched her. Smiling slowly and fully, Corabell shuffled to the well, where she poured water over her throbbing tissues. Abo left her in the shine of the moon when she needed more time to bathe.

Returning with the heavy bucket, Corabell noted the brightness of the night and strode easier when she saw Gerolf worked on the far side of the ridge. She poured water on the floor and worked the leaves free from the stones with the broom. Above her, the brothers pounded in fresh wooden shakes, working downwards, each plane fitting in under the former until the space in the roof had filled.

Corabell swept debris out the door and stepped out. The sensation of Abo's body within her unlocked a flood of concerns. Without a planted garden, how would they survive the winter? Elke had planted weeks ago. They'd have to board with the Gottschalks until the coming spring. Like children, she and Abo would need to abide their ways. Even as husband and wife, she wasn't sure this would change.

With her hands on her hips, Corabell walked until she spied Abo on the roof, his knees bracing against the slanted surface. "Abo!" He turned to her, smiling. "With no family to provide us with anything, we'll grow hungry and thin!" She threw her arms in the air and turned her back to him. Taking a breath, she spun to face him and exclaimed, "We lack seeds to sow a garden. We've no chickens, no cow or goat for milk." She lowered her voice, "Surely, the Gottschalks'll not allow me to bed with you. Not even when we're married . . . and I'll have to go to church every Sunday and listen to the strange German tongue."

Gerolf appeared from the far end of the pitched roof and belched loudly. He gestured to his brother with a curt nod, took several shakes and returned to the other side to tap them in. He came off the back of the roof and Corabell saw him striding away through the low grass.

Abo tapped the last shakes into place and climbed down the side of the wall, "This's why I work in the slaughterhouse, to be able to live without farming. A garden'll be useful, but my labor should provide sufficient coins to buy seeds and several chickens. We might buy dairy products from the trading post or from Elke." Abo dropped the tools in the leather satchel and helped Corabell collect the gear. "Leaving the Gottschalk house is important," he explained, "the sooner we leave; the sooner we can turn the garden soil. I hope Dietrich'll lend me the hoe and shovel. We'll need a fence, otherwise animals will graze there. And a chicken coop or the wolves'll eat the fowl."

"We could also use a skillet," Corabell added, "a cooking crane in the hearth, a tinderbox and another bucket to carry water. Oh . . . and a bed," she smiled as she mentioned it, "but I can make a mattress from pine needles. We'll need canvas to secure the stuffing, and a blanket too." As they spoke, the details seemed more manageable.

At the conclusion of Sunday morning service, Minister Schoenhofen spread his arms and with his palms raised to the congregation, announced there would be a wedding ceremony the following Sunday, the 29th of June. The entire congregation was welcome to attend as the young couple had but a single brother and no kin otherwise to attend the sacred union of matrimony. He reverted to German as he gave the final words. Lulled by the chanted notes of the mass, Corabell roused herself when she heard the invitation to the wedding, which would take place a week from that Sunday.

By the window light, Corabell turned the blue dress inside out. Elke threaded the needle with a similar shade of blue thread and urged Corabell, "Make your stitches as fine as you can." Several yards away Emily, her close friend Bridgette O'Shay, Eva and her older girls, Nola and Uta, gathered at the table to plan the meal and guest list for the wedding dinner. They invited Minister Schoenhofen, several friends from the slaughterhouse and the entire O'Shay family.

"Henry O'Shay's a Catholic." When Corabell looked up Elke explained, "They attend St. Patrick's Church on Adam's Street, in the center of town."

"Mm, and how many're coming to this dinner?" Corabell asked.

Elke's eyes met the ceiling briefly, before she addressed her spouse who read from the window light beside Corabell. "Dietrich, please add up the people who'll be coming to dinner." Dietrich shifted the newspaper gave his wife a short rumble and Elke shared with Corabell, "You know he keeps the books for the slaughterhouse. We profit well from his skills in mathematics." Corabell smiled weakly at her when she recognized Elke awaited some reply.

Emily and Bridgette decided to make a German wedding cake. Bridgette brought her thick cookbook to the table and opened it to the page she had marked. "Look here," Bridgette read aloud, "the recipe calls for eighteen pounds of flour, twelve pounds of butter, twelve pounds of sugar, six pounds of raisins, six pounds of currants, three pounds of citron, twelve dozen eggs, a half-pound of cloves, one quart of brandy and other spices to taste." She blew on a strand of blond hair and swept it behind an ear. Elke stood gazing at her, one hand on her hip, the other against her bosom, her jaw slack.

Sitting opposite Bridgette, Emily scrunched up her face, "Twelve dozen eggs? How many's that exactly?"

Elke shook her head, "But we've not sufficient pans to accommodate its baking. A half pound of cloves?"

Bridgette offered, "Aye, but it'd feed us, wouldn't it?"

"Yes, and all the town," Emily quipped, grinning. Elke shrugged and left the room, returning with a slip of paper, which held a German wedding cake recipe of more practical proportions. They would still have to obtain a bottle of brandy and two pounds of sugar.

Corabell removed the buttons in the waistband of the blue garment with brown stripes, repositioned them and sewed them back on so the skirt no longer sagged. Her favorite dress, she would wear it on her wedding day.

She had donned the dress earlier and stood on the table as Elke pinned up the skirt hem and shear cotton lining underneath. To flatten the new seams, Elke showed Corabell how to fill the iron with red-hot coals and press the fabric without singeing the cotton.

Abo stomped his foot exclaiming, "Ach, die Schuh!" Corabell looked up at him, her face blank. "Die schuh." He gesticulated, one hand sweeping to his head, "The shoes, I've not bought the shoes." He hit the floor again with his heel and paced through the house, his hands on his head while the floorboards creaked under his heavy footfalls.

Gerolf leaned against the side of the back porch with his bare feet outstretched and commented, "The girl's boots are finer than anything sold in town or at the trading post."

Dietrich looked up from the newspaper and cleared his throat before offering, "The shops downtown're open late on Friday evenings. You may use the carriage if you heed the road."

Corabell glanced up from her hem to catch Abo's response. He stopped pacing and thrust his hands in his pockets as he stared out the back door. Corabell spoke to his back, continuing to move the needle in her hands. "Nobody'll see my feet; the hem should cover my toes. I'd much prefer a cooking crane like Elke's than new English footwear." Dietrich grunted in reply.

"I think perhaps we can do without new shoes," Abo concluded.

Dietrich rattled the paper and turned the page. He gazed in Abo's direction and cleared his throat, "Ahem, Abo. A suckling pig would make a fine wedding meal. Why not purchase the swine from the slaughterhouse? The boss'll give you a better price. Mutter? Would that please you?"

From across the room Elke nodded, "Yah, that's a good idea, better than goose or turkey."

Abo lingered near Dietrich, "How many hours do you think it'll take to smoke?"

Dietrich paused to consider, "Hm. If you purchase the meat Friday we might begin smoking on Saturday eve. Depending on the size, eh? It should be ready the following noon."

After several more paces across the floor, Abo replied, "Herr Dietrich, I accept your offer of the horse and buggy for Friday evening. Corabell and I'll leave after dinner."

Gerolf's voice came from the open door on the porch, "I'll come as well. I've been to town once since arriving in this place." Dietrich nodded as Corabell smiled up at Abo.

"The suckling pig'll give the day a ceremonial feeling. A chestnut dressing will complement it, as will the red cabbage and creamed turnips. Emily's agreed to make tomato pies. Eva and Nola will bring vinegar pies. Corabell, you'll make a pumpkin cake, as well as carrot fritters and pea cakes?" Corabell nodded, smiled and Elke continued, "Freda's agreed to bring dried apple and cranberry pies, though her pie dough can be tough, but for the children I want to make doughnuts, they'll want wedding cake, you know?"

Each evening Abo sat at the table and sought Corabell's attention. "Writing your name," he reminded her, "is a symbolic beginning." Corabell would have preferred to give Abo her complete attention, but she was usually engaged in sewing, washing, or assembling and storing dishes in the cellar. Abo sat and asked her to spell her name, reminding her that the letters in words had different sounds than the actual name of the letter. "I would've spelled your name with K, as Germans do, but young Nola's corrected me. The English spelling uses a C for Corabell."

Corabell jerked her head up, "Nola corrected you?" She would always remember her name began with C, the sign of the half moon. To appease her spouse, Corabell memorized the other letters quickly, though she struggled to write them.

Chapter Six

Corabell

Dispersing fresh straw on the path to the outhouse, Corabell took the stack of old newspapers and left them beside the latrine's hole. Carrying a shovel, she headed back. Yarrow grew abundantly there, the heads delicate clusters of white and pink flowers. She divided the plants. Hoping they would withstand transplanting, she set a mass to each side of the porches and watered both locations well.

In the house, Elke made sourdough bread. When Corabell returned the older woman asked, "Can you bring out all the dinnerware?" Corabell looked at her flatly, and Elke explained, "I mean the dishes, bowls, glasses and steins. We'll need them all. Just set them on the table." The celebration had turned into a dinner for twenty-three adults and eleven children.

That evening before Gerolf hitched the horse to the wagon, Dietrich reminded them, "Mind the muddy spots in the road. Avoid them, or the carriage may get stuck. Or worse, you may lose a wheel. Eh?" Abo nodded while Gerolf brought out the gear.

Soon, the two mounted the carriage bench and directed the horse from the barn. Abo gave a hand to Corabell, and she took a seat between the brothers. Reins in hand, Abo dipped his head to Dietrich. Corabell wore the Sunday bonnet Dietrich insisted she don, though it obscured her peripheral vision and muted her hearing. Lacking something to grasp, she wound her hand around Abo's bicep.

The large shaggy horse needed little encouragement to trot. Abo remarked, "From Magnolia we turn down Clybourne, and run parallel to the river." A carriage whipped by them, causing the horse to jog suddenly to the right. The riders continued forward nearly flying from the bench. Corabell planted her hand on Gerolf's arm and did not release her grip until the wheels quit turning.

Aside the slaughterhouse, the river's edge held a handful of businesses. Some had felled the cottonwoods and willows crowding the banks. A public house had left trees standing and closely faced the street. Horses and a mule waited outside, the front door braced open with a large rock. Beyond the industrial sites lay plots of virgin pine trees and fields of corn, oats and wheat. Abo slowed for several goats who chewed weeds in the center of the thoroughfare.

"Clybourne turns into Division and we turn left, going east," Abo told himself. Old log structures appeared sporadically in various phases of repair. Moving closer to the town center, women with children in hand walked along the roadside. Corabell stared at their dresses and hats. Abo watched the street, which gradually declined in quality as traffic increased. They passed an abandoned carriage with one wheel embedded deeply in the dirt. Gerolf read the sign in front of the ruined coach, "Warning! Deep Mud".

A breeze blew and tugged at their hat brims, bringing dust from the street with it. "Must we take a ferry?" Corabell asked when she saw no obvious way of arriving on the far bank of the river.

"Nein. No. There's a bridge to the south a bit." Abo jerked his head upwards. "We turn onto Kinzie St. here."

Flocks of gulls made regular circuits through the air. Ducks paddled in lines and geese formed packs and meandered upright along the shore. The evening breeze filled the sails of a boat and the smell of lake life infused the air. Ahead, they spied the wooden bridge and followed the procession of foot traffic, carriages and horseback riders. Corabell tightened her grasp on the brother's arms as they took the incline and passed over the dark water beneath the timber surface.

"Look, the old fort," Gerolf pointed to a structure surrounded by shrubbery on the south side of the river. The square of military buildings, most of frame construction faced an open court.

Abo gazed at Corabell, "Dietrich said the brickwork's part of the old ruins the soldiers rebuilt in 1816 to serve as an armory." Her face obscured behind the brim of her hat, Corabell made no comment, but stared straight ahead over the brother's elbows she had drawn securely across her torso.

"The town improves the central roads with corduroy," Abo told her, and she turned her brim and met his eyes. "See how they've placed tree trunks horizontally across the street?" She nodded. "Older logs gather topsoil and the wheels of the carriage pass cleanly over. Newer logs that've replaced rotten wood create this steady rhythmic jolt to passengers." Corabell smiled as they jiggled and Abo stated, "The logs prevent trenches from forming when it rains."

Farther south, shops of three floors and more vied for attention. "We must be close," Corabell commented, "Certainly this's the village center."

Abo nudged her, "Read the street signs to me. Lake Street's the one we seek." She did not respond.

A block further, Gerolf pointed and exclaimed, "Bruder, it's there!" The street name hung from a gas lantern on the corner.

"Ya! This's it!" Abo turned into the road. Buildings of frame construction, most with large glass windows, displayed merchandise facing the street. Boarding houses announced vacancies with hanging signs and hitched horses loitered with carriages. They left the buggy tied at a post after allowing the horse to drink from a watering trough on the street.

On Lake Street, no boardwalks united the substantial porches. Jutting streetward, decks of businesses encouraged the passerby to come closer, away from the muck of the road and peer within. Homes with fenced-in gardens and wide patios stood between retail shops and other sites of commerce. Gray-haired women in rocking chairs tipped back and forth, making regular creaks on wooden porch planks. A baby's cries carried on the air and the scent of roasted beef emanated from a tavern. Abo reminded them, "We're looking for Church's, a two-story general store."

Wind blew the river smell that mixed with the fishy lake scent and the temperature felt noticeably cooler. Corabell pulled her blue shawl higher. She felt she walked in a dream.

The town's women were pale and wore their dresses precariously close to the filthy street. A dog trotted past, its tail aloft. In front of them, a fiddle's melody bounced from an open doorway. Two men wearing top hats entered the store, holding their brims as the wind threatened to loosen them. Abo directed Corabell through the open doors. Gerolf excused himself, "I'll meet you on the front steps."

Corabell withdrew the list Elke had written. They ambled to the front counter where a young clerk greeted them. Abo read the items and their quantities and the employee assembled the groceries.

Flour and sugar required scooping from larger barrels and weighing on a scale. The clerk dug walnuts from another drum. He emptied the nuts into a paper bag that store employees had cut, folded and glued. Allspice found a similar brown envelope. Paper wound about the lard made it portable. The man placed everything in a wooden crate.

Corabell asked whether they carried any native goods, specifically birch wood plates. The attendant raised a finger and stepped out of sight, returning with two. The larger was more of a platter, but the smaller ones would serve the dinner party well. In addition, Abo purchased six pewter cups and a plain, brass flatware set.

The shop clerk totaled their purchases. Abo read the sign above the stairs to the second floor, which directed customers upwards for "Instruments, Fabrics, Furniture, Hats, and Ready-Made Clothing for the Entire Family." Corabell smiled faintly and leaned against his arm.

Abo took her hand and led her to a viewing case with rings displayed. Wearing a long black apron, the assistant at the counter offered, "May I show you some of our finery?" and opened the glass. Corabell nodded. Abo picked up a silver ring with filigree swirls and delicate metal beading set in a slender band.

He slipped the ring on Corabell's left finger, "Ach, it's too big," he muttered and inquired, "Do you have this one in a smaller size?"

The man fumbled about under the counter, pulling drawers in and out. Extracting several other rings, he set them on the countertop. "I'm sorry, there seems to be only one like that."

Corabell took the loosely fitting band and placed it on the middle finger of her right hand, while Abo took her left hand in his and applied others. She watched him, intent and urgent, while her right hand wore the silver latticework. When none fit the left finger adequately, the clerk removed those they had seen, and set another score of plain gold and silver bands on the counter.

Corabell admired the ring with graceful ornamentation, holding it ever higher. A particularly wide silver band fit closely on her finger, so snug that it came off reluctantly. Abo sighed heavily.

Corabell lifted her left hand to examine the cool metal more closely. Her brow furrowed. "But Abo, it's plain, and so heavy. It weighs down my arm." She hung her hand by her skirt, and tipped sideways. Taking off the clunky band, Corabell handed it to Abo, who took it with a stony face.

"Now look at this one." She held her right hand up, admiring the ring's delicate charm. "It's so fine. Surely, this one's the best. Notice the detail?" She spoke slowly, bringing her hand closer for the men to inspect. The clerk nodded as the blond brother shook his head.

Abo gazed down his straight nose at the small woman who met his eyes as he spoke, "Nein, NO. It's the wrong finger, Corabell. It must be on the nach finger, the left side." He held his left hand out in front of her.

"Hmmm? . . . But all fingers are for rings!" Corabell threw her arms up while the blond head disapproved.

"No, there's but one finger for a married woman," he insisted. Corabell gesticulated for the words she failed to find and narrowed her eyes. She shrugged fiercely, her blue shawl rising just short of her ears.

Aside the front door, the musicians finished playing. In the sudden hush a woman glanced over at them, and a clerk at a nearby counter looked up to see who was involved in the dispute. Gerolf came and stood silently at his brother's side as others paused to watch. "Corabell, the wedding ring's a tradition, a symbol," Abo caught his voice rising and began anew, with a whisper, "We put it on the left hand, on this finger" and he held the digit beneath Corabell's nose.

"But what use have I for your tradition? Why should I abide these ways when I'm not a typical bride?" Corabell hiked up her dress hem to reveal her native boots, proving her words.

The act riveted the attention of those close by. They inspected the handiwork of stitching upon her toes. Abo's face whitened as Corabell continued. "This church where they speak a peculiar tongue, this's odd enough!" Dropping her skirt, she took the fancy ring and thrust it at Abo. A tear forced itself from one eye and she hissed, "I'm not sure I want any more of your ways." Corabell glared at Abo and stalked from the store.

Abo

Abo set the rings on the counter while the clerk and a circle of customers dallied and looked on. His heart beat loudly and he feared the worst. At his side, Gerolf tapped his shoulder. Abo fumed, baffled and speechless.

"Bruder, we're all tired," the dark brother commented and swept the two wedding bands from the counter, "Let me buy these." Abo strode off, retrieved the box of household items, balanced the crate on one shoulder and carried it through the store, chin high avoiding the gaze of all.

The temperature had fallen with the rising moon. Corabell resisted the swaying carriage, holding her body erect and stiff. As the horse settled into a trot, the movement of the buggy became regular. Abo felt her relax.

By and by, her head fell against him. Gerolf agreed to unhitch the horse while Abo sat unsure whether to wake or carry Corabell inside. Fearing she might rebuke him, he moved gently, easing an arm under her head.

The fire inside the house gave dim light to the main room. Abo approached the bedroom door. He stood and felt for the bedpost with a toe. Setting Corabell on the quilt, he knelt, fumbled for the ribbons and gently removed her bonnet. Loosening her boots, he thought to undo her corset, and untied the leather cords. Corabell rolled to one side. Her flesh, warm through the dress fabric aroused him. Slow regular breaths told him she slept. Retiring to his room, he lay awake beside his brother.

Chapter Seven

Abo

Gerolf roused him from the open doorway, a cup of coffee in hand, "Bruder, morning's come. Get up!"

Abo dressed in a hurry. Saturdays were hard, the most difficult of the week. All shipments had to be made. If they finished early they could leave, but all workers were compelled to stay until every order of meat hung in the delivery carriages.

Abo emerged from the bedroom unsure he would still be married. He approached the table barefoot and sought Corabell's side where he knelt on one knee, his hands clasped upon his trouser thigh, "Corabell it'd please me still to have you as my wife. Will you agree?"

She looked over the top of her mug and gave him an answer. "I will be your wife." Abo rose and kissed her cheek. Having had a fitful sleep and less than his normal amount he neglected to shave.

Corabell

Elke frowned, took another sip of coffee and glanced at Corabell. Dietrich paid no attention. Before Gerolf pulled Abo away from the table, Elke reminded him to bring home fresh sausage. Abo left, snatching a stick to clean his teeth and pulling his hair back into a tress.

The mass of flower blossoms had drooped since Corabell dug them up from behind the outhouse. She watered the plants again generously and waved farewell to the brothers.

Abo

As they strode to the slaughterhouse, Gerolf confided, "I'll be happy to be free of the Gottschalks, though they've treated us well." Abo eyed his brother, knowing what occupied his mind. The wedding would occur tomorrow morning, and Monday he would rise for work. The couple would sleep under their own roof, without a bed or pillow. With no tinderbox, there would be no fire. They owned no kettle and no coffee. Gerolf brought the facts to his attention, though Abo already knew what they lacked. He shook the contents of his pocket, "I've brought some silvers, brother."

On Saturday afternoon, the trading post would be open when they left work. Abo would buy the essentials even if flies hovered over his soiled clothing while he paid the bill. He and his bride would live without the Gottschalks. Gerolf pressed him asking, "Bruder, how long? How long before I may move in?"

Abo looked over at his brother, smiling, "A week."

Working absorbed their thoughts, energy and reflexes. At midday when the foreman called for a break, Abo conferred with Thomas Flaherty, who agreed to bring a keg of beer to the Gottschalk home at noon on Sunday. Nate, the olive skinned worker with glossy black hair, asked about the reception hour. Gerolf gave him directions, noting the time planned was noon. Abo bought a case of fresh sausage and the suckling pig, which Gerolf agreed to carry home.

In contrast to the downtown stores, the trading post was a whirlwind with an order that defied common logic. Finding and entering the establishment required diligent and conscious effort. The building sat obscured in a copse of trees. Abo was never sure which thicket it was; he normally wandered into several others attempting to find the business.

Two large dogs rambled about the periphery. The animals picked up the scent of anyone seeking to cross the threshold, gauged their intentions and allowed entry only to those they deemed harmless. They permitted Abo to pass with a cursory sniff, though two other men from the slaughterhouse were not as blessed. The workers backed up against a tree, as the beasts growled and flashed their gums and teeth. The men hollered, "Hello, the TRADING POST! Call OFF THE DOGS!"

An apron-clad clerk appeared promptly at the doorway and assessed the situation. "Brutus, Duke, COME!"

The clerk ignored the fellow who reeked of liquor and addressed the man clutching his weary hat, "YOU are welcome," and the man followed behind him, past the animals.

Outside, two horses stood tied to the lower branches of trees. A large metal water trough catered to their thirst. Without a front or back porch, inventory spilled into the pine straw. Woven native baskets held small items: soaps, hand knives, tin cups, children's moccasins and maple sugar candy. Inside, shovels leaned up against kitchenware that held floral soaps. Homespun fabric lay in a roll stuffed sideways within a wide copper pot. A crate of loose seeds rested under the counter, canvas cloth jammed behind it. Two burly clerks assisted the mostly male clientele.

The salesclerk packed the items Abo requested in a wooden crate: a tinderbox, kettle, skillet, coffee pot, sieve bag, milled coffee beans and a pot of honey took up most of the space. He also purchased several yards of tough canvas, a sewing kit in a small enamel tin, and an assortment of seeds for beginning the garden. The load required most of the coins in his pocket, which he parted with easily, pleased to pay for the items his new life required.

When Abo arrived at the Gottschalk home, he noted the flowers beside the porch. Circling the house, he entered the back, the crate balanced on one shoulder. Eva's girls helped their grandfather assemble a very long table on the straw-strewn ground near the back porch.

Abo pushed the crate under the bed, took fresh garments and headed to the pump. He passed Corabell, her hair damp with perspiration. Mounds of orange dough sizzled in the skillet. The smell of bacon fat filled the room and competed with the reek from Abo's clothing to dominate the air.

Corabell smiled and wiped her forehead, wrinkling her nose. Romy shrieked and flew down the porch steps into the corn rows in the garden when she spied Abo. Dietrich shuddered and pounded a fresh nail into the boards Uta and Nola held. Corabell appeared in the doorway with a dozen carrot fritters, the fat seeping into a cloth beneath them. She offered them to everyone and returned to the hearth.

Corabell

Emily and Bridgette arrived in the carriage. They carried tomato pies, dried cranberry and apple pies, fresh blueberry pies and the wedding cake from the back of the wagon into the house, covering most available surfaces. Hovering over their baked creation in the corner of the room, the two friends chatted in low tones while preparing the butter frosting. Bridgette blushed when Gerolf appeared, newly scrubbed with wet hair, wearing an old pair of Dietrich's clogs which added to his height. He bowed to the women and admired their baked goods.

Abo smiled and approached Corabell, who frowned as she tended the white parsnip balls that browned while she rolled them in a shallow pool of pork fat. One of the masses split in two, and she uttered a native word. With a long fork, she impaled the halves and lifted them onto the platter. "I'd gladly eat that for you," offered Abo.

"You'll burn your tongue. Stay a bit and tend these. Don't let them stick ... be gentle." Corabell gave him the long fork and hurried off barefoot, to check the oven. There, she extracted a tray of flat pea cakes, returning to set them on bricks at the table. The piglet, sausages, uncooked fritter dough, corn muffins, shelled chestnuts, cut green beans, a mound of rising dough and the finished red cabbage salad occupied the rest of the table space.

At the hearth, Corabell fed the split parsnip ball to the blond brother. Abo swallowed and mentioned, "I've bought some items for the house." Corabell offered him another. He lowered his voice, "We'll sleep in the cabin, after we're wed." Corabell looked for Dietrich. Failing to see him, she leaned into Abo and ran her hand over his uncombed wet hair. He bent and kissed her gently on the lips. The young women in the corner stopped speaking and stared. Abo slipped slowly away, stole a corn muffin and told her, "I must speak with Dietrich about roasting the spanferkel." Corabell frowned at him.

Outside, the dining table stretched across the grass. Two extra benches on either side would provide seating, in addition to all the chairs in the house. Dietrich and the girls had been working since morning. They thumped up the stairs. Abo asked about smoking the suckling pig, but Dietrich waved his hand and announced, "I can do nothing more until I fill my belly."

Dietrich stared at the table and countertops, heavy with food for the coming day. He called loudly, "Elke, mein Frau! There's no dinner for the head of this family? What's all this, and not a bite for me? Mein Gott." Dietrich took a fork from the table and jabbed a hearty portion of red cabbage. Corabell ignored him, busying herself with frying until Abo took a fork and followed the older man sampling items on the table.

Corabell quickly filled two bowls with Elke's vegetable and sausage soup that simmered at the back of the fire. She gestured to the table as she handed the men bowls, "The corn muffins are for tonight's meal." The older girls followed behind. Nola and Uta took their supper to the porch where they arranged themselves on the steps. Blond Romy clomped noisily past them to the hearth. Her disheveled, partially braided hair fell across her cheeks. She stood watching until Corabell asked, "Like a bowl of soup, too?" The child nodded, moving the hair from her mouth and leaving dirty tracks across her cheeks. Corabell frowned. "Oh no, go wash your hands and face on the porch, at the basin ... and use soap!" The child turned away. "Then I'll fill your bowl."

Elke took the white items from the clothing line. After serving Eva, Gerolf and herself soup, she sat at the table. In the corner of the room, the young women preened over the cake while the uncorked brandy bottle sat empty. They applied a thick white frosting to the sides, sporadically breaking into wild laughter.

Elke bristled and Eva reassured her, clasping her hand, "Mutter Gottschalk, they're young still. The horse knows the way and'll take them safely home."

Elke's eyes widened and she turned to Gerolf, "Won't you see them home? Emily, my tochter should be cooking for her husband, yet she's here, laughing over cake. You'll have to walk the distance back, you know?"

"Ya, of course." Gerolf replied and refilled his bowl.

Elke commented, "Henry O'Shay should be home now, surely wondering where his dinner is and where his wife's gone."

"Ach, Mutter Gottschalk," Eva soothed, "she'll make many meals in her life; allow Emily some frivolity! The man has five sisters cooking the evening meal and the parental home is but feet away."

Elke swept her hand from under Eva's clutch, and stood. "Emily, genug! You need food in the belly, to clear your head. Then you must be off." Elke stepped behind her daughter and grabbed her waistband, directing her to table.

"But I need to finish the frosting!"

"Nein, it's finished." Emily marched with a hand tight to her mouth, her eyes full of laughter. Behind her, Bridgette brought her lips into a determined line, though her eyes continued to beam.

With some nourishment, the two bakers became more sedate. Still, Gerolf sent them into fits of glee when he told them he was chaperoning them home. Elke shook her head, sighed deeply and gathered the dirty dishes to soak and the clothing to iron.

As Corabell finished frying, she remembered the pumpkin cake. She squealed, running to the oven. Whiffs of burning dough filled her nose. Dreading the sight of the bottom, Corabell stalked back and forth in front of the cooling cake while Eva whispered encouragement.

The sun had set and the temperature in the kitchen began to fall as a breeze blew through. The wind carried the voices inside and Corabell heard Bridgette ask Gerolf his age. His deeper tone answered; he was nineteen. The young women found that hilarious and the darkness engulfed their delight.

Chapter Eight

Corabell

As roosters announced the coming day, Corabell walked to the far side of the garden, and pumped to fill a pail. Everyone in the house stirred later than usual.

Abo and Dietrich had repeatedly checked the fire in the smokehouse and Gerolf wandered home late from the O'Shay home. Elke had heated the kettle for Dietrich's bath and pressed the white linens while Corabell attended to final food preparations and washed the remaining dishes.

Breakfast was rudimentary. It was too inconvenient to eat more than toast with butter and jam. Platters, pies and the final preparations for more complex recipes covered every available horizontal surface. Plates and Elke's fine china lay neatly piled alongside a variety of drinking vessels. The laundered and pressed table linens sat folded amid the dinnerware. Finding sufficient space for a coffee mug and toast required additional shifting and maneuvering.

Corabell slipped into the dress she had managed to adjust and wove two braids in her hair. Elke tied the ends with ribbon, then wound and fastened them low at the nape of her neck. Wearing the customary bonnet, Elke pinned yarrow along its crown. The household set out for church early.

On the morning of June 29th 1834, clouds masked the light. Dietrich walked with Elke at his arm. Abo wore a spray of yarrow at his lapel and a silk cream-colored stock Dietrich had lent him.

Inside the church, an older fellow opened the high windows. A white-haired matron swept the floors and placed a vase of flowers in front of the altar. The group sidled into the front pew.

Minister Schoenhofen, wearing a white gown with a thick cord at his waist, appeared through a side door and descended the steps from the altar, beckoning to the couple with a wiggle of his fingers. The tall man asked, "How are you, this Sabbath day?" His blue eyes took in their faces and he inquired, "For what purpose do you present yourselves?"

Corabell answered while Abo stood frowning. She exclaimed, "We're to marry, Sir."

He smiled lightly and nodded to Dietrich and Elke, who remained sitting with Gerolf. The minister probed, "And why is it you both lack parents to witness your marital vows?"

Abo replied, "My brother and I came to this country without family. Corabell stayed behind," he began to expound, but the minister turned to face Corabell, and Abo allowed her to speak.

Looking into the minister's eyes, she told him, "My people left our village. I came to Abo instead of joining my folk in the new lands where the white man's government sent them." His eyebrows lifted, and he nodded. Corabell glanced at Abo, fearing that perhaps the elder man would not perform the ceremony. His face wore no anxiety and he squeezed her hand gently.

When the minister appeared again, carrying a black book, he wore a green stole over his shoulders, the ends interwoven through cording at his waist. Motioning to Abo and Corabell, he directed them where to stand. Gerolf slid from the front pew and silently passed his brother the heavy ring. The man of the church made the sign of the cross as he read in English from the text.

The ceremony of Holy Matrimony continued with the wedding ring and exchange of vows. Abo placed the wide silver band on Corabell's slender finger. Asking the couple to join hands, the minister laid his right hand upon theirs and the ritual concluded.

Several younger parishioners arrived, filing in quietly and occupying the pews behind Dietrich. The minister stood with his head bowed, slowly closing the book. He took Abo and Corabell in hand and turned them to face the growing congregation, introducing them as newly married. Abo found Corabell's elbow, retrieved his hat and strode out the back of the church. They had several minutes before the morning service would begin.

Walking with her hand in his, Corabell stepped onto an old cottonwood stump and turned to Abo. She gazed into his eyes and silently wished the widowed sisters skies as blue as her husband's eyes. Abo set his hands on her leather bodice, sought her mouth and drew her against him. Corabell felt his yearning for her and nothing else pleased her so.

The sun appeared briefly before a bank of clouds obscured its light and turned the day into shadow. The organ began to play and Corabell jumped down, keeping Abo's hand. They joined Gerolf in the customary pew, where the brothers sang with the congregation in German.

Corabell gazed at the length of Abo's fingers. Thunder cracked and shortly after, rain fell hard and fast against the open windows, sending a fine spray inside. The temperature fell abruptly and the wind brought in the rain smell. Corabell closed her eyes, leaning on Abo's arm. She prayed the widowed sisters would arrive safely in the new lands for Mettawa's people.

In the pew in front, Willa the eldest Gottschalk daughter, sat with a baby over one shoulder. The baby's hand hung loosely, a delicate pearly-white fist. Turned to the mother, the cheek flattened against bones and flesh. Ages ago, her baby brothers had slept so soundly. With jet-black hair, they were cream colored then, never as fair as ivory.

There was little to do at the German service but surrender to the words. The minister chanted and made the movements he did every Sunday. Rain beat steadily on the windows. An occasional breeze blew through the rows and tilted the brims of women's hats, lulling Corabell into a stupor. She leaned against Abo's bicep, feeling the hardness of his muscle against her. She thought of him and how she would touch his skin and her eyelids dipped.

Soft baby hands clapped and clasped her finger tightly. The weight of the small body warmed her chest. A hot mouth sucked the flesh at her throat. Jaw piercing skin, she heard muscle rip and a rending pain shot through her neck. Thunder cracked, shaking the church and Corabell gasped, startled and pulled herself upright.

In Willa's arms, the baby stirred. The mother nudged the infant to another position. It would not be long before the congregation filed up to the altar for communion.

The parishioners stepped onto the wet grounds as the sun flickered through dark clouds. Abo offered Corabell his arm and pulled her close. Several couples congratulated them. A young man offered his service, should Abo ever need another hand in putting up a fence or such.

The couple walked behind the others, holding hands. Dietrich strolled in step with his eldest son Konrad. Abo explained to Corabell, "Konrad lives farther south in a house with land that fell to his wife Beatriz after her first spouse died. He farms with the help of Beatriz's son, Franz."

When they arrived at the Gottschalk home, Abo set out with his brother, Nate and Freda's boys, Rudy and Rory, to check the status of the fire and discover whether the pork had sufficiently cooked.

Corabell hung Elke's bonnet from the door handle of the small bedroom. She stood before the bed, considering it. Would she ever sleep there again? Checking that none of her hair had come loose, she strode into the main room of the house. Fiza, Beatriz's teenage daughter, without a corset or her shoes ambled barefoot around the table laden with dinner provisions. Corabell lifted a tray, "Like to try a spinach fritter?" The blond girl stared and chose the largest in the middle of the platter.

Corabell had a notion the youngest of the O'Shay daughters was about her age, "Have you been outside?"

"No."

Nola came and offered, "May I help with something?" She took the salver of fried parsnip balls to offer outdoors. Corabell thanked her and followed with another plate of prepared vegetables.

Patrick O'Shay arrived with his family and a barrel of homemade beer. Thomas Flaherty's wagon had pulled up alongside Patrick's carriage when Abo, Nate and Gerolf returned.

Gerolf brought out several glass steins, "Come and sample two ales. Made by different hands, Thomas Flaherty stored this in an oak barrel and wears the patina of time." Gerolf let out an inch of amber liquid, which he held up to admire the color. He passed the vessel to Nate, who dipped his head and sipped.

"Tis a recipe for ale from a German at the sawmill," Thomas told them, "made in early spring before the days warmed." The beer gave off white foam and Gerolf tasted it, nodding his approval. Gerolf passed a cup to Patrick who swallowed and nodded.

Gerolf continued, "Ya, and the second, made by the hand of Patrick O'Shay, a lighter ale with less foam at the head." Gerolf swirled it around and smelled it. When it hit his tongue, he muttered in German and drained the glass then thumped Patrick's back, as the older man filled a stein.

Corabell returned to the house as Henry and Emily approached in the two-wheeled gig. Emily found Corabell at the table in front of the unlit hearth. She hugged the bride, urging her, "Turn around while I tuck some flowers in your hair." Quickly standing back, Emily appraised her work.

Corabell found Abo beside Gerolf, Thomas Flaherty and Patrick O'Shay. Her spouse led her away from the house as the wind picked up and the sun moved behind a tier of dark clouds. Gusts assaulted them and Abo pulled Corabell close, protecting her face. Noticing the flowers in her hair, he smiled and told her, "We leave after dinner, before dark. Gerolf'll take us to the cabin in the carriage. Bring your things. I'll bring the box of sundries."

Corabell felt Abo's words reverberate through her forehead as she rested on his chest. She looked up. Abo pressed his lips to hers and a cold rain fell. The newly wed couple ran and resumed their kiss under the front porch roof. Wind blew rain against their shins, dampening their clothing. They opened the door and dashed inside. Their sudden appearance drew the heads of everyone who had taken refuge. Abo turned pink and Corabell glanced down and shook the rain from her skirts. They pulled off their sodden boots. Abo shed his coat and left the damp hat on the mantel.

Outside the rain fell heavily against the table Dietrich had constructed. Elke watched the clouds from the kitchen window, where the smell of lightning swept in with gusts of air. The youngest girls noticed hints of a blue sky behind the deep gray.

With scant space inside the dwelling, guests remained under the overhanging roof of the back porch. Patrick brought the keg in and served everyone of reasonable age.

The adults and older teenagers raised their cups in a toast to the bride and groom. Abo drew Corabell's hand in his and thanked them kindly. Subsequently, Thomas Flaherty raised his glass, "Come ye fellas, join me in a toast ta the women in our midst, who from the time of Eve 'ave made life interesting."

Bridgette made her way through the crowd of elbows to counter. "From all the lasses present to the men here this day... May they brew many more casks of ale!" Her blond curls and freckled cheeks tilted to the ceiling in salute to the brewers. The older and less spirited sisters joined in lifting their cups, and Thomas and Patrick O'Shay bowed in reply.

The rain cut off as rapidly as it began. Sunrays filled the blue sky and shimmered on the ground. Elke ventured out after the smaller children, inspecting the carefully ironed and soaked tablecloth. She took a towel and swept puddles from a bench, finding Corabell's pea cakes disintegrating in a platter of rainwater. Asking the young girls to mop the chairs and benches, Elke uttered to no one in particular, "What other calamity can occur?"

Elke and Nola removed the tablecloth and other linens and hung them to dry on the clothesline, while Corabell and Fiza brought out the chestnut stuffing and

German cabbage. Dietrich appeared carrying a platter of sausages, his gray wiry hair sprung loose without a hat to dampen its motion. Gerolf came from the direction of the smoke house, bearing the roast mounted on a plank of lightly singed wood.

As food continued to appear, guests left the house and gathered, taking seats. Eva poured water for the children as Thomas and Patrick refilled glasses, steins and pewter cups. Abo deferred to Dietrich on how best to cut the pork.

Before they began the meal, Minister Schoenhofen stood and said grace. He spread his hands and asked them all to pray in accented English, "Bless the pair who have become as one . . ."

At the minister's amen, Rory rose and speared a sausage from the platter. Dietrich pointed the carving knife at the youth, "Ach, sit! You'll be served in time."

Corabell and Abo sat next to each other in the middle of the table, as directed by Elke and Eva. Each received another cup of beer. Dietrich began cutting the pork Elke had seasoned with garlic, salt, onions and rosemary. As platters passed, people served themselves and their children. The guests grew quiet and only simple requests for chestnut dressing, green beans or the cabbage interrupted the silence.

Elke

Dinner passed without much dialogue as guests filled the hollows created by several hours of worship and morning chores. When conversation began, again it had a lighter tone. Emotions were less frayed and the children calmer.

Elke's frown dissipated as she wondered about Corabell. The young woman had worked tirelessly without complaint. She took the worst chores willingly and accepted Dietrich's moods without comment. At midday, the house would be empty once more. The housework would fall again to her.

Freda secured the seat next to her mother and whispered to her amid the voices made content by ample food and drink. "Mutter mein, with Frederick away, and you soon to be without help, I've wondered whether the boys and I might move back into the family house. Without an elder male figure to work with Rudy and Rory on discipline, education and labor skills, I fear they'll have clear disadvantages."

Elke stared at her daughter and asked, "Ya, Freda, but what'll Fredrick say?"

"Ach, Mutter. I've not heard from him in months. When he desires to rejoin his family, we'll return to our cottage."

Elke nodded before inquiring, "When had you thought of moving home, mein tochter? Young Gerolf'll leave soon to live with his brother."

"Soon," Freda replied, "Without Fredrick or close neighbors, I feel at the mercy of men passing by, searching for the trading post. If it were not for the dogs, I'd have asked earlier. I'll bring the dogs, laying hens, the rooster, goats and the horse and trap."

Elke nodded, surprised at how quickly the loss of Corabell turned into the addition of her middle daughter and two grandchildren. She doubted Freda would be the first to rise, light the fire and start the coffee.

Abo

The pork, cabbage and chestnut dressing settled the wedded pair and pulled them into family conversation. He and Corabell listened as Gerolf teased Eva about a particular widower at church with two small children, "The farmer juggled the child in his arm to extend his hand and bid you good morning."

Eva's eyes swept to her plate and she commented, "Not a year's passed. I'm still in mourning."

Dietrich assured her, "Eva dear, you'll always have a place at our family table." She nodded to him while he frowned at the dark haired boarder.

Gerolf persisted. Abo wondered how much beer he had drunk. Yet he did not appear noticeably intoxicated, merely persevering into a tender matter. In a lower voice, Abo heard his brother ask, "When exactly will the mourning period end?"

Eva asserted loudly, "My beloved Rurik returned to the arms of God the second week in advent." She met Gerolf's gaze with her own grief that vented in a flood of freely running tears as she continued, "There's no joy in the seasons. The girls and I live from the goodwill of my parents." Eva ran her hands over her cheeks. "I'm unwilling to hire a man to perform upkeep on the property. I'd sell the home, to be rid of it, but Rurik loved it so. Surely, we'd be better off living in town, or with my parents." Eva closed her eyes and wiped them with a napkin.

Abo explained to Corabell, "Eva's spouse Rurik worked at the steam-powered sawmill on Goose Island. Huntoon's Sawmill." Corabell nodded and passed Abo the bowl of red cabbage, waiting for the story.

"Rurik had experience working the double circular saw. The machine spins several hundred cycles per minute. When the saw bites into a log, it creates a deafening screech. Dietrich says it must have hit metal, perhaps a nail. The blade broke and razor sharp fragments flew through the air, impaling the walls and earthen floor. A shard struck Rurik through the chest, cutting cleanly through his flesh. He sprawled backward over the rollers. A fellow worker found him, split wide, lying in a pool of blood. Huntoon's Sawmill paid the widow for the burial expenses, and for a full ten-hour workday."

Corabell shook her head, "Mm, how horrible." She gazed across at Eva, who appeared to be recovering from the wave of emotion.

The widow smiled weakly at Gerolf. From across the table, he commanded, "Widow, please permit me to hold your hand." Eva glanced at Dietrich who suddenly stood. She quickly stretched a hand out to Gerolf. "Forgive me, dearest Eva." His brown eyes glanced sideways to Dietrich. "I merely wish to announce that when your mourning time's passed I intend to court you." Gerolf failed to see Dietrich raise the serving fork. The great thwack of fork tines against his skull silenced all.

Dazed, Gerolf fell off the back of the bench. He came to quickly, sputtering and coughing, as beer sloshed over his face. Abo pulled him back upright onto the bench. Gerolf sought the source of the assault and caught Dietrich staring at him, the tines of the long cooking fork in his left hand, the handle in his right.

Abo frowned at the older man. Elke glared at her spouse who seemed to shrink in size. Silence overwhelmed the table. Still, Dietrich was only half-cowed. He launched a powerful diatribe at Gerolf, in the tongue of the old country.

Taking the verbal attack in stride, Gerolf rose and circled the table to where Eva sat. There he dropped to one knee, "I ask for your most sincere pardon." Eva turned pink, as did Nola, who sat beside her. Then her lips spread into a smile and a deep throaty laugh escaped from her mouth. Eva quickly subdued herself behind the napkin in her hand when she glimpsed Dietrich in her peripheral vision.

Dietrich projected the fork upwards and slammed it tines down into the newly made table. Freda threw herself away from him and into her mother. Plates and platters rose and fell. Heads swiveled to Dietrich, who loudly demanded, "There'll be no more talk of my late son Rurik!" He bent and pounded the table once with his fist, "Rurik's widow!" Pound, "Or courting." Pound.

Still on one knee, Gerolf rose and bowed deeply to Eva. He bowed again to Elke and Dietrich. He strode to the porch where he filled another vessel with Thomas's amber colored beer.

Before Dietrich retook his seat, he set both hands on the table and dipped his head. Minister Schoenhofen quickly stood and bid Dietrich sit. The minister suggested, "Let's bow our heads and ask for God's mercy, that peace be upon this family and wedding party."

The pastor resumed his seat shortly after, asking Bridgette to refill his stein. The once-buoyant girl filled the vessel and returned quietly to her seat. Slowly people began to whisper, eventually daring to speak in normal tones. Dietrich resumed eating his meal.

Konrad sat across from Dietrich, and breathed a long heavy sigh. Filling his father's stein, he addressed him, "Vati, it's understandable you don't want to lose Eva to any young cad. It's been only months since Rurik's death and we hold Eva dear. But, I was the young one that married the widowed, land-holding Beatriz. Eva'll find her way. There're worse suitors than young Gerolf."

Dietrich appeared not to hear his elder son until he mentioned Beatriz. Then he raised his eyes from the pork and met Konrad's eyes. He finished his mouthful before he replied in a half whisper, "He tries me, as Rurik did."

Corabell

The gathering had an abundance of ladies, due mostly to the unwed sisters of the O'Shay family. To those unfamiliar with them, they appeared much the same age. Variations of blond hair, light skin and freckles, Bridgette had by far the most ample bosom and buttocks. Built more slightly, Mary was taller and had the largest teeth. Rachel's notable attribute were her very pale blue eyes.

Fiona O'Shay appeared a younger version of her older sisters. She paid little heed to the girls her age, Fiza and Nola. The cinnamon-skinned man opposite her at the dinner table intrigued her, his head a mass of dark, dense curls. When the girls called to her, she waved them away. She listened to the rhythm of Nate's speech, with accents in surprising places. She soon caught his eye. "Please pardon my forthrightness. Sir, where're you from?"

Nate set his dark eyes on her and swallowed, "What be your name?"

"Fiona. Fiona O'Shay, youngest daughter of Patrick O'Shay, the carpenter."

A while later, he answered her question, "Fiona O'Shay, I's born far away on a small island I'll probably never see again. Given my freedom in documents, I traveled up de east coast afore I made a turn and came west. Illinois' my home, now. The slaughterhouse's where I work and 'came acquainted with de brothers."

Fiona prodded him with questions to hear the lullaby in his voice. Before too long, Nate freed his legs from beneath the bench. He gave Fiona a nod as he rose and moved away from the table and retrieved his fiddle. He tuned the instrument briefly, finding the notes and adjusting the strings with a turn of a peg. Ambling to the porch beside Gerolf, Thomas poured him a few inches of ale.

Nate began a slow tune seemingly to himself. Then he turned to livelier melodies. The children flocked to the porch where they twirled and stomped on the wooden planks, mostly in time with Nate's boot that beat the rhythm on the bottom step. Bridgette's sisters tried to get her to come and dance, but she would have none of it. Corabell leaned against Abo, content regardless of Dietrich's hot tirade.

Emily

Inside the house, Emily and Bridgette began washing dishes. Without witnesses, Bridgette confessed, "I'd thought Gerolf had a fondness for me, especially when he sat between us, driving the carriage home the other night. It wasn't my imagination, his leg bounced against mine!" Emily heard the disappointment in her friend's voice, and understood how Bridgette would be drawn to Gerolf, his handsome features, dark hair and fun disposition.

"Eva's suffered so this year, with the horrible death of her spouse, my brother, Rurik."

Bridgette quickly looked up from the dishes, demanding, "What does suffering have to do with stealing the most fetching bachelor?"

"Yah, Bridgette, she's not stolen him." Emily countered. "Did you not see her laugh at the idea? He can hardly be her first choice. He's maybe ten years younger." There was no reasoning with Bridgette; she wore a wounded heart.

Eva appeared carrying the remains of pork and set the singed plank on the table with the half-eaten bowl of chestnut stuffing, red cabbage and fritters. Noticing Bridgette's steely stare at her sister-in-law, hoping to diffuse it and put her friend at ease, Emily asked Eva plainly, "Eva? Might you consider allowing Gerolf to court you? Once your mourning time's passed, of course. Have you ever thought of him in the way of a husband?"

Nola appeared carrying a stack of dirty plates, and loitered at the doorway. Eva shook her head. "Ach, no. He's far too young and such a dandy. He's more suitable for one of you girls, say Miss Bridgette, for instance." Bridgette's cheeks flushed and she smiled widely.

Nola stepped forward and loudly announced, "No, Mother. I'm going to be Gerolf's bride." Eva froze, gazing at her eldest daughter, still not fifteen. Emily and Bridgette turned and gaped. They shared broad grins before resuming work. Nola regarded their looks without comment. She submerged the plates in the soapy water, turned and stomped from the house. Fiza, bearing several dishes, passed her cousin on the way inside and appealed to her aunt Emily, "What's my cousin fretting for?"

"Nola intends to marry Gerolf," Bridgette replied quickly. Fiza pulled back the blond hair that obstructed her vision, securing the strands deliberately behind her ears. Her mouth dropped open like a fish and she leaned back against the wall. Moments later, her face shifted into a suspicious frown. Her eyes darted from Emily to Bridgette to Eva, who avoided watching her slow comprehension.

Eva perched her hands on top the washtub and asked the young women, "What do you think of me and Widower Amsel?" Neither was acquainted with the man. Eva confided, "In time, perhaps, I'll wed the widower. Sometimes sadness brings people together." She released the tub, and began drying dishes and stacking them in piles.

Elke
Nate's fiddle made movement easy. Feet made extra beats on the porch floor as music inspired dancing. Patrick lit his pipe and reclined against the side of the porch, his foot beating in time to the reel. His round yet surprisingly agile wife joined the younger sisters on the porch. They danced side to side, flashing straight legs and pointed toes, turning like the rungs in a cart's wheel.

Bridgette and Emily brought out the wedding cake and set it on the table. Eva carried a stack of newly washed plates as Bridgette and Emily reappeared, drying forks as they ambled closer. Fiza trailed behind them. Elke poised over the large fragrant creation and complimented the two bakers. With a knife, she made two decisive cuts. Extricating the first piece, she gave it to Abo.

Emily passed him a fork, and the women waited for some response as he chewed the yolk-rich, brandy-sodden cake. He nodded in affirmation before he spoke, his German accent strong. "Ya very, very good." The second forkful Abo offered to Corabell, who smelled the alcoholic spirits. The buttery sweetness of the frosting helped temper the brandy syrup that moistened the crumb. Even so, Corabell's eyes grew larger at the taste in her mouth. She covered her lips with one hand, her eyes watering as Elke, Bridgette and Emily stared.

"She must never have tasted brandy," Elke commented. Emily began handing plates to her mother who continued to cut. The youngest family members gravitated to the cake and when Elke mentioned it was for adults, their heads sagged.

Elke bid Fiza bring out the doughnuts. Sometime later the girl re-emerged from the house carrying the sugar-coated dough, and offered one to Willa's little boy and his slightly older brother. Fiza took one herself and gave the platter to her cousin Uta, who carried it among those her own age and younger. In this way, Fiona O'Shay had a piece of liquor soaked cake, which she ate slowly and completely. Though she had not managed to sit next to Nate, she settled with Fiza's older brother Franz, between them. Franz ate cake as well and asked Nate whether he could teach him to play if he acquired a fiddle himself.

Beatriz joined Elke as she returned to the house where they compiled items from the church parishioners. Most contributions to the wedded couple were utilitarian and many were handmade: a cooking spoon, a long-handled fork, an iron pot with three legs, a tin lantern, an ash burl bowl, a dented water bucket, an aged copper basin, bars of laundry soap and another of lavender for the hands. Beatriz added a white tablecloth and a half dozen pressed napkins, which she used to prevent objects from sliding around within the ample copper tub.

The sun dipped over the pines that bordered the far riverbank. Elke cut the remaining roast into manageable portions to provide the newlyweds with several meals. Mrs. O'Shay contributed a jug of preserves and a block of cheese, dipped in wax. Elke thanked her for her generosity and added the goods to the pot. A tomato pie remained and half the blueberry pie. Elke slid them carefully onto birch plates, along with a large portion of the wedding cake. Nola took over the washing while Emily and Fiza dried and packed the birch dishes, pewter cups and brass flatware into the sides of the washbasin.

Corabell

Corabell sought the outhouse before stepping inside to see what had occupied Elke for so long. Discovering the wide metal tub and its contents were destined for her cabin, her eyes watered. She thanked the women for their generosity, "One day, I'll return this kindness."

The wind picked up, heralding a change in spirit. Evening loomed. It was time to pick up the children, fasten horses to carriages and move homewards.

Franz shook Nate's hand, "I hope to meet you again when I've a fiddle, so I might learn from you." Nate nodded. Fiza shared something secretive in her cousin Nola's ear. Nola paid little attention. Gerolf heaved the copper pot onto his shoulder and descended the stairs carefully, while Nola watched through the kitchen window. Abo pulled the crate of home supplies from under the bed he had shared with his brother.

Gerolf

At last, Corabell climbed into the cart and scooted onto the bench. The space in back lay packed with the full copper pot, the crate of items from the trading post, a cage with a pair of pullets from Nate and another with a young rooster from Patrick. Thomas brought them a small weaned sow, which Corabell held in her arms. To herald their farewell, the rooster beat his wings and crowed and Gerolf began to sing. Abo gazed at Corabell. She smiled, closed her eyes and gently sank against his side.

When they arrived at the cabin, Gerolf helped them unload. He reminded them he would join them shortly and then directed the horse and cart in a circle, heading back to the Gottschalk home.

Inside the Gottschalk the house, Emily put food away. Henry sat at the table with Dietrich, a final mug of beer in hand. In the quiet interior, Emily remarked to Gerolf, "I noticed a particular girl has a hankering for you." He shot a dark eyebrow upward and gave her his attention. "The girl's still quite young," Emily continued to work, "too young for courting, but in a few years, her mother should allow a visitor."

"Her mother should allow?" He frowned, "Surely you don't mean Nola, a child!" Gerolf leaned against the wall as he watched her.

Emily smiled. "The girl claims she'll marry you, there'll be no other. Dear Bridgette was crestfallen at your display in seeking Widow Eva's hand."

Gerolf's eyes widened at his unintentional snub of pretty Bridgette. He sighed and turned from Emily. On the back porch, he raked a hand through his hair and sat on the top step, rubbing a stick over his teeth.

Chapter Nine

Corabell

Abo swept a hand over his head, "Can't recall if I bought candles." Corabell rifled through the copper basin and found the lamp, but no wick or oil. With no safe place to keep the piglet outside, they brought her in, confining her in a corner with the table propped sideways. The hens and rooster cages sat amid the table legs. By scarce light, they made their way to the well.

Corabell stumbled, "Agh!" She dropped the bucket and freed Abo's hand. "My foot!" Holding her wound, she perched on the stone surface of the low well wall and discarded her boot. Though she couldn't see the blood, she felt the sticky warmth of it.

"You found it, my Frau," Abo spoke other unintelligible German words and took her limb in hand. Holding her foot to his mouth, he found the source of blood and sucked, then ran his tongue around her toes, making her giggle.

Corabell let her spouse tend her wound before reminding him of the reason for the journey. Shedding her dress, she dropped her clothes where she hoped to find them again. "We've come to bathe. You need to undress. This isn't the way we did things in the village, but bathing's a more sensible symbol." She would wash and rinse him and he would do the same for her. Abo lost his attire faster than Corabell and set about bringing up water.

Small hands worked soap into a lather under his arms, across his back and up his neck and chest. Corabell doused him, the water so cold it fettered his breath. Her hands on his penis made him hard, but she paid no mind and continued until she washed his feet, rinsing him well. She ran a towel over his wet body.

Washing Corabell took half the time. Abo left her hair dry and pinned up. Securing her wounded foot in a cloth, Abo stepped into his boots. "Hop on my back, I'll tote you," he commanded. Corabell tossed her dress and underclothing over one shoulder and clutched her boots. Abo crouched and she scooted onto his back. With her breath on his shoulders, he took up his garments, grabbed the pail and headed back to the cabin.

Corabell slipped down as Abo swung open the door. The interior of the house was darker still. The piglet murmured, turning in her sleep. The hens resettled. Corabell asked about an outhouse and Abo answered with a negative; whether no outhouse, or not to go, she wasn't sure. She made her way outside to the corner of the cabin, relieved herself and hurried back.

Abo waited at the doorway. Corabell felt for the bundle that held the blanket. He leaned against her, cupping her breasts. Corabell felt his penis at her elbow. She took it in hand, as she once saw a village woman do, put the phallus in her mouth and marveled at how her body could absorb so much of him.

Abo's fingers between her legs made her aware of her breathing. She stroked the length of his flesh, feeling its turgidity and mushroom-like spread at the tip. He hoisted her up, bracing her against the door and moved into her.

Feeling a change in urgency, he quickened his pace. As she yielded, his movements gained force. Then at once, Abo freed her, setting her on the floor in front of him, his penis slipping inertly from within her. "Corabell? Are you well? Have I hurt you?"

Her reply, "Yes" held no anger, and she leaned against him, seeking his warmth and scent. He took her hand and explored the wall for the ladder to the sleeping platform above the hearth. Corabell took her bag and followed, her hips feeling generally wider.

She woke before dawn broke pink across the sky. Sleeping on hard, unyielding wood held no appeal; she needed to work on the mattress. Searching the crate, she discovered the tinderbox Abo had purchased.

The fire lit within the hearth, Corabell stepped out, scouting for branches to keep it alight. Brush and windblown boughs lay strewn through the grass and she picked up an armload for an adequate fire. Adding them to the flames in the hearth, she filled the kettle, set it to heat, retrieved the soap and damp towel and headed to the well.

The sky grew lighter as she walked. The river's mist lodged in the distant trees before the wind urged it onto open land where it rolled out in narrow veins. Corabell loosened her hair, finding crushed flower heads from her wedding day. In the few short weeks with the Gottschalks, she had appreciated the ease of the hand pump, though her village had used the old-fashioned pail at the well.

Corabell wet the towel and slid it over her face. She slipped the cold cotton between her legs and let it cool her tissues, then doused her head with more water. When she arrived at the cabin with a fresh pail, Abo squatted at the hearth stoop, pouring boiling water into the cylindrical bag heavy with coffee. Corabell did not interrupt him.

Abo noted the shadows from the morning sun and commented, "I can't be late." Corabell recognized his tension. Without bread, she sliced and fed a chunk of wedding cake to him. Pouring another stream of water into the milled coffee, he nodded to the pork Corabell uncovered. She cut a hunk of the pale meat and ladled spoonfuls of honey into a pewter cup as Abo swirled the pot, feeling it for fullness.

Corabell dipped a towel into the boiling water and pulled it out with the long-handled fork, waiting for the steam to dissipate before finding an edge. Abo watched her holding the cloth as he ate cake with his fingers. Her wet hair clung to her shoulders and back, her slip pressed against her breasts.

"What're you doing with that towel?"

"For shaving." Corabell patted her cheek with a free hand and wrung the fabric tightly. Abo took another sip of coffee and offered it to her, holding the rim of the hot metal vessel. He took the towel, warily laying it on his face.

With his face covered, Corabell pulled his cotton drawers low exposing his upright flesh. Abo slid the towel back over his head and watched her curvy upper lip take in the head of his penis. Her damp shift moved against his thigh and when her breathing couldn't contain the object in her mouth, she rose and slid the head of the organ between her thighs. She bent over holding the mantle, exposed her backside and guided him as her feet perched on the cold stones.

Hours later, she still felt him within her and longed for him to come home. Corabell arranged all they owned on the table, which she had repossessed from the pig. She gazed at the assortment of items and considered starting the garden. They owned nothing to turn the soil. The pig explored the cabin confines and piles of excrement perfumed the closed space. Corabell opened the windows, noticing the sunniest location was south of the house, far from the well. From the window, she saw the stand of woody growth growing amid calf-high grass.

Approaching with the piglet at her ankles, she trod on the small, scattered fruits the trees had cast off. Biting into one with few blemishes, Corabell noted the swollen embryo held only three seeds. She gave thanks for the apple trees and tended them, cracking the dead wood from the living limbs and pulling up the tall weeds that had crept beneath the canopies. She mounded the fallen fruits between the hooves of the piglet, which sank to its belly chewing an apple the size of an acorn.

Unwilling to leave the food pile, the pig watched her as she walked about. Among the rampant grass, Corabell found clumps of chive and dill in different stages of growth. Farther afield, she recognized perennials with fine spreading foliage. The feathery plant bloomed with small pale green, bell-shaped flowers. At the top where most sun hit, the flowers gave rise to swollen red fruits. Under the poisonous berries, upright stems of asparagus shot out from fresh shoots. Corabell yanked the grass out from around them.

Pulling foliage away, she spotted tiny yellow chamomile flowers, and thought of the two widowed sisters. They had been fond of the tea. Fennel grew some distance away. To its side, tendrils of goosegrass invaded the delicate fennel blossoms. Corabell picked the goosegrass stems and flowers for the hens, the sticky residue clinging to her hands. She opened her palms for the piglet to smell and it licked the sappy juice.

Corabell lugged the poultry crates outside and opened them. The pullets scrambled out, one bolting after a passing fly. She returned inside to wash her hands.

The sun was high in the sky. She had not eaten and still wore her slip. Her hair had dried loose around her elbows. For a time Corabell wondered what Elke would think of her. There was nothing to cook. Corabell stirred the embers, distributing them to the far sides of the hearth. She cut herself a hefty slice of tomato pie and pulled off a hunk of white pork meat. Opening the door, Corabell sat on the threshold with her plate and cup. The piglet approached and cried at her ankles. She pulled off a portion of piecrust and fed it, and the creature settled beside her with its rump splayed to one side like a small dog.

She would need to take the piglet along if she began work on the mattress. Straw was a suitable stuffing but Corabell preferred pine needles. The closest trees grew to the west, nearer the river.

Corabell donned her brown dress and corset, combed her hair and plaited the length into braids, pinning them up with Elke's pins. The hair off her neck felt considerably cooler. She pulled the laces on the corset, adjusting her breasts in front. Yesterday's abrasion had dried and a fresh scab had formed on her great toe. She tied the blue shawl at her waist and secured a ribbon around the piglet's neck. The knife rested in the pocket of her dress. She considered walking shoeless, but Dietrich's face came to mind. Before leaving, she drank from the green, moss-covered bucket.

Slightly to the north, a trail lead westward and Corabell walked with the piglet at her heels. She planned to drag as many branches as she could manage. Without a hatchet, she would use her knife.

The wild weather of yesterday left a steady wind in its place. Elke would be washing; the constant breeze would dry the clothes quickly. When Abo returned home, she would have her share of washing as well. Corabell made a mental list of items they lacked. They needed staples: flour, salt, cornmeal and oats. Coffee mugs would be nice. Candles and two chairs—no, three chairs. She had forgotten Gerolf. And for company? Four chairs, then.

Without a bonnet, the wind cooled her face and head. Allowing her eyelids to droop, she walked while the animal trotted silently behind. Corabell wished the widows full bellies and sufficient contentment to enjoy the wind. After walking a good distance, grass gave way to brush. Red and white pines became more common. Corabell sought the lower branches.

The river's scent mixed with the breeze, and the air gradually increased in humidity. The piglet sensed a change and began emitting a shrill cry every few heart beats.

The oldest trees soared overhead. Pine needles rained continually onto the higher banks below, their rich smell lingering between trunks before the wind swept it away. The dense carpet of needles gave gently under her feet.

Pines had fed her people in winter months, the pliable inner bark providing a source of flour and nourishment when dried and pounded, the needles providing nutrients when steeped as tea. As a child, she had chewed the sweet sap from pinecones. Village grandmothers made a drawing salve from the sticky exudate of the trunk, and another for chapped skin from the needles.

Corabell searched for smaller trees with branches she could reach. Picking up the pig to end its complaints, she secured it in her shawl, draping the wool across her chest and tying the ends. Inside the soft confines, the warmth put the animal to sleep. Soon the creature began to snore.

A group of pines grew at an edge of a thick copse. Corabell set the passenger beneath a tree and set to dismantling the branches. The weight of a large stone, brought down upon the back of the knife, worked better than the blade alone. Bending the split boughs, the wood gave under twisting. She longed for a hatchet; the knife was practically useless.

Accumulating branches longer and wider than her height, Corabell stacked them, and gave the mound a preliminary tug. Moving it was easy, but home lay distant. The piglet wandered amid the branches, whining. Repositioning the animal, she tied the shawl and dragged the pine heap into the cooling wind.

Had she come on the same path? The woods masked the tops of the towering cottonwoods that marked the lane closer to home. Amid the thicket of trees, she saw the roof of a wooden structure. Corabell dropped the load and bent her knee up to rest against a pine trunk.

Some yards in front of her, the carpet of needles erupted suddenly upwards. The bare head of a coal-black man looked around and locked eyes with Corabell, who startled. He placed a finger over his dark lips and his eyes softened.

Corabell forced her head to dip, in a nod. With that, the man threw a sack from the hidden hatch and scrambled out. He pulled up a small child and helped a woman dressed in a shabby frock from the hole. She hauled a load twice as large as the man's. Wearing a dull gray bonnet, a large brim obscured her eyes. With lighter skin than either adult, the child waited gazing upwards. The wind caught the small one and he teetered, unsteady, before the man scooped him up and they hurried westward to the river.

Corabell stood motionless, watching them depart. She left the boughs and walked purposely to the building, past the sleeping dogs and random items spilling out in front. Opening the door, she saw Nate leaning against the front counter, speaking with the man behind it.

Struck by the oddness of the threesome outside, and the lone dark-skinned man in the shop, her reason for entering evaporated. The clerk noticed her and asked, "May I assist you in finding something?" His gaze met her eyes and he paused.

Nate greeted her, tipping his hat, "Mrs."

Corabell hesitated, "Hm. I've wandered off course," she admitted, "and I'm hauling branches. Can you direct me to Center Street?"

Nate tipped his head to the clerk and motioned to the door. "Come, I'm goin' dere now. I'll show ya de way." Corabell turned and hurried to collect the burden. Dragging the weight with one hand, the creature cradled under her arm in the soft space between her hip and lower rib, she followed Nate.

The man did not attempt to help her. Her brothers would have behaved as though the freight was her work, they would not have spoken either. Along the narrow path, the branches battered up against tree trunks and exposed tree roots that had been polished smooth in places. Ahead Nate beckoned, urging her to hasten. He opened the brush to one side for her. Corabell glanced backwards at him and he tipped his hat. The path turned onto the much wider Center Street.

Abo

Abo stood beside the well, naked save for the drawers adhering to his buttocks. His discarded clothing lay in a heap on the ground and he worked a cake of lavender soap across his head. He smiled when he saw her in the distance.

Dragging a mass behind her, she bore something more at her side. Where had she been? No smoked curled from the chimney, no food scented the air. "Corabell, mien Frau! Come!"

She responded with a wave of a hand, and dropped the load at the side of the cabin. Her face lit with a wide grin, her pace quickened. Corabell lifted the shawl over her head. Unencumbered, she skipped to Abo and smoothed her hands over his soapy skin. Resting her cheek against his damp torso, Corabell shut her eyes, moved her hands to the drawers, bringing her fingers through the openings at his thighs, and then back to his buttocks. Abo whispered in his foreign tongue.

He stepped away and her expression registered the small betrayal. Poising the bucket above his nose, he rinsed the lather into the dirt at his feet. Spying her frown, he soothed her, calling her, "Cora," and the dearest of German niceties. Abo closed his eyes under the cold stream and doused his neck, chest, armpits, belly and groin. Corabell sank slowly into the grass, lifted her skirt and reached for him.

Abo tossed his sodden drawers and sank to his knees, setting his icy hands on her thighs. She squealed, rolled away and rose, taking his head in her arms. His mouth sought her breasts beneath her dress.

The couple heard nothing of the wheels or buggy until they returned to the larger world and lay on the grass. Noting the carriage and horse, they raised a fresh bucket of icy water, quickly rinsed themselves and readied themselves for company.

Abo walked the distance to the house nude except for the boots on his feet. Corabell bid him leave her there; she would rinse the foul work clothes. They had one bucket and the large copper tub. She would need that for dishwashing.

In the cabin, Gerolf poured wedding beer while Abo stood bare-chested in fresh underwear. Corabell motioned with her head to the piglet on her hip, "Gerolf, have you brought any tools? This one urgently needs a pen. I've carried it half the day, for fear it'll be eaten."

Gerolf swallowed his beer as Abo asked, "Where've you been? And what of the mass of boughs?"

Corabell met his eyes, "My husband, we're in need of corn meal, oats, flour and salt. I'd gladly cook if we owned some staples." Abo nodded. "We could also use an outhouse, a laundry line and another large pot for laundry," she added. Abo looked over at his brother, who watched them while he sipped beer.

Setting the pig on the floor and the dripping laundry aside, Corabell threw her arm wide in the direction of the limbs against the side of the house and informed him, "Our mattress requires pine needles . . . and a wooden frame I hope you'll construct." Abo gazed down at her and plucked several pine needles from her up-pinned braids.

Corabell turned to the remaining provisions as Gerolf remarked, "Elke made a rich stew of sausage and potato." Abo swilled his beer and foraged through the contents of the copper pot. He found the wheel of cheese, which he impaled, taking off a large fraction. From the mantle, Corabell unveiled the pork, set it on the table and pulled off a section of meat. Gerolf offered her beer. Nodding, she took her knife and cut her spouse a sizable chunk of the roast. Sliding a quarter of the tomato pie onto his plate, she told him, "The pie's good. I had some earlier."

The couple ate standing on one leg then shifting to the other while Gerolf commented on the burgeoning growth in Elke's garden. They still had not sewn seeds.

The men at the slaughterhouse had agreed with Dietrich's claim that the soil needed to be turned and left for a year. Gerolf preferred to begin planting, simply praying the seeds germinated. Corabell agreed with him. Finishing her mouthful she mentioned, "This morning, exploring the grounds, I'm certain I found the place of the previous garden. It's on the south side of the house," she waved her hand; "Some of the herbs still remain."

Gerolf grinned and strode to the door, "I've brought tools in the carriage. Join me when you've finished." Abo gave no response. The piglet cried at Corabell's ankles. She broke off a piece of piecrust and fed it.

Abo turned his eyes to his wife and she reminded him, "Abo, we need flour, dried peas or beans."

He gesticulated with his head, to the remains of the roast and bid her, "Cut me another piece, will you?" Corabell gave him a quarter of the blueberry pie as well.

With food and beer in his belly, Abo felt restored. He could not resent the intrusion of his brother, especially when he brought Dietrich's tools. He joined Gerolf, grabbing a hoe from the back of the wagon. Corabell had cleared the area surrounding the herbs she wished to keep. The brothers stripped the land to the south of the cabin of weeds, grass and thatch. Instead of turning and allowing it to lie fallow, they would plant.

Corabell

Corabell washed the few dishes with a bit of laundry soap, then headed to the well for fresh water. Rinsing the plates and table, she poured the rest of the water into the copper washtub. Adding Abo's work clothes turned the liquid red. She set out again for the well, hoping it would be the last trip of the day. With a fresh bucket of water, the garments exuded a lighter shade of pink. She wrung the clothing as best she could.

In the dimming light, the silver spangled hens returned to their cage, raking the earth as they ambled to the side of the cabin. Relieved, Corabell saw the men had saved the goosegrass. The young leghorn rooster trailing behind the hens crowed suddenly, thrusting his beak to the sky and his wings downward.

Corabell meandered closer to the men to avoid having to repeat herself. She spoke with her hands on her waist, "Gerolf, you'll need someone to attend to your laundry. I'd gladly take the duty, as we'll soon live under the same roof," she began. "Today we own a single bucket and wash tub. Without river sand, a scrub brush or washboard, I can't say how much of the mire from the slaughterhouse will remain in the fabric. If you want your clothing as clean as possible, you need to think of purchasing a large cleaning tub and some tool to loosen the grime."

Abo smiled as he worked the hoe. He bent to fling root debris into a pile at the southern end of the garden and stones into a heap at the end of each row. Corabell relaxed her shoulders and rocked back and forth. "It'd also be helpful if you'd make a watering system so I might avoid having to tote water from the well."

Gerolf stood and gawked at her. He brushed a thick strand of damp hair behind an ear. Then he replied to Corabell, who stiffened under his tone. "Woman. I agree to buy the items you may need for washing, but you'll receive them only when you've written them down in a list." Her eyes grew round, reminded of how her brothers and uncles had addressed her. Abo glanced over at his brother and whipped several stones through the air.

Before Gerolf left, he gave Corabell a short pencil and a card from the slaughterhouse for her to write on the back of. He handed it to her gravely, watching her eyes. Glimpsing beauty in her brother-in-law, she turned away wary that her appreciation showed. At last, the dark brother leapt into the carriage and turned the horse around.

Silence surrounded them. Before the sky turned completely dark, Corabell planted a row of spinach. Abo constructed a rudimentary cage for the piglet by pounding branches into the ground. The wind blew and Corabell smelled rain, she retrieved the pine boughs and dragged them into the cabin. The gusts flattened her dress across her when she dashed out the door. The needles had to dry for the mattress.

Abo took off his clothes and submerged a cup in the bucket twice. He drank, and frowned when Corabell brought in the piglet who had whined mournfully from the new pen outside. She set the animal against the southern wall and blocked its exit with pine boughs.

The darkness inside the house hid her body more than Abo's. He stood in front of the half-open north window, his light skin partially illuminated by the night. Corabell took the pins and braids from her hair and stepped into the rain to pee. She returned with damp skin and desire for her husband, who stood silently at the window, in the breeze and spray of rain. She brushed her nipples against his back and caressed his rounded buttocks. Still, he did not turn to her.

When he failed to respond she addressed him, "I thought of you, golden haired one, in the days after I bought meat. I wondered how you smelled, how your mouth tasted and how your hands might feel against me. Abo. I've gone without you and I want you joined with me as a husband should love his wife." She waited for some reply.

"I will not share you," he told her while facing the pelting rain.

Corabell drew herself around to the front of his body, "Wives aren't shared, unless asked to do so." Abo shook his head no and bent to kiss his wife.

Chapter Ten

Corabell

She washed briefly as the first rays of light worked through the sky. Breaking daylight illuminated the animal prints in the damp earth. Corabell reckoned a wolf or coyote had passed in the night and she thought of her wolf dog companion.

The agreement with Gerolf occupied her mind. She would ask Abo for help in spelling the English words. Pouring boiling water over the milled coffee, Corabell waited for the water to trickle through. She pulled out the wedding cake and smelled it. The weather had not been overly warm; the days hot enough to curdle milk had not yet arrived. She cut two slices of cake. Pouring coffee, she stirred honey into each cup.

The piglet squirmed loose from the pine boughs and Corabell caught her, confining the creature with an armful of plucked greens in the temporary enclosure outside. She opened the chicken's cages and they sprinted out. Returning to the cabin, she called, "Abo the coffee's done," and heard him shift on the platform above the hearth.

With the pencil in hand and Abo's past tutoring, she felt confident about the word "tub," but the word "wash" troubled her. Could a single letter make a wah sound? If so, what was it?

At last, Abo's bare leg dangled over the ladder rungs. Tossing a napkin in the simmering three-legged pot, she bent over the table, chin resting on her palm, holding the short pencil. Abo passed her, lifting her gown. He stroked her backside, rearranging the her breath pattern. Turning to the table, he took a sip of coffee and broke off a chunk of the egg-rich cake. He murmured an appreciative note and Corabell caught his eye. She watched him before asking, "Abo, what letter makes a "wah" sound?"

"You must mean a W." Corabell looked at him as if he'd spoken German. She wrinkled her brow and repeated what she heard him say. He nodded. Corabell abruptly realized she knew the letter and wrote it carefully, following it with the others she figured made an "osh" sound. With a grunt of satisfaction, she looked down and read the word to Abo.

Corabell adjusted her shift down around her legs. She checked the water, which boiled steadily. Taking the long-handled fork, she fished out the cloth, letting the steaming water drain. She told Abo, "You must shave or the men at work'll think your wife doesn't care for you." His eyebrows lifted and he muttered something. "Abo, this English is difficult enough," Corabell objected, "I don't know that other tongue. Please check my word." Corabell pointed to the table. Abo glanced at the slip of paper and shook his head. Her face fell.

"You want an "A", not an "O"," he explained.

With a small exclamation, Corabell discarded the steaming napkin and marked the paper accordingly. She asked, "Ready to shave?" Patting the edge of the table, "Come, sit." Abo obeyed, taking the plate and cup with him. He breathed deeply, inhaling the steam from the fabric on his face. Corabell gathered the shaving tools and set them at his thigh.

He wondered, "What'll we do when my brother occupies the house as well?"

"I'll do twice the work with half the privacy, until Gerolf weds."

"Mhm." Abo worked up lather with the shaving brush.

Corabell considered the word "bucket", and with deliberate care wrote the first letter. She wondered how much help her husband would give her or whether he had aligned with his brother. She tested him by spelling the word. "B . . . U . . . K . . . I . . . T." Abo frowned. Unsure of the spelling, Corabell waited, the pencil poised in hand. Studying the word, she pondered how it she might spell it differently, before Abo guided her to a different vowel before the final "T." She would speak with Nola about the skill of spelling. Perhaps the girl would teach her some rules.

Though she needed to write several other words before Abo left, the vowels toyed with her understanding of their sounds. Corabell used an "O" instead of the letters "AU" in laundry and failed to include an "E" at the end of "line." She wrote the last word, "brush," entirely on her own, showing it to Abo for correction.

He smiled at her work and Corabell beamed. She put the pencil and paper aside and focused on her spouse, rinsing lather from his face. Combing the blond hair back behind his ears, Corabell secured it with a leather strap. Stepping away to assess her work, she smiled as Abo stared downwards at his alert penis. She pulled her shift over her head. Abo ran his hands over her breasts, and helped her up onto the table where she tentatively sat astride him.

Before leaving Abo recalled the food staples, reciting them aloud. He would pass the trading post after work. With a hand on the pocket where he kept the list, Abo assured her he would pass it to Gerolf.

In the garden, Corabell planted the seeds Abo purchased, and watered the earth mounds and sprouts daily. She washed clothing in piecemeal fashion, pulling wrinkles from the fabric, as they owned no sad irons. She kept the animals fed and content, though the piglet loathed the temporary sty and preferred to follow at her heels. Corabell had no market day; she owned no coins and Abo offered none. They had no oven; Corabell cooked corn bread in the iron skillet on the hearth.

After some days, Corabell prompted Abo to bring meat from the slaughterhouse as he had done at the Gottschalk's. "Otherwise," she told him, "I'll become thinner than when I met you in front of the cottonwood tree."

Abo paused at her words and turned to face her. Cupping her cheeks in his palms he replied, "I hope to fatten you."

The sincerity in his face made her eyes well with tears and she confided with downcast eyes, "I still lack my monthly flow."

Abo's brows shot high, "But when did your cycles cease?"

"In the winter. The widows and I ate through the stores of food. Spring being the thin season, we found little to eat. My womanly flow still hasn't returned." Embracing her, he kissed her tenderly before he left.

Corabell

Henry O'Shay delivered a load of lumber before Abo returned from work. Corabell peered out the front door, "What's all this for?" she asked while he stacked the planks alongside the door.

"Gerolf mentioned an outhouse, pigsty, garden fence and front porch."

Later that evening, Gerolf appeared carrying a washtub across one shoulder. The supplies she had listed shifted inside. Corabell thanked him with some reserve. He tipped his head in response. The list he had insisted on still roiled her.

The wood delivery surprised Corabell and motivated her to finish the mattress. She returned to the pines near the river, hauling home branches longer than she stood. Exuding the essence of pine, the needles would run in one direction beneath the canvas, forming a dense, tough pad. When Abo crafted a bed frame and wove a rope through alternate holes, the mattress would lie atop. It made no sense to hoist both cumbersome loads up onto the sleeping platform. They would claim a space to the side of the hearth, along the southern wall. Gerolf would take the sleeping platform away from sight, above their heads.

The imminent arrival of the younger brother put the couple on edge. The piglet wandered into the garden and upset a row of seedlings. Corabell scolded the animal and set it inside the crude pen, while amending the damage. She noticed the footprints of a large beast on one of her many trips to the well and it added to her apprehension.

Abo arrived home with a long sausage and two flagons. One held dark ale, the other hard cider. Soon the piquant aroma of cooking sausage filled the air. While asparagus boiled and honey-sweetened cornbread cooked in the skillet, Corabell tasted the ale and commented, "I think I prefer cider." Rather than stand and use the table, they perched on the door's threshold and ate dinner.

Abo used the very last illumination of the sky and Dietrich's shovel to continue digging the outhouse pit. By necessity, it had to be as far from the water source as possible. The well lay at the northern edge of the property, and Abo had begun excavating near the southwestern edge, beyond the garden, behind the cabin.

Beyond the newly planted vegetable rows, clods of earth landed beside the hole at regular intervals. Sometime during the week, the ditch had grown deep enough to hide her spouse from view. Using a makeshift ladder, he emerged from the hole and began stomping down the earth, flattening the surface.

Corabell peered into the abyss. Abo noted, "I'll plant a black alder tree nearby to keep the flies away." Corabell cocked her head and looked at him from the corner of her eye, and he smiled nodding. "At home, the tree towered over the outhouse. My grandmother made an ointment from the bark she used on chilblains."

Corabell frowned, "Chilblains are what?"

"Ach, you know the itchy welts you get from being too near the fire."

She nodded, "But have you seen this black alder tree growing in this land?"

"Nein, no. Not yet."

"Maybe this tree grows only in your old country, and our soil won't nourish it. It may never have a home here." Abo sank down beside her on the grass. She gazed at him in the darkness, his skin easily discernible, while the flesh of her arms lay hidden in shadow. "Elke brought her beets and you'll seek out this foreign tree, while soldiers push the Bodéwadmi and other clans farther from their homelands."

"Mhm but your father, a French trapper came from afar, as well. Would you prefer I return home?" Abo gave her a tentative smile.

Corabell paused before she shook her head no, and commented, "My people don't have that option." She sighed deeply and lifted Abo's head into her lap, unknotted the leather tie and released his blond hair. "At the Gottschalk house, it's bathing night," she reminded him. "Gerolf probably stayed for a hot bath, knowing he wouldn't get one here without a tub."

In the darkness, Corabell urged Abo to rise. He should bathe; she would wash and comb his hair in preparation for church. Abo moved slowly, the week's work making his limbs heavy. Corabell pulled the shovel up and held her husband's hand. As they walked to the house, she mentioned the footprints she had seen. Abo commented, "Hm, my brother'll help me build the sty and chicken coop."

The cold water made his body quiver, but Corabell would not relent. The soap had to come out, otherwise his hair would be sticky and impossible to comb. His golden head would not be dirty for church. The second bath of the night, he had no energy for it. "If I was at the Gottschalk's, I'd have beaten the dirt from my clothes and gone to bed."

"Yes, but you're not." Corabell combed his wet hair, pulled it away from his face and squeezed it dry.

They found their way to the loft cleaning their teeth with sticks of fennel. Soon after lying down, Abo curled against the warm body of the woman and slept.

When she woke, Corabell extricated herself from Abo's limbs and went directly to the well, taking the lavender soap and bucket with her. The first day of church without the Gottschalk's guidance, Corabell wanted her hair clean and pinned up. The morning dew wet her feet and ankles on the path she had made well trampled in the first days at the cabin. She saved her boots for the trek to church.

From the corner of her eye, she sensed movement. Turning quickly to see, she stopped to listen. When nothing shifted in the distance, she continued on. Wolves moved through her mind with memories of her dog. She made herself pour the icy water slowly over her head. Shuddering she ran the soap bar over her scalp. Pouring again, she rinsed the lather down the length of her hair. Throwing her shift on, she took up a freshly filled bucket and returned to the cabin, spotting a fresh paw print in the damp earth. Corabell quickened her pace, fearing the hens and pig had been devoured in the night.

The black and white feathered pullets pecked at the corners of their cages while the young rooster stood idle. The piglet began crying when it saw her. Corabell gathered a quantity of goosegrass for the young sow, opened the poultry cages and returned to start the fire. With the kettle on to boil, Corabell began combing her hair as she gazed out the open door. Across the field, she recognized the animal's gait. The tail flicked upwards with the familiar loping stride. She dashed outside, calling to him. The wolf dog lifted his head but turned away.

Rebuffed, Corabell returned indoors and took up combing again. Finding the white shirt and trousers Abo wore on Sundays, she hoped they were flat enough to keep the churchwomen from concluding they lacked an iron. Corabell feared they waited for her to fail so one might assume her position.

Preparing coffee, she glanced out the door seeking her animal companion. Combining ingredients for corn cakes, Corabell set the pan to heat. Abo rose. He poured coffee and grumbled about the lack of a chair. Naked in front of the open door, he gazed out and asked, "I heard you calling. You saw the tracks?"

Corabell nodded and patted the table, "Come and shave."

The day would be hot. Sweat rolled off her breast, and caught in the fabric along her waist, dampening her dress. She wrung the shaving cloth and handed it to Abo. Tilting his head up, he draped the cloth across the stubble on his cheeks and chin.

Her gaze shifted through the window facing east. Some distance away, the canine sat facing the cabin. Again, she called to him from the threshold and he watched her, immobile.

Abo lowered the cloth and saw the animal through the open door, "Before we leave, I'll bring in the piglet and chickens, though they'll make a mess."

"The wolf dog's been closer. I saw the tracks. He's not harmed the rooster or hens." Corabell checked the skillet, melted a dollop of pork fat and ladled in a scoop of batter.

Abo's neatly combed hair of the previous night swept in all directions. He submitted to the comb in Corabell's hand. Gazing appreciatively at his nakedness, she told him, "Grandmother would be pleased with my choice of husband."

Abo smiled gently and dressed. Corabell relented and helped corral the unhappy hens back into their cages. Abo caught the rooster. Before leaving, they confined the pig to a corner of the room with the table, setting the chicken cages nearby.

As music flowed from the church, they quickened their pace, joining Gerolf in the pew next to the Gottschalks. Corabell covered her head with her shawl when she glimpsed Dietrich's expression from the corner of her eye. She understood none of the words, yet appreciated the sacred essence of the ceremony. The gestures of the priest, with his upward stretched hands appealed to the Great Spirit she knew.

Without the bonnet to obscure her face, Corabell felt it rude to close her eyes. At first, she focused on the minister's motions, but Nola in the pew in front diverted her attention. With her brown hair pinned up under a straw bonnet, the girl clutched a mirror in her palm, which she held shoulder height and tilted, as if trying to locate something.

Settling into a stable position, Nola gazed steadily at the image in her cupped hand. Corabell watched as her sister Uta whispered a query, which Nola ignored. Uta feigned a reach for a hymnal and peered into the mirror. She rolled her eyes and looked behind at Gerolf, who sat focused on the minister, oblivious.

Eva eyed her daughters. The eldest sat motionless, captivated by something she clasped in her hand. Uta looked at her mother and shook her head in contempt. Spying the mirror, Eva gazed over her shoulder at Gerolf, Abo and Corabell. She flushed and jostled her daughter's arm, demanding the looking glass. Nola gripped the mirror to her heart before relinquishing it without a glance at her mother.

Corabell had seen enough. She closed her eyes and gave thanks for being at her husband's side, with food in her belly, a home with two fancy hens, a proud young rooster and a growing sow. They stood to sing a hymn Corabell had heard before and Abo ran his finger over the German lyrics. It was enough for her to try to learn English, but Abo's effort charmed her. The cleric spoke the closing phrases and they bowed their heads in final prayer as the attendants extinguished the candle flames and the minister opened the doors.

Gerolf gathered a sack from underneath the pew. Eva attempted to deflect Nola's advance toward Gerolf, but her daughter pulled her arm free and strode away undaunted, taking the forearm of the dark haired brother.

Widower Amsel approached with one child in tow and one asleep on his shoulder. He whispered loudly. Eva glanced at him and gave him a small smile. His deeply wrinkled shirt smelled strongly. A wild beard covered his cheeks and chin; his brown hair hung loose and his trousers draped loosely from his frame. He wore no hat. He bowed to Eva before speaking to Dietrich, "Sir, may I have a short audience with you?" Dietrich nodded to Elke and waited in front of the disheveled parishioner. "I'd like to introduce myself. I'm Amsel. A widower, you see." The wild father extended his hand to Dietrich who shook it, nodded and turned away.

Corabell glimpsed Gerolf waiting under the shade of a tree, Nola clinging to one arm. Eva approached, greeting them. For Eva, Gerolf dropped the sack. He bowed, took her hand and kissed it, while Nola tried to maintain contact with his moving limbs. Corabell turned her head, not caring to see the distress on the girl's face. Abo did not favor the drama either and hastened his brother along with a curt word.

Gerolf held Eva's hand briefly before he let go and caught up with them on the path to the cabin. Carrying the satchel across his shoulder he asked, "Bruder, what tasks do I begin?"

"I've just finished the hole for the outhouse. We're likely to catch something in it if we leave it unattended much longer," Abo noted.

Abo

Since announcing his intention to broaden Corabell's delicate figure, Abo visited the trading post nightly after work. On various days, he returned home bearing a bushel of potatoes, a basket of onions, a jug of cream or a pound of cheese. Lacking a pantry or root cellar, Corabell stored the food on the mantle above the hearth.

Abo called to her from across the plot, "Corabell! Bring the water bucket! She waved in reply. The men had stripped off their shirts, coats and hats. Corabell set the water pail on the grass and they passed it between themselves.

Four beams stood vertically in the soil. A pitched roof with birch bark shingles would top the privy. One side would have a door, the other a platform with a hole. Having purchased wood and nails from the lumberyard, they still used Dietrich's tools. They needed to buy their own. "Corabell you've less structure to your days than either of us. Elke usually goes downtown on market day; you should go with her and purchase the gear we need," Abo commented as he held a horizontal support that Gerolf nailed to the vertical corners.

"Do you know what to look for in a quality hammer, saw and screwdriver?" Gerolf asked and looked at her squarely.

Corabell shrugged, "I'll know if you tell me."

Abo pulled the hammer from his brother's hand, "Feel the weight of this. A good hammer'll have some weight and a handle that won't rip your hand. See the leather on this?" Corabell nodded and gave the tool back to Gerolf.

"I'll write you a list." Gerolf told her.

She stared back at him, swallowed and volunteered, "We need a hatchet." She started back to the house before turning to suggest, "And a shovel." Gerolf looked at his brother who met his eyes steadily.

As the smells of cooking food emanated from the house, Abo finished hanging the outhouse door. Gerolf left his brother and strode to the cabin bearing the saw, hammer, nails and unused lumber. Not long after, Abo heard the sounds of his brother's industry. When he entered, he saw Gerolf had knocked together a sturdy bench.

Gerolf ate his first meal in the cabin, sitting on a bench. While serving the pounded pork and slivers of potato and onion baked in cream, Corabell commented, "You work so capably, I hope you'll make another for my side of the table."

"Yes, surely. I needed somewhere to sit, you know." Gerolf glanced at Abo who stood, plate resting on the mantelpiece. "Come, there's enough room for two," Gerolf told Corabell and slid aside.

As Corabell ate dinner, she informed Gerolf, "There's no mattress up on the sleeping shelf. It took some days for the pine needles to fall from the drying branches that I used to stuff the mattress with." Gerolf nodded but made no comment. Corabell offered, "I'll make you a mattress like ours, if you purchase the canvas."

Gerolf turned to her, "Write me a list of what you'll need."

Abo saw his bride turn her eyes to her plate. He took his dish and wandered to the southern window, where he regarded the planks and posts for the garden fence. Turning to Corabell, Abo asked, "I have to gather birch bark for the outhouse roof, care to help me?"

He returned to serve himself more potatoes from the table and Corabell met his eyes, "Let me wash first. There's an area just north where a stand of trees grows to about so round," and she demonstrated the girth with her hands.

Abo hoisted his Corabell onto his shoulder, making her squeal and grab his neck. On the way to the birch trees, he held her buttocks, as she straddled his waist and he leaned her back against a maple tree and ran his tongue down the side of her neck to her breasts. The world wore him with irritants and fire smoldered within her. Given a chance, he would live there. Their time together passed too quickly. The sky darkened and they still had none of the bark they had come for. Abo followed his wife to the colony of trees and they filled a tablecloth with strips that peeled from the tree trunks. As she bent gathering bark, her backside beckoned. He took her again from behind. They arrived on the property as crickets chirped, and washed at the well before crossing the threshold.

In the diminishing light, Gerolf huffed at the lack of an oil lamp or candlelight. He pulled the clothing from his sack, waving his trousers in the air to ease the wrinkles. Giving up, he folded them over the rungs of the ladder to the sleeping platform. His shirts bore more creases and he groaned when he saw them. Looking to Corabell, some hope in his eyes, she told him, "Sorry but we've no iron." As darkness cast the interior in deeper shadow, Corabell undressed.

The first night they shared the cabin, Abo whispered to Corabell in bed, aware his brother lay overhead. He heard Gerolf turn and sigh before drifting to sleep.

Corabell

As Corabell walked barefoot on the trodden path to the well, she saw fresh paw prints and called, "Nemoshe!" Listening, she heard only the wind sigh over the grass. Corabell bathed and dressed, tying the leather corset laces to restrain her breasts. She headed back to the cottage with two pails of water lengthening each arm.

The water had begun to boil. She prepared coffee, while an animal's cry sailed on the air. The wail made her pause. She waited for another cry, but there was nothing more and she went to feed the animals.

The morning mound of goosegrass made the hens twitter and they tossed the stalks left and right. The piglet appeared satisfied with the greens and Corabell returned to the house as her husband rose with a full bladder. He gazed at the distance to the outhouse and pulled his penis from his drawers. Corabell directed him to the heap of drying weeds and organic debris explaining, "Urine helps the composting process, you might share the secret with your brother." Abo shook his head no. The larger of the two hens had laid her first egg. Corabell eagerly took it from the cage.

Her mind wandered, recalling the dark-skinned people who appeared up from the ground. They were Nate's people. She and Nate were alike, seemingly caught between two worlds.

Looking for the pencil on the mantel, she reviewed the sounds of the words she wanted to write. "Canvas" was not too hard to spell. She showed her list to Abo, whose smile confirmed the letters were correct.

Corabell made oatmeal. Abo ate warmed potatoes from the previous night. She tossed two cloths into the pot to heat for shaving and sat beside her husband on the newly made bench. When Gerolf finally stepped down the ladder, Corabell poured him coffee, passing the honey. She asked, "Would you like potatoes with cheese? The oats need more time to cook." He nodded and Corabell served him, passing a fork. Abo collected the shaving gear from the windowsill and went to use the outhouse.

She could do little else for breakfast. Corabell attended to her hair, brushing it back from her face, and into a tress she secured above her neck with Elke's pins. She felt Gerolf's eyes on her and withdrew to the mattress side before she recognized Abo's feet lumbering back from the latrine.

Stirring the oatmeal, Corabell asked, "Ready for hot cloths?"

"Ready," Abo replied.

"Yes, certainly." Gerolf retrieved his shaving equipment and sat on the bench beside his brother to share the bowl of steaming water.

Corabell plucked a cloth from the pot and held it aloft, as an animal's cry sounded again through the air. Her gaze darted to Abo, who remarked, "Sounds like the slaughterhouse." She had seen the wolf dog, sitting and gazing in her direction. "Frau. Don't be rash," Abo turned to her, "He knows you're here." His eyes met hers as he shaved under his jaw.

Corabell began the task of the day: washing. Soiled work clothes soaked in cold water to rid the fabric of blood. She offered a cup of the liquid to the piglet. Droplets of red sprayed along its pale snout as the animal lapped it up. She returned to the house to find that the oatmeal was finally soft enough to eat. Spooning oats onto a plate, she wound a stream of maple syrup on top and handed the portion to Abo.

Gerolf shaved his face carefully and commented, "I'll buy a mirror." Corabell pointed to an area he had missed along his jaw. He thanked her, amending his stroke pattern, and asked with shut eyes how it looked.

The brothers' faces were similar in shape: wide through the cheeks, broad brows and straight noses though Abo's blond hairline peaked downwards in a V-shape. Corabell scanned their features for whiskers they had missed. Gerolf opened his eyes and Corabell stepped back, feeling too close. He rinsed his face and asked, "Would you do my hair as well?" Corabell shook her head no, but offered him the brush.

Chapter Eleven

Corabell

She ran her hands behind the wolf dog's ears, thumped his shoulders and the pale flare across his chest asking, "What did you bring me? What of the widows?"

The animal freed the fur ball to her open palms and Corabell felt its heart pounding through its downy hide. Inspecting the small creature, she recalled how he had once brought her a rabbit and a mole. A span of white fur circled an eye. She recognized it was a pup and wondered what to feed it.

The sun mounting in the sky overhead reminded her of the wash. She would have preferred to work in the shade or near the river, but neither was close. Corabell drank, loosened the laces of her corset, pulled the dress over her head and knotted the slip up around her thighs.

When she finished scrubbing the second pair of trousers, she noticed Nemoshe again. He came straight to her, relinquishing the object in his mouth easily and left promptly afterwards. Unlike the first, no heartbeat hammered through its fur. She nudged the creature, feeling sick for it and set the small body inside the front door.

Resuming work, she pondered a suitable burial site. After emptying the vat of discolored water, she checked the living pup. Crouched upright in the crate where she had left it, its torso rose and fell with each breath. Corabell offered it a cloth sodden with bloody water, stroked its warm head and returned to the laundry.

Her slip stuck to her back, shoulders and breasts. When the soapy trousers gave off no hint of pink stain, Corabell poured another kettle of simmering water over them to let the suds seep from the fabric. She breathed a sigh of relief, knowing she had finished the hardest work of the day. Her empty belly ached and she went inside to find something to fill it.

The cold oatmeal had thickened in the three-legged pot. Scooping a portion for the piglet, she topped her own with preserves. As she sat eating in the doorway, Nemoshe trotted towards her across the grass.

Corabell feared the next pup would be dead like its sibling, but this one struggled, its white paws kicking as it dangled from the skin at its neck. It yelped when released into Corabell's lap. Without the bloody water or cream, she watered down a spoonful of oats, adding honey. With minor coaxing, the creature began sucking and licking. When the pup's belly had swelled and it nodded off, she laid it beside its littermate.

Corabell wrung the trousers one leg at a time, and then tossed the shirts in the basin. With the brush and soap cake, she began to scrub. Rinsing shirts required considerably less muscle, though she was grateful when Nemoshe nuzzled her back.

Corabell opened her hands to receive another furry figure. Its limbs sprawled haphazardly in her palms. The wolf dog nudged it and watched the stillness before moving away. Corabell placed the awkward form beside the dead sibling.

The sun had moved far across the sky before all the garments either swung in the wind from the clothesline or lay flattened, buttoned and stretched on the grass. Corabell went inside, mixed cornmeal with flour, salted it and worked in a dollop of pork fat and a bit of water. She fed the fire and set the skillet to warm slowly while she set out for the well, empty buckets in hand.

Nemoshe found her there, a pup balking under his clutch. The big male followed her to the cabin where she set the pails and lowered her palms. With a white blaze across the chest, the brown pup quieted when freed. Corabell searched for sustenance, deciding on a mashed corncake.

She dropped a dollop of pork fat onto the hot pan. It sizzled, melted and turned clear and she poured in an ample cup of the corn-wheat mixture. When bubbles covered the dough, she lifted the mass, turned it and cooked it slightly before transferring the patty to a plate. Eating half, Corabell softened the remainder with honey and water, and offered it to the pup. The creature tasted the mush on her finger and began lapping up the paste.

Nemoshe appeared at the open front door and dropped two more pups inside on the stones. The newly delivered ones were smaller. One furry, flattened body appeared trampled. The other failed to suckle on Corabell's finger and breathed intermittently, its ribcage rising and falling in an odd rhythm. She placed the dead pup with its mates and dipped a napkin in the corn mush to persuade the other to open its mouth. When the pup failed to eat, Corabell donned her corset and placed the small body against her skin in the pocket between her breasts and shift.

From where he sprawled in the sun, Nemoshe sat erect. His ears perked up and he growled. Corabell looked off to where the bending grass threw long shadows and surmised it must be the brothers. She took the wolf dog by the fur at his neck and showed him the crate where the three breathing pups slept. He came willingly, sniffing the small ones and the mattress, where Abo lay at night. She released her grasp and the animal left the cabin, but remained on the grounds outside.

When Corabell peered out the door again, she saw two familiar figures approaching from the south. She stoked the fire, stirred the grain and made several more patties.

The wolf dog sniffed and licked Abo's trousers while he embraced his sweaty, smiling wife. Her hands took in her spouse's fresh head, kissing him deeply. Though her breathing leapt, the scent of the slaughterhouse repelled her. Abo pulled back when he spotted the creature at her bosom.

Corabell motioned to the three pups in the box near the mattress, "The wolf dog brought them." She turned to the others lying in a row in the shadow of the door. "He brought them all, even the dead ones." She extricated the pup at her breast, noting the absence of a heartbeat and set it with those on the floor.

Abo set the burlap sack of meat and a basket of onions on the table. He squatted near the row of lifeless bodies and ran a finger over the furry back of one, "Ya, I'll dig a burial pit." He carried them against his belly. The wolf dog strolled away from the cabin and sat some distance from the door.

Abo called to Gerolf, who halted before the entry, "The wolf animal's a friend of Corabell's. Bruder, kommen, we need to dig a hole."

Gerolf set a large cut of canvas on the table, "I'd be grateful if you'd craft me a mattress similar to your own." Corabell stirred the contents in the pot and nodded. She felt his eyes watching her, lingering over her slip and she turned to the fire though sweat dampened the hair at her temples and neck. Abo motioned from outside the doorway, "Bitte, bruder!"

Returning, Abo threw a towel over his brother's shoulder and emptied the water pail into the kettle. They headed to wash at the well.

Corabell fried more dough to hold the men until the beef had cooked. Stacking the patties, she stepped outside to collect the dry clothing. The sun-starched cotton shirts she folded in half and slung over an arm, the trousers over the other. Inside, she draped them over the ladder rungs, passing the brothers who sat side by side, clad in cotton drawers, eating corn patties and drinking the last of the hard cider.

Corabell reappeared with more clothing over her arms. The wolf dog followed at her heels. The large male nudged the pups until they mewed and then licked their faces and heads. He allowed Corabell to rake her fingers through the thick fur behind his ears, before loping through the open door without a glance at the men watching from the table.

Gerolf stood and perused the stock of wood, cup in hand. Not long after, he was measuring and sawing wood for a second bench.

He asked Corabell, "Do you need more counter space? I could make something for you; say to the side of the hearth to aid in cooking."

"Oh yes, to this side here." Corabell waved a spoon in the span between the stones at the foot of the hearth and the logs of the cabin wall. Abo lounged by the flung open door.

Passing her spouse, with a battered basket on her arm, Corabell cut stalks of asparagus and a sizeable mound of goosegrass. She wanted greens. Grandmother had counseled village women to eat plant matter for a healthy baby and plentiful milk. Corabell tried not to think of pregnancy. Her monthly cycles had still not begun. They would return soon, she reassured herself. She had grown plumper; she knew by the fit of her corset. How could she be a wife to Abo without bearing his children?

Abo

Abo wanted the animal shelter far enough from the house to not smell the muck, but still close within the sphere of cabin safety. Gazing at the garden, trying to decide its location, he listened to Gerolf pounding sporadically inside.

Corabell worked her way back to him through rows of germinating plants. The beans had been first to produce shoots, thrusting pale green tendrils on sturdy stems, inching upwards each day. Abo looked down at her, "This garden and all your labors could easily be lost, torn through and eaten to the roots by deer, cows or pigs."

She volunteered, "I'll help you if you'd protect the area with a fence." Abo pulled her to him. Corabell leaned back and he wound his arms around her. He knew if his brother were absent, he and his wife would not be considering a garden enclosure.

Abo dipped his head to her neck and tasted the saltiness of her skin. Releasing Corabell, he called to his brother. Gerolf appeared, pushing strands of sweat-soaked hair behind an ear. "If you don't object, I mean to use the remaining posts to build a fence for the garden." Corabell returned to the house and hearth.

Corabell

Re-emerging from the cabin and grabbing a shovel, Corabell joined Abo, who directed her to the farthest corner, where the outermost post would lie. She threw her weight on the shovelhead, urging the sharp point into the ground. Her mind ran to Abo, whose own stiff tool sought her yielding flesh. When he came to inspect her progress, she pulled him away into the tallest grass.

The couple worked with new vigor. In time, two posts stood upright at the far corners of the rectangular plot. While Abo sawed the last post into two equal pieces, Corabell dug holes nearer to the cabin sides. When she finished the last one, she set the shovel against the cabin and dashed inside to check on dinner.

As she feared, the potatoes had absorbed the liquid entirely and begun to scorch the sides of the pot. Onion-infused vapor furled across her lashes, making her eyes water as she loosened the meat with the long handled fork. The onions released their outer sheaths to the hardened brown juice at the bottom. Gerolf loitered at her elbow.

A spark of self-consciousness slid through her when she smelled Abo's body on her own. A married woman should be perfectly acceptable smelling like her husband, she told herself. Corabell set the caldron squarely on the hearthstones leaving the lid askew and fork within. She turned to the door, though Gerolf's question made her pause.

"But where're you going?" Gerolf glared at her departing form.

Corabell smiled faintly at him and hurried out. She reappeared smelling of lavender soap, her frock damp at the neckline. Serving Gerolf a generous portion of roasted meat, onion and potato, she told him, "Until the garden begins to produce, these greens and asparagus'll be the only vegetables we have, unless you purchase something from the trading post."

The younger brother inhaled the steam rising from his plate and nodded. Corabell served herself and looked through the window for Abo. He set a post in the corner hole nearest the door and tamped down the dirt around its base. Neither brother remarked on the well-done nature of the roasted meal. They ate silently, having second helpings and finishing the meat.

A pup mewed and crawled over the side of the wooden crate, falling onto the stones. Moments passed before the mewing began anew, the white-footed pup wandering across the floor. Corabell stood, scooped it up, sought the others and cradled them in her lap at the table. Gerolf watched her intently, "What'll you do with the wolf pups?"

"Nurture them, of course."

"No! You think it's wise to shelter wild animals where you'll have children?"

Corabell met the brother's eyes, "Wild animals? The wolf dog was my companion! When the Great Spirit grants me babies, I'll protect them." Gerolf shook his head and looked away while Corabell sat speechless, and gazed from Abo to his brother.

Abo pushed his polished plate to the middle of the table, "I need to set a few more posts." The younger brother cleaned his plate with a chunk of potato, "I'll help you." They left Corabell to the dishes and the three hungry ones.

Before feeding the puppies, Corabell secured the spotted hens and rooster in their crates. The piglet gave her small grunts of satisfaction as it chewed the carbonized potato and onion she had scraped from the blackened pot bottom.

Corabell prepared a fresh cornmeal paste adding a discarded lump of beef fat and stirred it until the mixture thickened. Pulling it from the heat, she let it cool on the stones. After a time, she spooned the mixture onto a plate, thinned it with water and sat with the pups near the mattress where the sky darkened though the window.

The coffee-brown pup with the white blaze across its breast needed little prodding to eat. It waded into the mixture and lapped the mush, sending bits through the air. After some coaxing and encouragement, the two others understood the idea.

As she began washing at the basin on the table, Corabell watched the dark pup drift to sleep across the plate; the siblings dozed with their heads between their paws. She lifted them one at a time and cleaned their faces and feet, picking corn meal, burrs and grass seeds from their soft fur.

The boiling water failed to dislodge the burnt remains of dinner, but the heat made washing more pleasurable. After feeling Gerolf's disapproval, Corabell appreciated anything soothing. With the soapy liquid, she rubbed the sweat from her neck and underarms, then sat to clean her ankles and feet.

In the distance from the direction of the well, Corabell heard the tones of Gerolf's voice. Abo gave no reply. When Gerolf yowled loudly, exclaiming in German Corabell smiled. She stepped into Abo's work boots to empty the scum-filled water on the nearest plants in the garden. With a tooth stick in her mouth, she drew off her gown and stretched out upon the pine-filled mattress, pulling the box of pups closer to one side.

Corabell woke when two hands moved from her waist to the flesh of her thighs, parting her legs and playing against her with a taught erection. Abo bent over her and kissed her neck as he found her entrance. She gave thanks for her husband, for the darkness of night, and for the mattress she would not move from until dawn.

In July, the corn stalks pushed higher daily. When out seeking pine needles, Corabell collected acorns to feed the piglet. To avoid trouble, she left the pups barricaded in a corner with the table turned sideways and hoped they would not tip their water bowl.

Corabell made the second mattress without an ax. The process blistered her fingers, and made her impatient for tools. Her list of items to purchase had grown.

Elke and Corabell planned the excursion into town on the approaching Saturday afternoon. Dietrich opposed the two women traveling alone with so many coins and they had yet to resolve the shopping issue. They stood together watching families spill from the open door of the church. Elke confided to Corabell, "I'll ask Konrad to accompany us, he may need to make a trip to the city."

The Widower Amsel approached, his children in tow and dipped his head, "Frau Gottschalk, how're you this morning?"

Elke gave a slight curtsy, "Well, thank you, just seeking a suitable escort to accompany us on a mission to town."

"You've found your man, here before you, at your service."

Elke blushed abruptly and seized Corabell's arm, "Oh no, I'd thought I'd catch my son Konrad. No. I'm afraid I can't impose. With young ones to care for, surely you've more important things to do." Amsel wore his customary wrinkled shirt, worn coat and beaten hat and hung back when Dietrich approached.

Dietrich shook his head when Elke reported Amsel's offer. The rumpled father, holding one child over a shoulder and the other by the hand, drew closer, "Sir, I'd have the hand of the beautiful widow of your past son, but this isn't the time to speak of such things." He shifted the baby to his chest. "It'd please me to have a spell with adult company, and perhaps the women'll direct me to suitable behavior for a widower seeking to remarry." Dietrich wrinkled his brow and Eva, standing at his elbow, flushed when Amsel mentioned her.

As Dietrich faltered, Abo encouraged him, "I've instructed Corabell to buy the best quality tools, but I'd trust a farming man's opinion over hers." Corabell narrowed her eyes. Dietrich relented and agreed.

The following Saturday, the widower arrived at the cabin soon after the brothers left for the slaughterhouse. He drove the wagon up Center Street to fetch Elke. Waiting on the front porch wearing her russet colored bonnet, Elke waved when she saw the buggy approaching. Amsel had flattened his own misshapen hat down to his brow to avoid losing it to the wind.

The women sat beside the widower watching all they passed while the wagon creaked and jostled over uneven streets, creating a swirl of dust that swept out behind them. Those walking beside the road averted their faces to avoid temporarily blindness, though the fine soot of the street hailed over them nonetheless.

Widower Amsel helped Elke down from the wagon in front of Church's General Store and proposed she remain there while he and Corabell sought out the tools. After the purchase, they would store the heavy implements in the wagon and return to buy the rest of the items.

The widower picked out various tools, allowing Corabell to choose from the variety that he deemed the best quality for the money. She paid for the gear at the counter, drawing some interest from the store clerk as she pulled coins from the pocket of her dress.

At Church's, Corabell bought a copious quantity of inexpensive factory-made white cloth for sheets and underwear. For men's shirts, she found several yards of linen in bold, deep blue and picked a coarse linen remnant in a similar blue for herself.

The store sold high quality homespun cloth, purchased from enterprising women. Corabell felt the fabric, imagining the time spent creating a yard of the material. Not even her grandmother had made cloth; it was far easier to trade or purchase from the white man who usually carried a surplus.

While the trading post had only a whim of organization, Church's General Store was light, colorful and artfully decorated. One area of merchandise flowed into the next. Four bathtubs of different quality designated the bathing section. Metal mesh shelving hung suspended between the sides of a porcelain-coated tub. In its depressions lay small implements—brushes, scissors and pumices.

Spider-legged stands displayed a variety of towels in various hues and sizes, along with a variety of long-handled scrub brushes. An arrangement of shallow bathing bowls with matching pitchers in assorted sizes had been positioned on a low chest of drawers. Bars of J.B. Williams shaving soap sheathed in fine white paper lined the bottom of an open chest drawer. A sign advertised the local business of Charles Cleaver, his rectangular slabs of hand soap perfumed the surrounding air. Smelling several, Corabell chose bars with scents of birch, cedar wood and balsam fir.

The women wandered, remarking on the color of a horn spoon and design of a bread trough. A mahogany sideboard displayed redware cups by color. Corabell found coffee mugs near the fine English transferware plates, platters and tureens. Checking prices, she chose an ivory-colored, sturdy functional design and carried the matching bowls to the counter rather than walk with them. Before leaving the area, Elke hoisted up a single ten-pound sad iron and wondered aloud, "Corabell's it time you invest in a set of irons?"

Corabell distracted her, "Elke, look at the thickness of this feather bed! Wouldn't that be warm on a wintry night?"

Corabell set her shopping basket on the counter. She requested five pounds of dried beans, a pound of milled coffee, a tin of compressed tea pellets, a pound jug of honey and vial of salt.

Amsel wound his way through the domestic area. He picked up a cake of the laundry soap and headed to the counter, where the clerk arranged Corabell's purchases neatly within a wooden crate. The farmer suggested, "Perhaps a drink before we head back?" He set the crates of purchases in the back of the wagon and covered them with a worn tarp before offering an arm to each woman.

With noon approaching, they walked up the dusty street and stopped at the first public house. To catch a breeze off the lake, the proprietor had thrown all the windows wide. They found benches at a table that caught a cross breeze. Amsel requested three glasses of cider from the maid, who brought them a basket of the morning's biscuits, compliments of the house.

The widower smiled deeply, "What opinions have you on how best to win Widow Eva's hand?"

Elke adjusted the brim of her hat, "Speak with Dietrich directly, ask his permission to court the widow. Eva regards her father-in-law highly. Though my husband may seem crusty, he knows Eva'll either remarry, or sell her property and live with her parents in town."

Amsel choked on the dry biscuit and took a large swig from his glass. Elke recounted the drama at the wedding dinner, Gerolf's pledge to court the widow and Dietrich's response to the German boarder. She continued, "Eva's girls need a father. Young Nola's set her own heart on wedding Gerolf; the entire matter might be brought short with a marriage between the adults." The widower nodded silently and looked to Corabell, as did Elke.

Corabell nodded, "Marriage makes life happier for most. Life's daily work is too much for one, alone. My own mother married several times. Her first husband returned to his own country, the second died in sickness and the third in gunfire. When my mother passed, she was married to her fourth husband and had borne four children." Corabell looked into the blue eyes of the widower, "Eva might be content with you and your boys, but I'd act quickly . . . They're babes now, and'll easily accept a new parent."

They stepped out into the bright summer afternoon. Whirling through in sudden bursts, the wind carrying debris and sand hailed over their exposed skin. They clung together.

Elke brought her hat brim down against her cheeks. The widower squinted, clutching the hat to his head and Corabell covered herself with the shawl. Circling and whipping against them from a different angle, the wind flattened their clothing against their bodies, pelting them again with chaff. They huddled as they strode to the wagon. Upon reaching it, they rode northwesterly, away from the center of commerce, approaching fields with stands of trees, where homes became less frequent, thoroughfares increasingly overgrown, and lanes bore fewer markers or went unnamed.

As the wind changed again, rain fell in large pelting drops. Elke took the horse's reins and Amsel reached into the wagon's back and pulled up the heavy tarp. Though the covering helped protect them, it rested heavily on their heads. Their clothes were soon sodden from the blowing, shifting downpour.

Rain dripping from the brim of his mussed hat, Amsel offered Corabell his hand when she stepped down. He unveiled the contents beneath the tarp and passed her the crate of purchases. Shielding the box with her shawl, Corabell hailed Elke from the open door of the cabin. Amsel deposited the heavy tools at her feet. Retaking his bench seat, he waved a hand in farewell, bidding the horse move on.

Behind the sideways table, the pups barked heartily, carousing in their enclosed corner.

Chapter Twelve

Corabell

The brothers arrived home soaked, cold and hungry. Not amused by the pup's interest in his blood stained trousers, Gerolf swatted the brown-furred creature away. He stood to one side of the door and shed his outer clothes, leaving the heap. Abo added his trousers and shirt to the pile. Soaked and pungent, the mess beckoned to the pups. They pounced on the sopping clothes, assessed the stains and lowered their bellies as they licked.

Corabell uncovered the beef Abo brought home, noting wide streaks of fat and sinew. "Such poor quality meat . . . for a butcher to bring home."

Abo spoke over his shoulder, "It was destined for the river Frau, and free." A breeze blew through the slits between the timber walls. Intermittently, a squall brought a shower of fine rain along with it.

Corabell felt Gerolf's eyes watching her as she shifted between the hearth and the newly constructed countertop. She commented evenly, "Such meat'll only serve for stew. We can eat it with potatoes and onions, but it needs cooking for some time." She looked to Abo, "Those with root cellars have space for storage, and come home to smells of dinner bubbling in a pot." She handed Abo a mug of hot black tea with honey and offered Gerolf a cup. The men sipped quietly, their noses dipping into the rising steam.

The hot tea restored some life to Abo and he noticed the wooden crate on the righted table and the new tools on the floor. He rose and felt the grip of the handles and the weight of the metal. Testing the hammer, he banged in several wooden pegs that had come loose in the wall.

Gerolf and Corabell gave him hard looks while the clamor caused the pups to scuttle defensively into a corner, fur standing on end. Abo gazed out the window into the downpour, "Ach, mein Gott, I've left Dietrich's tools out in the rain."

To construct a root cellar, they would have to break through a wall. The choices were few. The garden lay to the south of the house, the hearth and new countertop took up most of the western wall. The window and door occupied the east side, leaving only the north wall of the house free. The coolest side with the least amount of sunlight, nothing directly encumbered the outside space. Abo stood in front of it, gazing at the stout logs that extended far above his head.

Corabell had used the corner to keep the pups, and two deposits of dung and urine filled depressions in the stone floor. Gerolf rose to join his brother as he assessed the wall and stepped in a fragrant mound that oozed between his toes. He exclaimed loudly in short Germanic syllables.

Corabell rushed to Gerolf, who hopped on one foot, nose wrinkled and lips pulled up in disgust. Bounding up and down, he landed squarely in second dung pile, lost his footing and threw both arms up. Falling heavily on the cold stone Gerolf swore.

Abo smirked. Corabell frowned at her spouse and offered a hand to her husband's brother. In a fury, he warded off her advancing aid, pitching her backwards over the bench.

Face blanching, Abo rushed to his wife's side. He threw her damp petticoat over her outstretched legs as she lay prostrate and wide-eyed. Abo helped Corabell to her feet and she glared at Gerolf and straightened her bodice.

On the floor Gerolf ranted, his foreign words thick and angry. Abo turned and sprang at him, bare feet landing beside his brother's head. He thrust his face just short of Gerolf's nose and growled a short comment as the younger sibling righted himself.

The dark-haired brother stalked from the cabin, leaving a trail of dog shit. He flung the door wide and walked into the pouring rain, his German tirade growing fainter. Corabell silently picked up the refuse and washed the spots from the floor. She gathered up the rag and pile of soiled clothing and threw the heap away from the entrance.

In time, Gerolf reappeared. He stood at the threshold naked, wiping dripping hair from his eyes, his underwear in hand shielding his groin. He scowled silently at his brother. Corabell turned and looked at him squarely, hands on her hips. She pulled the swath of fresh cotton from the crate and flung it open, presenting it to him. Without a word, he dropped the sodden drawers, took the fabric and wound it around himself. Retaking his seat, he shivered on the bench before the fire.

Abo

Having decided the appropriate site for the root cellar lay along the north wall, the brothers recruited slaughterhouse workers Nate and Thomas for construction. Henry volunteered to assist after delivering a fresh load of lumber.

The sawmill worker thought little of Abo's rudimentary design with cellar access down an outside stairway. Henry agreed though, the northern wall seemed the best location. He argued, "Your construction efforts'd bring greater benefit if you'd provide access and storage space to the cabin, with a pantry to the area above the cellar."

"We could use another room," Corabell agreed.

The men arrived early on a Sunday morning. To Dietrich's chagrin, the brothers missed church service. He softened when the brothers promised they would return his tools after construction.

Corabell stayed home to attend to the men. Emily accompanied her spouse, bringing a flagon of hard cider and a basket of green beans. To cool the flagon, Emily submersed it in the pail hanging at the well. As the men cut through the northern wall, the women grilled the beans, cooked sausage, and prepared potatoes with onions, fresh chive and dill.

When evening muted the daylight, the men beat the dirt from their clothes. Having hewn through the cabin wall, they excavated deeply into the soil and dug a rectangular pit that extended northwards an ample distance. Within the sunken space, they set supporting wall timbers regularly, topping them with square-cut beams that received the pantry flooring. The floorboards served as the cellar's ceiling and ran from the northern boundary to just short of the cabin wall, allowing space for interior stairs.

Henry fashioned a hinged access door that when pulled upwards from the pantry floor, revealed the way down to the cellar. He set planks horizontally for steps while the others framed the room, creating a pitched roof. Assessing their feat, Henry pointed to the pantry's tightly set wooden planks, "Most of the frame houses my father builds still have no flooring. The housewife spreads sand upon the floor, creating swirls or patterns. When enough refuse gathers, she sweeps out the floor and begins fresh."

Corabell nodded, "The homes in my village were all that way, but I prefer a solid floor." The brothers thanked their friends admitting they were in their debt.

Although the most demanding work was complete, details remained for Abo and Gerolf to finish. The roof lacked shingles and was prone to rot until it received a proper crown. A door would close off the pantry space from the main room, and both rooms needed shelving to make them fully functional.

The brothers worked on the finer details in the evenings and on weekends after church service. Gerolf took time for distractions. Abo excused him, enjoying his brother's absence by romping with his wife.

Abo and Gerolf hung the pantry door with brass hinges, completing it with a decorative brass knob, the first in the cabin. The scent of fresh wood lingered inside. Corabell collected birch bark and Abo secured the shingles on the roof of the addition.

Corabell
Vegetables matured and ripened. The pups began tussling. The sow grew more interested in rooting for grubs and the hens began laying eggs reliably. By August's middle, the garden yielded vegetables for most meals. Shadows lengthened through mid-September. Corabell noted the weaker, gentler sunlight.

The scent of the wind changed, and though days could still be hot and dry, nights grew cooler. When the wind whipped between the cabin's logs and blew out the candle's flame, Abo remarked, "We've got to work on the cabin walls." Gerolf lit the wick at the hearth while his brother cleared his throat, "After dinner, I'll take a shovel and find a vein of clay. I know it's there. I hit clay after working through a layer of drier loam, when digging the outhouse pit."

Abo softened the clay with water in a crate. Corabell contributed the box of ash aside the hearth and Abo mixed it into the pliant mud. The three began chinking the cabin's horizontal cracks with materials they found—dried leaves, straw, bark pieces and withered plant matter from the compost pile. With the dry, rigid material in place, they daubed on the yielding clay mix.

Gerolf
Smoothing the remaining clay on his fingers into the dried material, Gerolf gazed at Corabell. Her leather bodice fit snuggly, making her breasts rise, and though her waist still appeared narrow, her brown skirt splayed across her hips and buttocks. She noticed his attention and smiled. A glossy sheen covered her hair and eyelashes. Her cheeks seemed wider; the smooth caramel-colored skin of her arms and neck appeared succulent and ripe.

He cleared his throat, and Abo looked over at him. Gerolf held his brother's eye, "Bruder, I believe dein Frau is with child."

Abo looked at him sharply. "Huh!" Corabell uttered. Her forehead wrinkled and she cupped her breasts, confronting Gerolf admitting, "Yes, I'm larger . . . but then I'd been near starving when I came to this side of the river. If you don't approve of the flesh on my bones, you might avoid gazing my way."

"My pardon dear woman, you're mistaken. I approve highly of your more feminine form." Gerolf smiled easily. Abo clipped him lightly on the head as he strode past him. With a hand at her waist, Abo urged Corabell away with him.

Corabell

Heading to the well, Abo told her softly, "Corabell, unhand your bosom. This gesture excites me." She threw her hands away with a sharp exhale and huff.

Autumn despair surged mixing with anguish of the banished clan, the death of her grandmother, and separation from family and the widows. She worried the women had never made it to the tribe. Why else would the wolf dog reappear? He had plainly forsaken them.

Sorrow swept over her and spilled on the grass. She choked on her sobs. When Abo held her gently, Corabell gave up pretenses and cried. Her nose ran with her tears. With belly and chest heaving, she heard her own sadness and her mind quieted. Moving away from Abo's comfort, Corabell lowered the pail at the well. Winding the laden bucket up, she turned, hiding her remorse.

Corabell splashed water on her face, wetting the hair at her temples and soaking the material at the front of her dress. Without a petticoat, the fabric clung to her. Abo sat on the low ledge of the well and reached for her as her breathing settled and all that remained was an irregular hiccup spasm.

"Corabell, have you had your monthly flow?" Not responding, she looked away. Abo hung on to her waist and pulled her between his legs so that her bosom fell at his face. He inquired, "How do you feel? It's true, you've become rounder," he cupped the fabric covering her breasts. She smiled and ran her hands upward, behind his ears. Untying the laces of her bodice, he loosened the leather and unbuttoned the front of her dress, spreading it, bringing her breasts forward. He noted, "Your nipples have darkened and spread wide as saucers," Abo opened his mouth and sucked in her teat and the surrounding flesh.

Corabell shut her eyes. Moving his hands across the skirt at her buttocks, Abo pulled her forward. She smiled as the final spasm of crying left her. They settled low in the grass. With hands clenching her buttocks and steadying her rhythm, she slipped from pity to pleasure.

They returned to the cabin in darkness. Gerolf sat at the table near the hearth. A single candle lit the area dimly. He worked, carving with a hand knife. Gazing up at them, he scanned Corabell's features.

Abo noticed the glance and approached his brother deliberately, speaking in German. Gerolf rose slowly, so the two brothers stood nose to nose. Corabell shifted from foot to foot, knowing only the language of their bodies. German came off their tongues and neither backed away. Gerolf ran a finger over the corner of one eye and Abo responded with a hip thrust and a single syllable. Gerolf stared before the very limits of his lips turned up and he snickered. Abo kept his face icy, then relented and smiled faintly, shrugging. He stepped back. Taking a stalk of fennel from the mantelpiece, he began cleaning his teeth as Gerolf pulled out the bench and returned to his craftwork.

Chapter Thirteen

Corabell

Corabell broke eggs onto the mass of sliced potatoes and onions browning in the skillet. Gerolf handed her a slip of paper, "Read this list of words to me." Holding an eggshell, she gazed up at him, sighed and took it. He must have planned to ask her to read it; he had printed neatly, rather than use his loose natural script.

Corabell pronounced, "Dub, dab, daauub?" trying to make sense of the letters. She turned the eggs and potatoes and finally stood with the long fork in hand and spoke the strange word, "Daub." Gerolf smiled into the small mirror he balanced between knees while he shaved. Corabell frowned and served breakfast. "I don't know this word and you can't make things up!"

Abo chuckled, "Perhaps we should add to the list, a new bedroom for Gerolf."

Corabell set aside the empty skillet, took a sip of black coffee, and stood with a hand on her hip. She was not sure what Abo intended, but she was ready. She had heard Gerolf at night, his rhythmic motion reverberating down from the sleeping platform above. It coincided with the times Abo took her as she dozed. She felt the younger brother's activity related too closely with her own wifely obligation.

Abo took a long sip of water. He used his hands to draw in the air a woman in the last months of pregnancy. "Surely," he turned to his brother, "you'd like to be far from the sound of a wailing baby."

Corabell's face fell; her hand gripped the edge of the table. With flushing cheeks and thinning lips, she struggled to harness her fury. "Gyagwades ne?!" She screamed, hitting the table with her hand.

Through a wave of revulsion for the conduct of the white brothers, she spoke clearly, "May . . . be!" Corabell asserted louder than she had ever addressed either one. "Maybe" she restated, "I'm with child, and maybe . . . not."

The brothers exchanged flat stares. "If you speak of the baby before it moves inside me, I must leave. Your senseless, loose words threaten its life. Chipiyapos, the dark twin'll come and steal it away." Abo watched Corabell. Her volume dropped slightly, "Only after the child moves is it safe to speak of new life!"

Gerolf quickly wiped the lather from his face. "But where would you go?" Abo stared at them.

Corabell roared, "Anywhere!" and strode suddenly bending into Gerolf's face, "To the empty village!" Her arms flew up. "The Gottschalk home! Wherever no foolish talk fills the air."

"You'll go nowhere. There'll be no more talk of this," Abo stated and rose. Facing Corabell, his blue eyes calming, he clasped her shoulders, "We won't speak of this until it's safe. We won't provoke a dark spirit." Under his hands, her tension ebbed, allowing her to smile faintly.

The garden called to her. Apples hung heavy in the trees and each night deer, raccoons and other forest creatures liberated them. Birds pecked at the sweet fruit, taking minor snips from numerous apples and left them still hanging. Squirrels feasted and the wolf pups stalked them, chasing them madly until they found refuge in the branches beyond reach. Below the three stood vigil, scouting beneath the high branches, barking sporadically at any squirrel that dared stray from the uppermost limbs.

The rodents and yapping pups attracted birds of prey. Corabell noticed a pair of swallow-tailed kites gliding over the tips of pines farther away near the river. They circled closer, their long black forked tails weaving and diving.

Corabell gathered the best apples, filling the large washbasin. Only the finest fruit remained tasty when dried. Dragging the full tub to the house stoop, she sat in the shade and cut the cores free for the piglet, hens and rooster. The apples would dry in the sun on a string of twine, assuring a source of sweetness through the winter.

Out of Corabell's sight, the golden eagle hunted, spying the pups that raced after furtive squirrels. It descended, swooping over the branches of the apple trees, a dozen feet above the plump flesh below. Only when it dove, swift as a bolt of lightning, did she hear the terrified cries. With her knife in hand, she leapt up and darted through the garden side to the sounds of horror.

As she advanced, the huge bird released a raspy cry. With brown and black feathers flocked in purple iridescence, its wings spanned seven feet. Sharp and harsh, the bird's shriek met the pup's yelps.

It barely held the white-bibbed pup in its talons. Corabell ran at the bird. The wolf pup fought, its razor sharp teeth seizing the blue-gray beak that sought to pluck out an eye. The bird called again, releasing a talon. The pup flailed against the claw that held it, fell into the grass, and bounded away, fur on end.

The predator circled back over the garden and cabin, while Corabell stood with her knife in hand. The bird gazed down, its round brown eyes searching. Sailing overhead, it circled lower for prey. Currents of air rushed past her. Its yellow toes and black nails clutched the pup with white feet.

Corabell gasped and ran at the winged animal. The grass impeded her stride. Air swells from the beating wings sailed over her. The pup squealed, squirming and kicking furiously under the raptor's firm grasp.

Corabell shrieked wildly and the hunter responded with its own call. The thrashing pale-footed pup lifted higher, paws beating the air, cries growing ever fainter.

In the tall grass, Corabell stopped and stood panting as she watched the predator and prey gain elevation. The young animal released its bowels and bladder while the wind obscured its wails. The bird flew higher, calling strongly.

Corabell prayed for the white-socked pup; breathing into her cupped hands, she sent her breath into the air above her head. Turning, retracing her steps to the cabin, she spent the rest of the afternoon cutting and coring apples. Though her tears quit flowing, dirty smudges marked her cheeks where she had wiped them away.

Her forehead and eyes pounded. She yearned for the Neshnabek, the True People who would console her, tell her their stories of the great bird and determine what meaning the golden eagle held for her.

She carried the strings of apple slices out to the laundry line, and hung them loosely, spiraling them upon the taut rope. The sun's rays would dry the fruit and the breeze would keep most insects from landing. To dissuade flies, Corabell tied strips of cloth at various intervals between the slices. As the wind moved, the fabric fluttered above and below the apple segments.

Corabell called the pups. When they did not come and she failed to hear them, she began to search in familiar hiding places. Some time had passed since the attack. Their bellies would be urging them home.

She circled the cabin, making ever-larger circles around it. Her voice rang into the grass and across the vegetables in the garden, where she forbid the dogs play. Pangs of worry shot through her, and her tears began, altering the tone of her voice.

When Abo called to her, she turned homeward. From afar, she saw he held something at his chest. Hope quickened her pace. Perhaps he had the pups, though

Abo never held them; that would be unusual indeed. She trotted, wiping her flowing nose. Then she saw Gerolf come around the side of the house, carrying the shovel. All her fears spilled and she raced to see what had occurred.

Abo held the brown pup against his chest, its head buried in the armpit of the filthy shirt. The pup with white fur circling an eye lay flattened along his forearm, its body deeply traumatized, eyes open, blood leaking from its open mouth.

Corabell gasped and took the wounded pup in her arms. Cradling it against her torso, she hummed the death song she had sung for her grandmother. She walked with Abo to the spot north of the chimney where the brothers had buried the others, months ago.

Gerolf worked, digging a hole deep enough to discourage animals from unearthing the body. Corabell kissed the creature, smelling the scent of its soft fur. She set the limp dog in the ground and went to wash and prepare dinner, avoiding the brother's eyes.

Abo sat at the kitchen bench, the head of the brown pup still buried in the safety of his armpit. The smell of putrid clothing filled the warm room but Corabell made no complaint. She stoked the fire and added two new logs.

While she prepared dinner, Abo recounted, "Gerolf and I saw the dogs at the side of Center Street. The white-eyed pup shot into the street, racing to us, not heeding the on-coming carriage. The wheels and horse hooves trampled it lifeless." Corabell sniffed as her nose ran along with her soundless tears.

When Gerolf appeared back from the well, bare-chested and freshly clean, he sat on the bench and motioned for his brother to give him the brown sibling. He rubbed the grime from its fur and swaddled the animal in the damp towel he had used.

Corabell boiled the sausage in the same pot as the potatoes and onions. When the tubers had softened, she spooned the mixture over a bed of newly washed spinach that wilted under the heat. The three ate silently. The scent of food roused the remaining pup and Corabell fed him a piece of sausage cut up amid potato and cornbread.

Sated, Corabell took an apple and cut it in quarters. The men continued eating as Corabell provisioned them with more potatoes, onion and sausage. She swallowed a bite of apple and revealed in a hoarse voice, "The golden eagle swept low over the apple trees, found the pup with white socks and stole him away."

Confiding the incident brought new tears to her swollen eyes. Abo sought her hand and she moved away, heavy with shame for the care of Nemoshe's pups and feeling unworthy of consolation.

The change in weather came incrementally, every day bringing fresh signs of approaching autumn. The brothers worked with full bellies until the final illumination of the sky dimmed into shadows, daubing the areas of the southern cabin wall where Corabell had previously chinked.

Corabell washed the dishes. She brought the strands of apple into the cabin, noticing how the sun and air had browned the exteriors.

The pup with the white blaze on its breast curled up beside the mattress in the crate he had slept in with his littermates. After a few days of acute lethargy, the lone whelp regained some spirit. He walked without continually lying down, though he followed Corabell everywhere she went. The animal began to anticipate the arrival of Abo and Gerolf and waited for them at the end of the lane, on the corner at Center Street.

As summer came to an end and the trees turned colors, Corabell noted how her lower belly suddenly grew taut, revealing a mound between her pelvic bones. When Abo noticed her growing orb, he planted his large hands over it. "Surely," he confided, "this mound's new." Corabell smiled and whispered that perhaps Gerolf had been right.

Her desire for Abo did not abate, though her taste for him changed. When his flesh hit the opening of her uterus, she winced and wailed. When he repeatedly beat on her innards, Corabell cried out, waking Gerolf above them, who insulted his brother and pounded the floor with a boot. The wolf dog pup, sleeping on the floor at the foot of the bed, barked as Corabell swatted her husband's moving body. Abo quickly learned to work within the limits of decency and Corabell's body when he sought satisfaction.

When the first cold winds hit the cabin, the walls contained the warmth within. The animals had to wait a few more weeks until the brothers completed their shelter from the cold.

Corabell worked in the garden gathering herbs and tying them into swaths she hung from the cabin rafters when she could put off other chores. She dried basins full of apples and squash on bright days with the aid of the sun. When frost seemed certain to come, Corabell picked the last fruits from the trees and stored them in barrels below the house. Potatoes, turnips, carrots, beets, purple cauliflower, cabbage and spinach would be content for some time outside in the colder soil. She would pick the crops eventually and store them in the dirt floor of the cellar. In time, they would pucker losing moisture, but would maintain enough flavor to be suitable for stews and soups.

The maples turned shades of orange and red, and the cottonwoods turned creamy yellow. The leaves of the apple trees turned less glorious hues of mottled amber, russet and copper. As crisp days replaced the summer heat, the wolf pup stalked imaginary enemies, and then careened in circles around the cabin's perimeter.

Chapter Fourteen

Abo

The slaughterhouse of Archibald Clybourne ran on the efforts of a few skilled butchers and a dozen laborers. Adjunct industries promptly set up businesses nearby. The tannery bought hides. Pig fat became lard. The slaughterhouse sold it during cooler months when heat did not threaten to turn it rancid. Soap and candle makers bought suet, the hard fat surrounding kidneys. Clothing factories sought horns, hooves and teeth for buttons and certain long bones for women's corsets. The slaughterhouse retained a small fraction of intestines, blood and organ meats to use in making sausage.

The riverbanks accumulated piles of animal heads, their faces stuck in fearsome expressions. Coyotes, foxes and opossums made pathways through the pale grass to the edge of the waterway where they crunched through bones to get at frozen marrow. The water roiled about the parts stuck in its flow. Swarms of ravens, crows, herring gulls and black-backed gulls picked and brawled over available entrails. Bald eagles and red-tailed hawks were fewer, though they descended too to take an easy meal from the feast.

In winter's deepest days the banks froze and in extreme cold, the entire waterway solidified. On such occasions, the men of the slaughterhouse expelled refuse onto the icy surface, where blood and entrails quickly congealed. Mounded litter merged with snow and ice, awaiting the first thaw when viscera and errant parts would begin to decompose.

Old Gepperth, the head butcher, found less stressful work in a shop downtown, leaving the Bachmeier brothers and Nate as principal butchers. Slaughterhouse labor weighed heavily on Abo. The cries of animals awaiting death, their panicked eyes and the stink of fear ate at his spirit. He felt certain the details of the trade would horrify his wife.

By the final days of October, Corabell's round belly showed beneath her frock. In the pew beside Abo, she pulled her shawl past her eyes, so no one might guess her eyelids drooped, fluttered and shut. At home, mere moments after sitting comfortably, she drifted to sleep. Abo often found her bent over the table, head resting on an arm, an uncooked mound of dough in the skillet. She spent no time before the fire mending clothes. When the dishes were clean and stacked, she bathed, scraped her teeth and slipped into bed, leaving the brothers at the fire to talk of finding other vocations.

Corabell

Fatigue followed her through November. Laundry days were hardest. The men's soaked trousers were far too heavy to lift. Even when squeezing out one leg at a time, the effort made her belly contract and harden. Sitting to recuperate, Corabell nodded off, so she persisted struggling to rid the garments of blood, urine and liquid stool.

The chill made washing more of a challenge. Corabell boiled water continuously. Heat dissipated in the nippy air and the cold well water made her hands numb and clumsy. She scrubbed, hitching her skirt up to the lower ends of her corset to keep it dry. With the breeches stretched flat upon the dry grass, the shirts pulled free of wrinkles and fluttering from the laundry line, she finished the most grueling work of the day.

The scented memory of warm apple bread haunted Corabell. With two apples and a cup of the sour dough starter Elke had given her, she began preparing sweet bread. Coating the skillet with lard, she sliced the apples, offering the cores to the curious dog to chew. With the dough and fruit arranged in the skillet and the lid secure, she settled on the bed and closed her eyes.

Corabell woke to the sound of rain and the smell of baking apples. Hustling from the bed's warmth, throwing her shawl over her head, she ran into the growing evening dimness. Picking up the trousers, she tossed them inside. Freeing the last shirt from the line, she hurried back. Before attending to the damp laundry, Corabell peeled off her wet dress and petticoat and pulled on her deerskin breeches, boots and a woolen undershirt of Abo's. She slipped her corset back on and pulled the laces snugly. The corset bowed, accommodating her belly's expansion and supporting her heavier bosom. Corabell hung the trousers in the pantry, setting the waists on the shelves and pulling the wrinkles from the hanging legs.

The brothers appeared drenched. Corabell directed them back outside, requesting they disrobe and throw their garments over the clothing line, where the rain might shed some noxious filth. Assenting grudgingly, they moved to the northern side of the cabin, returning later in underwear and boots, hair darkened and slick to their scalps.

Corabell removed the skillet from the hearth. Her nose was correct; the loaf had browned lightly. She turned the skillet upside down onto a birch plate and Abo took her arm, "What're you wearing? Turn around." Gerolf watched Corabell spin in a circle. Abo directed several curt foreign words at him. The dark brother responded with a wave of his hand.

Corabell guessed her husband's thoughts, "I got wet in the rain, rescuing the wash," pointing to her wet, hanging dress. "We need a line that runs across the room, so the shirts can hang and dry." Abo glanced at his brother, who stood appraising Corabell's form and restated the curt expression, causing Gerolf to avert his eyes. Standing on a bench, Abo tossed a length of cable over a cross beam and fastened it to a joist on the opposing side. Corabell smiled faintly. A fresh wave of weariness washed over her, but she made tea and bid the brothers dress in something warm as the smell of cooking beef and onions melded with dough and apple.

Abo

In December, slaughterhouse work fell to a few hours every weekday morning. On his first free afternoon, Abo purchased provisions needed to plaster the interior walls, construct a wooden bed frame and build a wardrobe with interior drawers. He hauled the materials home on his shoulders over the subsequent week.

Gerolf set out to call on the Widow Eva. The weather remained damp and chilly. Frigid cold had still not swept south, down from across the Canadian plains. Corabell anticipated the arrival of bone-chilling days by hanging double layers of thick, homespun woolen fabric from a branch fixed atop each window. In the morning, she pulled the curtains back to let in the warming sunlight. Abo brought home a white oak barrel, normally used for wet contents—brined pork—but rejected due to a gash at the top. He intended to fill it with water, should the well freeze over in the coldest months.

Gerolf returned to the cabin in a bitterly black mood as light sent long shadows across winter-dormant grass. He would not speak or respond to Corabell's inquiry of Eva's girls, but set to chopping wood for the fire.

Corabell

The younger brother bought several cords of firewood from the lumber mill in early fall. Henry delivered a fraction of the order, needing a draft team to pull the rig. It took some time for the men to unload and stack the wood.

Overhearing their intermittent banter, Corabell learned the depth of Gerolf's fancy for Eva. It was not just the widow he hankered for, but the instant family he would acquire when he married her. Gerolf imagined the widow would be flattered by his attention. He knew Nola favored him, though having him as a parent might be difficult for her. The younger girls might even prefer the unkempt widower for the two playmates they would gain.

Corabell made bean soup with sausage, carrots and onions. The iron skillet on the hearth's railings held a baking loaf of sourdough cornbread. She listened to the steady thwack of the axe and the abrupt parting of logs, while the brown dog barked sporadically at Gerolf.

Abo drilled holes for rope in the bed frame that would support their mattress. Corabell worked at the fire, knitting a woolen sweater from sheep's wool she had found at the trading post. She admired the mottled gray wool for the natural lanolin and sheep scent the fiber retained. Elke had taught her a basic stitch, with her own needles. Working with the yarn, a trace of oil remained on her fingers. Getting to the end of a row, she set the work down and checked the bread.

Corabell ventured outdoors, "Gerolf!"

There was no reply and no sound of the dog. Abo shook his head at her concern, "He'll be in when he's hungry and his outlook more civil." They spoke quietly as they ate.

Not long after, Gerolf and the animal charged through the door, breathing heavily. Corabell served him soup and he sat for supper.

Gerolf could not contain the story. Ladling himself a second bowl he related, "I arrived on foot, finding the widower's harnessed horse outside. Amsel and a fellow I didn't recognize carried trunks to the waiting carriage. I inquired from Eva, 'What was the purpose of their visit?' She confided she's to marry the widower come the New Year."

Gerolf spoke slowly, seemingly listening to his words, "I asked Eva to delay her commitment, to let me court her. Surely, she'd see I'd be a better choice than that farmer. She shook her head at me. Told me I was far too young. Too young and inexperienced, she said. She wants to marry Amsel. They have losses in common. They need one another. She put her hand on my shoulder and told me, I don't need her as Amsel does, and I'm lucky it's so. I'm a handsome young man with a skill to earn a living," Gerolf sneered at his last words as he took a piece of bread and cleaned the remains from the sides of the bowl.

Abo listened without comment. Corabell thought how different men and women are, when a man can fill his belly heartily after an upset of the heart.

Gerolf took several breaths before he continued, "Nola had been listening. She came in, stood at her mother's side and announced she'd recently had a birthday." Gerolf looked to his brother, "She stands at her mother's shoulder and still lacks a bosom. She's a child!" He gazed into his bowl, shaking his head. "Nola announced she'd be available for courting and would proudly call me her husband. Eva supported the idea. How could she?" He flung his arm, the spoon in hand. Pointing the utensil at his brother, Gerolf jabbed it in the air as he spoke, "I called on her, not her girl."

Gerolf lowered the spoon, "Eva stood, her shapely body," his cheeks flushed, "next to the slightness of her daughter, and she listed Nola's talents: a wonderful sourdough bread, the finest of stitches, good with numbers and she'll make a capable mother." He shook his head, "Does Eva think me a fool? It appears she has no feeling for me."

Heavy with food and warmed by the fire, he recited the widow's words, "She wants to marry Amsel. Christmas approaches and my dreams've died."

Preparing to wash the dishes, Corabell positioned the basin on the table. Gerolf, sitting on the bench facing the hearth, looked to her abruptly and asked, "Corabell, do women find me attractive?"

Corabell smiled tipping her head, "Yes." Abo looked up from his work, gazing at his brother. Gerolf stood and began to pace.

Corabell considered her words, "There're several women who find the Bachmeier brothers pleasing. I know Bridgette fancies you Gerolf, and there's a woman at church who sweetens when Abo's near."

Abo met her eyes. Corabell nodded and continued, "Minister Schoenhofen's younger sister, Catharina Heck. Widowed in her far country, with two children, rumors say her husband drowned in a vat of pickles. On her brother's advice she came to these lands, hoping for a suitable spouse and new life."

Abo turned to his brother, who passed him as he paced, and commented, "Mm, perhaps there's another widow to consider." Gerolf stopped and gawked at his brother, and Abo said her name, "Catharina Heck."

"She's quite pretty," Corabell conceded, adding, "Her golden hair's a bit darker than Abo's."

"She has a pleasing smile." Abo added quietly.

Gerolf's eyebrow shot up. "But why does she smile upon a married man?"

"Perhaps," Corabell quipped, "you should ask her."

There was no denying or disguising her pregnancy. Corabell's dresses expanded across her hips. Her favorite dress of blue and cream stripes fit her former slender figure. To wear it again she would have to pluck out the stitches she made when she sought to impress Elke with her sewing ability. Instead, she wore the purple gown with repeating hyacinths to church. Abo especially liked it on her.

Corabell preferred her brown linen frock. When the temperature dipped, she wore her breeches underneath and felt honest.

"When do you think the baby will come?" Abo asked.

"Not too soon. I've seen bellies out to here." Corabell swept her hand out in front. "Mine's still a reasonable size."

With no beef until the cattle arrived in spring, and no gun for hunting, Abo asked Corabell to fashion several baskets to serve as traps. He showed her one he acquired from the trading post. It had a dome of thick, loosely woven mesh and a substantial rim with sufficient weight to thwart a bird's attempt to escape.

With little green material available for constructing baskets, Corabell agreed to see what fiber she could find, nearer the river. Pleased with the prospect of variety in their diet, she dressed warmly, wearing her breeches, boots and dress with layers of shifts underneath, her deerskin coat on top and shawl over her head.

The wan light of winter filtered dimly through the overcast sky, and Corabell set out westwards towards the river. The young wolf dog bounded side-to-side. Corabell hoped to find sweet grass. Though individual strands were thin, she could braid or twist them in bundles, creating a stronger fiber.

Before reaching the boggy edges of the river, she found American bittersweet covering a strand of young pines. The woody winding vine had dropped all foliage, revealing poisonous berries in shades of yellow to brilliant red. The vine would give under pressure and conform well to the demands of a basket. Corabell cut twelve strong strands, focusing on the more pliable ends. The dog smelled the cut branches and ambled ahead. Gathering the bundle up, she slung it over a shoulder and walked west to the river.

The pines along the riverbanks retained their needles; all other trees stretched denuded branches to the gray sky. Corabell crunched through damp leaves as the dog picked up his pace, holding his nose to the air while he trotted. Ahead of her, the animal caught a scent and disappeared farther up the bank. She heard raucous gulls farther south, where the slaughterhouse lay, and saw the birds circling. To the north, Corabell heard the dog barking and she stopped, listening. She knew that tone. The barking quieted.

Corabell trotted along the riverside path, calling the dog. Splashing ensued, and then yelping. Striding nearer, she saw something in the water, a wet mound. The animal gave it a tug. A small brown foot bobbed to the surface.

Corabell gasped and bounded into the shallows. She grabbed the sodden fabric and towed it to the bank. The face of the child rolled upwards. Corabell whooped, let go and fell backwards. The dog reared, barking. Cold water reached through her layers, icing her flesh before she heaved herself up.

Corabell shuddered, took a breath and hoisted the body from the river. The head fell loosely forwards, against her. She wrestled the wet weight into her arms, finally carrying it across her chest. Her mind ran to the child she had seen, appearing suddenly out of a hatch in the ground.

Near the trading post, Corabell considered what to do. The dead child needed a send-away, a prayer to drive its spirit along. The dog stayed close, leading the way along the animal trail to the cabin. Corabell felt river water stiffening to ice in her boots before her feet numbed. Her heart beat against her ribs as she pondered: I'm in trouble. The whites have slaves. Nate's helping them flee. Where does this put me? Will they uproot me? Make me live with my real people, away from my golden hair? We're married, with a paper. I learned to write, so I could sign . . . The white world, where Nemoshe brought his litter. Corabell pulled the body closer and hastened.

Abo was home. He had fed the fire; white smoke ran into the gray sky. Corabell rushed, ice solidifying her outer clothing, heat from exertion warming the fabric against her skin. She kicked at the door, and Abo opened.

His hair mostly loose from the band tenuously holding it back, he looked at her vacantly. Then his expression stirred. He set the hammer down and flew to take the child. Corabell stepped back, shaking her head. Her lips were purple-blue.

"No, No, the child's dead, cold dead. Will you help? He needs prayers. At the water's edge, the dog found him . . . freezing, alone." Corabell clasped the body closer as water drops fell from the tender fingers.

"Gerolf!" Abo called. His brother appeared at his elbow. Abo nudged him, "Bring Corabell inside. I'll take the child." Corabell let the body go reluctantly. She had found him; he was her responsibility.

Gerolf

Gerolf pulled the vines from her shoulder and led her to the hearth, wet skirts clinging to her legs. Corabell extended her hands to the fire as her clothing began to steam. Her hands went to her belly and she shuddered deeply.

Gerolf noted her blue lips and offered, "Let me take your boots." Corabell shifted to lift each foot. He pulled off the hardened leather, leaving Corabell standing in wet woolen hosiery. A violent shiver set her teeth chattering. Walking gingerly to her bed, she shed the wet deerskin coat and left damp footsteps on the stone floor. Jerking loose the corset, she fumbled with the buttons of her dress, stepped out of the garment, and then out of the leather breeches. Drawing the slips over her head, she dropped the woolen leggings and sodden panties, leaving her bare and blue. Corabell rifled through a stack of Abo's underwear searching for woolens as Gerolf gazed at her.

He knew it was wrong, his brother would pound him, but felt compelled to watch. When he glimpsed her skin, his eyes would not move. They lingered on the orb of her belly, her buttocks and her slight hips. Her breasts hung round and wide, the nipples deep purple turning slightly up.

Gerolf felt his brother's knuckles across his skull and he turned to face him, fearing Abo would darken his eye. "Out! Leave the house while my wife changes!" The dark brother quickly acquiesced, bowing his head as he grabbed his coat and shut the door.

Corabell

Abo stood with one hand on the windowsill fixing her with a red-faced stare. "Why shed your garb in front of my brother?" He demanded.

"I'm wet, cold . . . and need warm leggings," Corabell explained, in fierce truncated words. Groping for dry woolens, her belly contracted, abruptly revealing the curvature in her abdomen.

Abo noticed the sudden change and reached out, wary something was awry. His warm hands invited Corabell to lean into him, her mouth blue and teeth quaking spasmodically. Picking her up, noticing the dusky purple shade of her face, Abo set her on the bed where he enclosed her in his arms. She nestled into his warmth, placing her icy hands on the insides of his thighs, seeking his chest on her face and his flesh on hers.

The comfort of his body gave her heat and courage. She donned dry woolen hose and a dress, worked an old pair of Elke's clogs onto her feet and left the wet attire, taking a sheet outside to where Abo had laid the child. The earth rested, frozen. A pickaxe might get through it, but they lacked one. Corabell wound the sheet tightly around the small form while she hummed the death song.

"Should I fetch Nate?" Gerolf wondered.

"The dead are fine outside. There's work in the morning," Abo added, "There's no emergency."

Corabell knotted her final stitches, "Can you set the body to one side of the pantry roof? The Great Spirit'll see it and no coyote or wolf can reach it. Please speak with Nate; the child can't stay here."

The following day Gerolf reported to Corabell, "I urged Nate aside and conveyed the news. He agreed to pass by later and thanked me for the kindness we've given his folk. I told him you plucked the child from the river. What Nate'll do with the body, I didn't ask. The ground lies hard as rock."

Corabell learned of Christianity from the missionaries Mettawa allowed to stay in the village. Abo explained the Christmas celebration, "Like the three wise men from the East bearing gifts of frankincense, myrrh and gold for the baby Jesus, Christians bestow gifts on those they adore."

With gifts in mind, Corabell sought Elke's help in piecing together the sweater she had knitted. For those who washed daily, she crafted a soothing salve to heal the most chapped of hands. Corabell knew the wood of the ivy vine would stop itching, reduce swelling and soothe the pain of split knuckles. She would need to gather a mass of plants to transfer the subtle woody scent and active properties to the grease.

Abo left the cabin to check the trap. Gerolf went to visit the carpenter, Patrick O'Shay. Returning from the well, Corabell noticed Nate approaching quickly. The dead child lay bundled upon the pitched pantry roof.

Pulling the body from the roof, he balanced the frozen load, and scanned the distance he came from, "Have you told anyone?"

"The brothers."

"What part of de river did you find him?"

"The shallows, north of here."

"Why put de chile on de roof?"

Corabell bowed her head, "The Great Spirit needs to come for the boy; hidden away he won't be found and'll never find peace."

The brown of Nate's eyes flickered some comprehension. He took her hand, "I's grateful to ya, dere's no speaking of de shadow folk." Corabell nodded and Nate turned and strode away.

Gazing up into the cloudless blue sky, Corabell reckoned she had time to cut a fresh load of ivy. She called the dog, threw on her deerskin coat and draped the blue shawl around her head and neck.

In the crisp air, Corabell thought of the widowed sisters while she snipped the trailing stems. Had they reached the clan? With an abundant supply, Corabell slung the vines around her shoulders. She sent prayers for the widows as she walked, breathing into her cupped hands and extending that breath to the sky.

Returning to the cabin, she hailed Gerolf, who turned and offered her an arm. They walked in silence before he began to sing. Corabell smiled and he lifted an eyebrow in response, not breaking the tune.

She imagined this was no hymn. A courting song, she guessed, by the swagger and the tilt of the head. Still walking beside her, Gerolf freed her arm and dramatically spread his hands.

From across the field, Abo watched his face stony and tight. He met them halfway to the house, a young turkey in hand. When Gerolf glimpsed his brother's expression, he broke off the melody and strode into the cabin, taking the ladder to the sleeping space.

Abo attended to the bird with tight, thin lips. Sulking beside the table, it tore at Corabell. He must have been pleased; the trap had worked. When she ran her hand up the back of his neck, he yielded but said nothing. She failed to know how to comfort him. Fishing the turkey from the near boiling water, Abo began to pluck, releasing the feathers into a crate. When Corabell offered to do the work, he paid her no heed.

A pale plume escaped. Caught in an updraft, it floated in a current of rising heat. The white down descended in front of Corabell's face. She blew at it, watching her husband doing woman's work. With a glance at the sleeping platform and no sign of the brother, she took the turkey from her spouse, lifted a leg and straddled Abo's lap. Taking his face in her hands, Corabell opened her mouth, penetrating him with her tongue until he felt hard under her buttocks.

Chapter Fifteen

Corabell

On Christmas morning, Corabell slid from the bed's warmth onto the cold stone floor. The hand-stitched underwear felt as chilled as the fabric of her dress, though the thick woolen tights warmed quickly against her skin. She had made the leggings the way Grandmother taught her, using a single needle.

Wearing the leather bodice, shawl and boots, she moved soundlessly to the hearth to rouse the fire. The flames tempted her to stay. She threw on her deerskin coat and secured the shawl over her head and neck.

Members of the clan had bathed outside year-round, but she was clean from the night before. The German brothers were making her soft with their ways. She threw a handful of well water on her face and filled the buckets. The cold took her breath and her belly constricted into a tight barrel. She returned to the cabin where the fire sent a steady column of smoke through the chimney.

Gerolf purchased a large tin bathing tub and pulled it in front of the hearth on Saturday evenings. Corabell filled their largest vessels with water, though the tub was far larger than any quantity of water she could heat. At best, several inches steamed from its depths, the temperature cooling quickly. Throughout the week, they bathed beside the fire with water poured from the kettle.

The eve before Christmas day, Corabell sought to bathe and wash her hair after the men had done so. Abo brought home a flagon of hard cider, which they had all enjoyed. It was late, dark and cold and Abo did not ask his brother to leave.

Gerolf worked by the light of a dim oil lamp, constructing slides for the inner drawers of the wardrobe. He sat with his back to Corabell. Emptying the boiling kettle into the soapy water, Corabell shed her clothing and got in. She washed, relishing the heat warming her flesh. Soaping her hair, Corabell bid Abo, "Will you fetch me the pot on the fire? I need to rinse my hair." Abo poured according to her directions as she closed her eyes and murmured about the marvels of hot water.

With a towel, Corabell dried quickly and donned a shift and her deerskin coat. She sat by the fire combing her hair and worked a greasy pungent ointment onto her legs and belly. The heat of the fire caught the aroma of woody ivy and sent it throughout the cabin.

The hens adapted to shorter days and frequently laid no eggs. Inside the animal shelter, the fowl huddled, their feathers fluffed outwards as they perched on top of the pig's body. The sow nestled into the dry straw. She snored lightly, her breath vapor rising through the stalks. Awakened by the dog's bark and Corabell's presence, the animal stirred and skirted farther beneath the bedding. The hens ruffled their feathers and flew onto the perching rod, emitting small familiar noises as Corabell sprinkled feed below.

In her satchel, Corabell stowed the four lard tins she had cleaned and filled with her own skin ointment. They would be away from the cabin all day. She took the compost bucket with scraps, added a scoop of corn and some bacon grease, and returned to feed the pig.

Without gloves, her palm burnt on the pail's metal handle and her toes ached from the cold. She hurried back to the cabin and stood near the fire, rubbing her hands before making breakfast. When she turned the bacon with the long-handled fork, Abo rolled over in bed and inquired, "Coffee ready?" The water roiled in the kettle.

"Soon," she replied finding the container of milled coffee.

Abo dressed quickly, donning his German woolen underwear then his outer clothing. He wore the undyed sweater and the first pair of long socks Corabell had knit under Elke's directions and guidance.

Gerolf wore his usual Sunday best, having neither new socks nor sweater for the Christmas celebration. The dark brother smirked at Abo when he spied him wearing the sweater. Abo donned a necktie at his collar and a deep blue shirt beneath the sweater's bulk.

The three walked to church with Corabell in the middle taking their arms. "I once had a pair of buffalo pelt boots. They were given to my grandmother with me in mind. I wore those boots through winters until my toes grew cramped. Grandmother asked me to part with them for fear I'd never marry." Abo looked down at her, "We could go to town to look for boots."

Corabell smiled, envisaging the products the stores sold. She shook her head, no. She imagined a boot with no semblance to the Victorian woman's boot of the day, bearing multiple glass buttons requiring a special tool to fasten closed.

"Perhaps someone at the trading post knows where I might find a warm boot of hide and fur."

Abo gazed down at her, "We'll go together." She pulled him closer and agreed. Corabell coated all their footwear with tallow that offered some degree of waterproofing, but she had no remedy to render her deerskin boots warmer.

Abo adjusted the pack, which bore two brined geese for the Christmas table. Wary of confinement, the larger Canada goose had fought hard. Abo gutted the creature, and soaked the carcass in brine. Preparing the snow goose in the same manner, he noted the birds without feathers were considerably less impressive.

The white frame church blended into a gray sky and snow covered ground. The three stepped inside, scanning the entry. Pine boughs, branches of bittersweet and holly decorated the lintel and sides of the front door. Heavy incense melded with the smell of the fireplace. Young male assistants wore white robes with elaborate silver and gold embroidering. Metallic needlework adorned the altar's white cloth. Corabell noted the women's endeavors to enhance their hair and apparel. Finely embroidered woolen shawls draped over several shoulders. Ringlets bounced beneath fine hats, while jewels, feathers and furs embellished other attire.

Gerolf

Gerolf strode to the customary pew, unbuttoned his overcoat, and took off his hat. He genuflected and entered, glancing back at his brother and his sister-in-law. Elke welcomed them quietly. Dietrich nodded and smiled, bidding them all a Merry Christmas. Corabell returned the greeting and took her seat at Abo's side.

On the festive morning, Widower Amsel arrived carrying one pink-cheeked child, the second followed at his side, bundled in several colors of knit wear. The noses of both ran with green snot. Instead of sitting at the customary bench on the right side of the church, Amsel found the Gottschalk family and joined them, taking the seat beside Eva. Gerolf eyed the man in front of him wondering how Eva could prefer him.

Abo

The organ began to play and everyone stood to sing. Abo held the hymnal. Gerolf's voice rang in his ear as they sang a carol they had known since childhood. He thought of his parents in Germany and wished them good health, hoping they had received his letter. As the liturgy continued, Abo noted Corabell responded with the congregation to the minister's chanted verse. Her cheeks and the tip of her nose remained flushed from the cold; a northern Madonna, Abo reckoned. Warmed with contentment, he gave thanks with closed eyes.

Corabell

Sleep could not pull her away; the incense hung thick in the air and the finery of the parishioners drew her eyes again. The service retained a subtle mind altering aspect that none of the flock was immune to. The children in the pew in front gradually slumped onto each other, a parent or the bench railing. Amsel's babe in Eva's lap twirled a curl of her brown hair while small Romy leaned against her mother's shoulder. Uta's head lay against the back of the pew and Nola wrote in a small book as she stole glances back at Gerolf. Corabell reclined against the warmth of Abo's shoulder while sensation returned to her toes.

Those taking Holy Communion formed a line leading up to the altar where they knelt to receive the wafer and wine. The parade of people gave Corabell an opportunity to observe the fashions and footwear of the congregation.

Those who could afford woolen dresses donned them; those who could not wore their heaviest brocade with a multitude of petticoats beneath, though all wore flat thin slippers, wooden clogs or leather boots with sturdy heels. Only the youngest children wore soft boots in the style of moccasins. Not a soul donned an animal fur boot.

Returning to the pew after communion, Abo's eyes swept over the congregation as the fireplace logs settled in a large crunch. Sparks flew through the screening and an usher brought up a fresh piece of lumber.

Full of halleluiahs, the last hymn rose to fill the frame structure and seeped out through the drafts into the bitter winter morning. The sun, obscured by the overcast sky, lent only the slightest illumination to the day. Heavily bundled parishioners shuffled through the open doorway, wishing each other a Merry Christmas. They presented the minister modest parcels, containers of jam and rounds of waxed cheese.

Dietrich inevitably got involved in conversation. Elke knew her children waited. She dressed, preparing for the numbing cold. She and Dietrich had arrived with the horse and buggy, though Elke told Corabell on several occasions, "I'm not certain the carriage's better than walking; the wind's so cold, it frosts my eyelashes and near freezes my eyes."

Konrad and Beatriz swept Elke up and she patted Dietrich's shoulder as she left her spouse. He glanced at her as the children drew her away.

Abo shook the pastor's hand, and Corabell smiled while the elder praised her health. They bid him Merry Christmas and stepped into the biting chill. Outside, they waited pressed together for Gerolf and members of the Gottschalk family.

Abo asked Konrad to allow Corabell a space in the coach. Konrad nodded and Abo nudged her along with Beatriz, who put a gloved hand on Corabell's shoulder. They did not speak; the cold pressed the flesh on their faces, sending stinging needle pains through the skin.

In the buggy, sitting so close, Corabell felt every inhalation of the bodies beside her. Konrad tucked the buffalo pelt in around their shoulders. Warmth gathered quickly between the thickly clad forms, though the rushing wind sliced at exposed skin. The horse snorted and threw its weight against the harness and the wheels began to crunch over the frozen ground.

Gerolf

Gerolf tipped one shoulder, "Quick, Romy, jump on my shoulders. Hold on to my head . . . Not my ears! We'll beat them all home." Abo offered Uta a place on his back. She resisted, waving his offer away as she dipped her face and trod along with her mother. Abo offered Eva his arm, which she took. The group walked together as swiftly as they could, to be done with traveling and be within sitting distance of the hearth.

Corabell

Konrad's buggy arrived at the house first. Shortly after, Silas delivered Willa and their four young ones to the front porch. The children flung the door wide open, letting in a gale of cold air. Elke urged, "Children! Shut the door!"

Corabell unwound the shawl from her head and neck, and offered, "May I take your cover?" Willa ignored Corabell, though her daughter heeded her and quickly attended to her buttons. Elke assigned simple Fiza and Romy the task of tending the mulled hard cider while she added a handful of raisins, currents and several whole cloves.

"May I take your wrap?" Corabell asked. Elke smiled and kissed her cheek, thanking her. With tears in her eyes, Freda shed her coat and shared, "It's been over a year since I've had word of my husband." Corabell tipped her head in reply, adjusting the armload. Willa's baby sat on the floor, legs straight out in front, staring at the fire, seemingly unable to shift due to the clothing encumbering any movement. Corabell watched the child, wondering whether she dared disrobe her to some degree. She thought no and left with the garments over her arms.

Gerolf

Gerolf arrived with Romy high on his shoulders, her cheeks rosy and face frozen in a smile. She raised her arms grasping the lintel above the front door as Gerolf walked through the entrance. The sudden reduction in weight made him turn to see her hanging from the doorframe. He lunged to grab her as she giggled. Eva smiled at their antics, while Nola exclaimed, "Romy! No horseplay at Grandmother's house!"

Undaunted, Romy stuck her tongue out when her mother turned away. Abo leapt up the front porch stairs, carrying Uta over his shoulder, her feet tucked inside his overcoat. She had yielded, letting Abo carry her like a sack of flour. He entered the house and stood at the hearth holding the sobbing girl with numb toes.

Franz, Rudy and Rory followed closely behind Abo, kicking the door closed behind them and jostling for space in front of the crackling blaze. Those recently outside wore a mantel of frigid air. Stomping their frozen feet and stroking iced ears, they began to relax. Abo sat on the floor and eventually Uta sat beside him with her boots extended to receive the hearth's warmth.

After regaining his senses, Abo offered Corabell the bag with the geese. Before the three boys began to disrobe, Elke asked them to warm themselves and fetch more firewood.

Elke

Dietrich stood in his coat, close to the hearth where he turned slowly, letting the blaze warm him. Elke offered him a hot cup of cider and stood in front of him as he blew at it and took a sip, "The horses could've stayed in the barn, if I'd known I was going to drive an empty carriage home!"

"And how are the Nogly's?"

"They're expecting another grandchild, I gave them a ride. I had so much space!"

"Ach, you did a good thing. Merry Christmas mein Herr." Dietrich kissed her forehead.

The table extension accommodated many, and the women turned to assist Elke in dinner preparations. Corabell lit the candles she placed in saucers on the table and window ledges. It was past noon, and the daylight ebbed outside, the gray sky signaling snow.

Elke rinsed brine from the geese before stabbing the skin and filling the crevices with chopped onions, apples and sprigs of mugwort. She set the birds on a grate within a cast iron pot, covered the top, and stationed the vessel within the roaring heat. The turkey roasted, impaled on a spit to one side of the fireplace.

Corabell worked on the sideboard, washing and cutting potatoes. At her side, Eva worked lard into the salted flour for biscuits as Nola creamed sugar into butter for gingerbread men. Uta stood watching at her elbow. Romy sat on the floor beside the bundled baby. The infant slumped against the chair legs, her eyes partially closed as she dozed.

Gerolf

Emily and Henry appeared, vaguely distinguishable below their wraps. In their arms, they bore cranberry apple pies.

Directly before dinner, when platters and side dishes cluttered the table and Dietrich readied himself for the blessing a loud knock sounded at the front door. Gerolf answered.

He frowned and swallowed at the thoroughly bundled, uninvited guest with two babes before him. Silent, Amsel met his eyes, an infant in one arm, a side of smoked venison in the other, the elder child gripping the corner of a coat pocket. Dressed in an assortment of knitwear and animal pelts, the youngster at his side shuddered violently and cried, "Papa! My feet!"

Amsel's blue eyes went to his offspring. Gerolf stepped back, opened the door, and extended an arm to the warmer interior. He bid the man, "Merry Christmas, I'll see to the horse and buggy." The burly man stepped inside and stood before the hearth. Gerolf eyed Dietrich as he passed to retrieve his coat and the house fell quiet. Grandmother silenced the children, who were not as wise, with warning looks.

Dietrich rose from his accustomed chair in front of the flames. With a tight jaw, he extended his hand, "Welcome to my home, Merry Christmas." He shook the farmer's calloused hand and asked Eva, "Widow Gottschalk, come receive our guest and his children."

Eva wiped her hands as the widower unwound the garb from his small ones, making a pile of knitwear in the corner of the room. She gave the father a small smile and took his beaver skin hat.

People settled into their former tasks and tension dissipated like the cold that swept through the front door. Gerolf returned from the barn. Watching Amsel, his sentiment softened when he saw the farmer attending his children. Warming again, Gerolf wondered if Eva would have chosen Amsel if he had fathered no children, and then he sighed, shook his head and turned to the flames.

Elke

Before Elke served dinner, Dietrich stood at the head of the table and rapped on a water goblet. Silence spread and faces turned to his angular cheekbones as he declared, "Let's pray." He opened his hands as the German words flowed from him. A succession of, "Amens" followed, softer voices pronouncing the word seconds later.

Elke, Eva and Corabell rose to serve the poultry and venison. When every plate had a serving of meat, Emily made her way around the table with potatoes roasted in duck fat. Freda followed serving red cabbage. Konrad filled pewter cups with the amber lager he had made for the season. Nola offered a plate of warm biscuits to all.

Amsel crumbled a biscuit and cut morsels of goose for the baby, who sat in his lap. The older child perched on the bench beside him. Blond hair curled around the large head of the infant. The round face and large cheeks had no resemblance to the hairy, worn man. Wiping trails of green snot that ran from the older child's nose, Amsel tasted a forkful of dark meat, "Mm, I miss a woman's cooking."

Dietrich seized the moment for a toast. The tongues had returned to the table and people spoke amiably. He tapped on his water glass, commanding attention as he stood and raised his pewter cup. "The time's come," he cleared his voice, "to put away the concerns of the old year and focus on the New Year upon us. Among us are a widow and widower that will join their lives in marriage."

The youngest members looked at one another, lifting their eyebrows as they chewed. Eva put her fork down and glanced at the widower. Amsel looked at Dietrich when he was able and smiled. "Let's wish them the happiness of this world, and fortitude for the times that'll try their spirits. To Eva and the Widower

Amsel!" Dietrich held his cup up and everyone followed, even Gerolf, though his hand was lower and he kept silent.

Romy requested someone pass the biscuits. Fiza stood at her stepfather's request, and made her way around the table refilling beer steins, pouring a half-cup for her brother Franz. Konrad whispered in his wife's ear and she blushed before cutting into her dark turkey meat.

Konrad stood, raised his cup and gazed at his dark haired wife. "I've a happy announcement to share. My wife, Beatriz's with child. I wish to toast mein Frau, who grows more beautiful every day. To her health!" Konrad raised his cup to the ceiling and most drinking vessels hailed her. Elke congratulated her as Freda patted her shoulder.

Gerolf

Sitting on the bench beside Gerolf, Henry told him, "Three of my sisters've begun an enterprise baking for the town folk. They load their pies into the wagon and sell them at Church's Market on Saturday mornings. They convinced my father and me to build a larger oven onto the side of the house. We used layers of firebricks, Portland cement and sand to enclose the heat source and the chimney in a room that accommodates a large washing basin with piping from a cistern we constructed outside."

Gerolf listened as Henry talked, nodding his head as his mind wandered to his parents and the farm in the state of Baden-Wuerttemberg. Henry continued, "The oven keeps its temperature for hours, and puts out more heat than any hearth. 'Tis a wonderful thing to visit a truly warm room, though I doubt my sisters've thought of how it'll feel in July." Gerolf smiled, imagining shapely Bridgette O'Shay clad in a damp chemise.

The widower put the baby on the floor with the older child and turned to the dinner on his plate. He asked for biscuits, potatoes and more turkey. Konrad filled the man's stein with beer and the widower thanked him kindly.

Corabell

Corabell rose to use the outhouse. When she returned, the babe on the floor gave off a foul stink. Dietrich turned, "Thank you Corabell," as she took the child away.

"Sir, have you brought baby linens?" Corabell inquired quietly.

The grizzled man shrugged. Willa avoided Corabell's eyes when she handed her a fresh cloth. The baby's damp woolens smelled of ammonia, but before Corabell moved away, Dietrich told her, "Wait, Corabell. Stay."

Dietrich rose and spread his hands as he had done at the beginning of the meal. His expression had softened noticeably. His jaw slack and hands loose, he thanked God for the food and the health of the family. Dietrich retook his seat and asked, "Konrad, how much beer's left?" The eldest son poured the last of the beer while Fiza filled Willa's cup with hard cider. The family lingered, picking on the remaining food, while Emily cleared the plates, and Gerolf listened to Henry expound on the latest home innovation.

Corabell cleaned the baby's bottom, discovering the baby a boy. The skin of his buttocks, penis and scrotum was inflamed and red. She tied the edges of a fresh cloth, pulled on the blue woolen leggings, and set the soiled diaper outside the front door.

Returning to the bench, Corabell set the baby in her lap. Without the foul pants, the child exuded mold and worse. She held his small warm hands, noticed his long dirty fingernails and then scooted him to the edge of her lap, away from her body where he had settled. He balked, repeatedly tossing his head back. Wet heat soaked her thighs and she scanned the table for someone who might take him.

The widower glanced over at her, then rose and took his son. Holding the small one across his chest, he saw the dark damp circle on her skirt and told her, "Come, stand by the fire. There's no sense in trying to keep a baby clean, or dry." He turned to the warmth emitted by the flames, exposing his own urine-stained clothing. They stood while the wetness evaporated, emitting a rank stench. The widower commented quietly to her, "Five mouths, I'll soon have three more girl children. Five children to feed every day."

Corabell wondered if she heard him correctly. Meeting his eyes, she frowned and asked, "But what man doesn't want the largest possible family? True, they'll hunger like anything that lives, but they'll tend the garden and animals, sew and laugh and make a larger life for you." She did not wait for a reply. With her final syllable, she moved away, closer to the women, where she busied herself drying wet plates. Her brothers would have called the widower an English weasel.

Corabell commented softly to Emily, "I don't like this Amsel." Emily stared at her. Corabell leaned closer, "Eva shouldn't marry this one. He's stale and bent, too old for Eva. Better she marry young Gerolf."

"But Eva needs to marry. Her girls need a father. Her parents won't always give her the support she needs. Gerolf? He's a boy, still." Emily brought the dessert plates to the table and Corabell shook her head while she dried silverware.

Konrad's stepson, Franz, coated his bow and tuned his newly acquired but well-worn fiddle. He stepped away from the dining table and nearer to the younger women who washed dishes and utensils at a side table. There he began a slow melodic version of "Greensleeves," and the children who were not asleep drew closer.

Corabell sought the outhouse again. Without Abo's coat, her flesh stood on end. The reek of the baby remained with her. Trying to rid herself of the odor, she blew her nose. Inhaling the arctic air, cold bit her lungs, making her trot the last paces to the cabin.

Abo stood at the window. Corabell rushed into his radiant warmth. With his arms down her back disrupting the cold cloak over her, she felt his body harden. Yearning to be home and alone with him, a wave of sadness broke over her. Feeling she might cry, Corabell pulled Abo to the far cabin window, where fewer people would see them. "You ready to leave?" Corabell nodded, afraid if she spoke, her voice would waver.

Emily exclaimed, "Everyone must stay until all have sampled my pie."

Abo kissed her forehead, "We'll go soon, after pie." He led her back to the table bench. Elke filled mugs with warm eggnog. Emily sliced and Eva served the cranberry and apple pie, which silenced all who held a fork. The youngest among them drifted to sleep and those who sat at the table asked for seconds.

Corabell sat beside Abo; the widower on the opposite side and a few seats down from her. She felt compelled to gaze at him, noticing his hands and split dirty nails. He lacked several side teeth and those he retained were brown near the gums. Surely, Dietrich would not let Eva marry him.

Dietrich

Widower Amsel finished a second slice of pie and worked his fork back and forth over a dollop of thickened juice on the plate. Dietrich contemplated the unfamiliar parishioner and glanced at the older child lapping at the sticky saucer.

On Christmas Day, the man had neither shaved nor attended to the state of his fingernails. Dietrich chastised himself for not seeing the obvious; Amsel had little respect for the occasion. He thought himself a fool for praising the impending union with Eva, and then he admonished himself for judging the man by his appearance. Taking the mug of eggnog, Dietrich rose and ventured down the lengthy table to sit before the widower. Gerolf watched his growing interest in the unkempt church member.

Glancing at the head of the household intermittently, the grubby man secured the hair behind his ears and pushed himself back on the bench. He turned to Dietrich and gave him his full attention. "How long's it been since the wife of your babes passed on?" Dietrich waited for an answer, his tall stature slumped, the vertebrae of his bony back pressing through layers of clothing.

"The birth was in spring, she passed in birthing. Too much blood lost. I had the babe with no mother to suckle. But he drank goat milk and grows, though he pisses, pisses a river. But the older one uses the pot and totes water, too."

Dietrich looked over at the quiet child close to the fire. "How old's the eldest?" A strip of woolen knitting bound the head above the ears. Leggings ended at the knees, the sleeves at the elbows and the sweater strained to cross the torso.

"About three years now." The widower glanced down at the younger child at his feet and allowed his eyes to drift to the women who gathered behind Dietrich. Dietrich turned to see Emily and Corabell whispering in discussion. Speaking face to face, the outline of Corabell's ample belly was plain on her slight figure. Emily had always been a pleasure to behold.

Abo joined Dietrich on the bench; in turn, the widower fixed him with his blue eyes. He raised an index finger to Abo. "Take heed she doesn't leave you with the babe. Birthing's a hard business for some, and your woman's small, it won't be easy getting the head out. If she starts bleeding, best she take the babe along with her. Child rearing's not a man's job. It makes him small, small and hard, something I've become." He looked down at his plate with the confession.

Dietrich gazed into his mug. With an urgency to set things right, he cleared his throat and asserted, "Feeling the way you do about family, I'm reluctant to entrust my grandchildren to your keeping. Better they make their home with Elke and me."

"The girls are older. They'll be fine; they'll care for the babes, bring water, tend the animals, cook and clean. I've been in need. Eva and her girls'll solve many problems." He paused and added, "I could hardly put in a crop with the children at my heels. At last, I tied 'em both in a tree, up so high no wolf or coyote could get 'em. They stayed in that tree while I worked and returning to the cabin, we ate cold oatmeal for supper. Every day I tied 'em there, way up high until I finally got the field planted."

Dietrich sighed and gazed at Abo who shook his head. Then he exclaimed in a voice all could hear, "I'm afraid, Sir, I've misspoken. I cannot let you marry our Eva."

The women turned and moved silently to the table. Eva smoothed several loose hairs and set her hands on her hips. The widower frowned, bringing his thick eyebrows together, "I believe the widow's willing and in need of a man."

"I don't trust you with my kin. My granddaughters are learning to read, sew and bake. Though they're no longer babes, they'll try your patience and still need a father. You admit you've no calling for child rearing. I'll not pass my grandchildren to your care."

Eva came and sat at Amsel's side, her elbows pressing into the wooden table, "Father Dietrich, do you not see this man needs a woman to tend his little ones? To wash, mend clothes and sew fresh garments for the young ones?"

"Yah, this's so. He also needs to shave and bathe."

Eva took Dietrich's hand in her own and met his tired eyes as she explained, "He's broken like me." A tear ran down her cheek.

Dietrich sighed and withdrew his hand, "You may be broken Eva, but my granddaughters are young and healthy and I'll not have them growing in their womanly duties with Amsel as their guardian. The man hangs his own small ones in a tree. What'll he do when Nola sasses? They'll live with Elke and me, if you choose this man."

Amsel rose abruptly and withdrew his legs from beneath the bench. He patted Eva's back and moved away. Dietrich withdrew from the table, took his pipe and tobacco from the mantel and sat in his favorite chair in front of the fireplace, his eyes on the flickering light. Elke made her way to him and kissed his temple whispering, "Merry Christmas, my love." He took her hand and held it at his cheek as he stared into the flames.

Eva remained on the bench. Her head drooped. Corabell appeared with Amsel's hat and coat over an arm, and he addressed Eva in a loud voice, "Will you have me, Widow? I'll take you still, even without your pretty girl helpers. You may visit them on Sundays. It's Christmas, it'll be my gift to you. A generous man I am."

Aside the front door, Widower Amsel accepted his coat, scarf and animal pelt hat from Corabell without looking at her. He gazed at his offspring. The youngest lay sprawled on the warm floor near the hearth; the older sat with heavy eyelids. Amsel gestured to the door with his head. The elder child stood and scrambled through the scruffy pile of knitwear discarded in the corner of the room. "Your answer, good woman. What'll you say? Will you be mien Frau? If you agree, we'll visit the minister in the morning."

Eva pulled her feet out from under the table and bench and strode to her abashed children who gathered in Elke's embrace. With her gaze on the floorboards, she appealed to her mother-in-law, "Dearest Elke, please care for the children, as Rurik would've wanted." She strode to Dietrich's chair and knelt.

Eva addressed his feet, her arms limp at her sides. "Dietrich, there's no other way for me. Without Rurik, I'm nothing. I'm not a strong woman and they need me. The girls will behave, I trust. You'll see this's the better way." Eva rose. She walked to the bedroom and reappeared shortly after wearing her black coat, hat and shawl. The household watched her silently.

Amsel quickly lifted the child from the floor, and bound the fur around his head and torso while he startled in his sleep. He tied the scarf ends vigorously at the belly, so the rise and fall of breath were the only signs of life. The older one donned a small knit coat, and then wriggled into a thick woolen sweater that fell to the ground. Winding a fur hide around the shoulders, the child secured it with a scarf on top and the father pulled its ends tight.

Elke

Eva took the bundled baby from beneath Amsel's arm, and the child's hand. The man opened the back door and closed it forcefully after them. The three girls peered through the side window at their mother, who disappeared into the barn. Elke gathered beside them and spread her palm across Romy's forehead. She spoke softly, "Remember girls, they're babies without a mother. You're older with a mother, grandmother and several aunties."

"Momma?" Romy's panicked voice rang through the quiet home and she clutched her grandmother's arm. Nola set a hand upon her sister's shoulder. They watched the carriage emerge from the barn, their mother on the riding bench beside the man and his children.

Romy broke from her spot at the window. She threw the back door open and ran into the lane, Nola and Uta lengths behind her and Elke paces behind them. Moments before the carriage picked up speed, the girls gaped at their mother with the two other children, one on her lap and the other at her side. When the buggy turned away from them, Romy sprinted beside the moving cart yelling hard, "Momma! Momma! Mom . . . ma!"

Eva turned to her daughter as Romy's feet hit ice and she skidded. Her legs shot out behind her and her arms thrashed forward. She landed solidly on her belly, forcing the wind from her chest. Face down on the hard frozen ground, her hot tears met the ice. Sobs made breathing difficult and she gasped. Nola eased her sister up and held her hand and they strode back to the warm cabin, where everything had suddenly changed.

In the main room of the house, family and guests spoke quietly, bringing forth the gifts they had worked on in previous months. Beatriz opened the crate Konrad brought inside and handed boxes of homemade cookies to all. Elke had dyed and knit woolen sweaters for Willa's children. For Eva's girls she had dyed and crocheted woolen shawls. In evenings void of her spouse, Freda had sewn white linen aprons for the married women. Emily dispersed rounded loaves of raisin stollen to those present and Corabell passed tins of hand salve to Elke, Emily, Freda and Willa.

Nola presented her crocheted scarves for the men with a determined greeting of, "Merry Christmas." Her salutations to Henry and Abo were more subdued and when she offered the last scarf to Gerolf, her eyes teared. She wiped her cheeks with the backs of her hands, opened the folded rectangle and swung the scarf over Gerolf's head. He stooped to receive it and she whispered her greeting.

Gerolf set a hand on Nola's shoulder as she moved away, sniffling. He drew her close and held her. Nola's sobs muffled against his shirt. When her weeping failed to abate, Elke pulled her away into a bedroom and her younger sisters followed.

The girls shed their dresses and shoes, filling the hooks against the wall with their attire. Elke brought in two pillows and a feather comforter for the bed. Her granddaughters would stay with her.

Willa, Emily and Beatriz kissed Dietrich, bidding him farewell. The men shook his hand and pounded him on the back before turning for the door. The cold air seeped in with the exit of each couple and family, making the cabin's interior suddenly cool.

Corabell

Abo and Gerolf brought out their overcoats and dressed. Corabell fed the fire, replenished Dietrich's drink and thanked Freda for the apron. She donned her coat and hastily kissed Dietrich as Gerolf stepped outside.

The cold air settled her mind as she closed her eyes and clung to Abo's arm. They listened to the trees cracking along the lane as they walked. In the darkness, an owl called and a more distant bird responded.

Ahead, Gerolf sang. When she and Abo caught up with him he confided, "I misjudged Eva. The abrupt passing of Rurik sunk a hole through her heart that only two dirty children could fill. She doesn't want another man. Rurik filled those shoes and the small ones need her."

Abo patted his brother's back. Corabell pulled Abo's arm as she hastened her pace to a trot, telling him, "I'll lose my toes to the ice." Abo looked at her, gauging the extent of her suffering and picked her up. With a belly, she no longer bent as she used to. He cradled her in his arms, opening several buttons to allow her feet within his overcoat.

Inside the cabin, their breath made white streams while they worked to start a roaring fire. The dog followed Gerolf in and sat on the floor in front of the hearth. Corabell wondered, "Do you think Eva and Amsel'll be in church on Sunday morning?"

Gerolf nodded. Abo opened the bottle of spirits, "Yes, surely." The brothers sat on the bench before the flames and leaned back, their elbows on the table, pewter cups in hand. Corabell brought her shawl over and sat on it, leaning on the warm dog that smelled of straw.

When Corabell woke, the brothers had threaded cording through the holes of the bed frame. Breaking into guffaws every few minutes, they attempted to maneuver the stuffed padding onto the cables. Corabell rose and set her hands on her hips, watching them. They gazed over at her and grinned when she offered them her aid. Soon after, she lay in bed, elevated off the cold floor on a platform of taut rope.

Chapter Sixteen

Corabell

The temperature rose; clouds blew in and settled before they opened. By Sunday, snow lay at the height of her boot tops. She waited at the window beside the door for the brothers.

The walk to church took longer due to the snowfall, which turned ordinary trees into phantoms. Parishioners stomped excess snow from their boots and brushed it from their hems as they climbed the stairs to church. Damp and steamy inside, water darkened the floor planks.

Corabell loosened her shawl and followed Abo to their customary pew behind Eva's three girls. Dietrich must have warned them not to swivel in their seats seeking their mother. They sat facing forward holding hands. Corabell touched each of them and whispered a greeting as she passed. Abo quietly hailed Elke and Dietrich.

Eva appeared with one child on her hip, the other holding her hand. She took her customary pew urging the child at her side along so she could sit next to Romy, her youngest daughter.

Beneath their heavy cloaks, Amsel's scrubbed children wore clothing suited to the season. A black bonnet covered the blond curls of the young girl. She pulled her heavy chambray dress up around her knees when she sat. The boy, clad in a pinafore and dark leggings appeared heedless of the change in his attire.

When Amsel arrived with a cleanly shaven face, people stared, not recognizing him until he joined Eva and the children. Beneath a dark frock coat, he wore a pressed white shirt and gray tie. His wavy hair flecked with white, lay shorn against his skull, revealing his blue eyes while Eva's brown ones bore dark circles beneath them. Several strands of hair had fallen out from under her black velvet bonnet. Her emerald dress came from a time when she had worn colors.

Prior to beginning service, Minister Schoenhofen asked the newly wed couple to approach the altar. Amsel took Eva's hand as he stood and she strode with the babe on her hip. The minister asked them to face the congregation. "Please welcome this couple that God has brought together. May they grow in their appreciation for one another." They walked back to the pew amid applause and congratulations. Eva was smiling when the sermon began. As it wore on, her eyelids dropped and her chin sank to her chest.

Against the din of the German language, Corabell wondered about securing a pair of fur mukluks. How far would she have to go to find a shoemaker familiar with such footwear? The boots had been worn throughout her village. Her clan had been a mobile people, leaving for winter hunting grounds and visiting surrounding villages. Memories of her kin were a well of sadness. Corabell preferred to watch young Nola in the pew before her, taking furtive glances at Gerolf.

Winter wore slowly on. Corabell's belly swelled until the growing fetus changed the manner of her gait, throwing her feet outward. Moving became more laborious and she welcomed the brothers' shorter work hours. She could ask them to fetch water.

With half days of work at the slaughterhouse, the brother's clothing was less vile to wash. Most laundry hung in the pantry froze. Though Corabell avoided creating a laundry maze in the cabin's interior, they lacked another area warm enough to dry their garments when the temperature dipped to bitterly cold.

Elke confessed certain church women delighted in seeing Corabell's pregnant state from week to week. They whispered wagers on when the baby might come. Under her clothing, veins ran along the taut skin of her belly and breasts. The baby moved daily, pushing up against her insides. She felt the shifting position and when wearing only a slip, showed Abo the protrusion of an elbow or knee.

On a cold morning in April, Abo noted a change in Corabell's shape. He told her, "The baby's dropped low between your loins, making you the shape of a sweet pear, mien Frau. It shouldn't be long now."

For weeks, Corabell had been sewing small baby clothes. She held them aloft for admiration and even Gerolf thought them dear. Abo constructed a rocking cradle. Church members brought her other basics: rectangular swaths of thick cotton, small crocheted blankets, hats and a white baptismal gown. Corabell thanked them for their generosity and sought Elke's ear to confide her fears about delivering a child, "In my village the grandmothers assisted with births. I'd feel more at ease with you and Eva attending me."

Elke promised, "When Gerolf brings me the news, I'll come without delay. Ready yourself by boiling your linens and towels. Birthing can be a bloody process."

Eva

The morning rays softened the heaps of snow. Slush and puddles filled every pocket in the ground. They left church quickly so Uta could show her how well she was reading. Carrying the youngest child on her hip, Eva held the hand of the eldest while Romy followed closely behind. Uta opened the volume of rhymes and began reading in a loud voice so her mother, walking behind might hear.

On the higher ground beneath leafless cottonwoods, Nola explained she and Grandmother had begun sewing a summer dress. From her pocket, she pulled a square of blue cotton fabric, which her mother took in hand to feel the weave. "How do you fare, my girl? Have you had your monthly flow yet?" Eva gazed intently into her daughter's eyes as her cheeks flushed.

Nola's eyes met the earth, "No I've not."

"That's good. There's no rush to be a woman." She brushed her daughter's cheek.

Amid the cacophony of people hailing each other and the plodding gait of horses and buggies approaching and leaving, Corabell hurried across pools of melting snow to Eva and her children. Amsel sat several carriages behind in the queue waiting for passengers. When she got within hearing distance, Corabell explained herself plainly, "Dear Eva, might you assist Elke as I bear this child?"

Eva shifted and glanced at the wagons waiting in line. "Corabell, I'm sorry. "I hardly think I'll have the chance."

Corabell's face fell; her hand met her lips and she nodded. Nola stepped forward, "Mrs. Bachmeier, I'd gladly be of help."

Corabell's gray eyes darted from Eva to Nola. "If your grandfather allows it, you've my permission," Eva said and met Corabell's eyes, "I wish you a fast and easy labor. Goodbye, my dear ones." She kissed Nola's forehead, brushed Uta's cheek and squeezed Romy's hand. Eva turned and waved as her children raised their hands in reply.

Corabell

Corabell felt a hand on her arm. "Don't worry, Mrs. Bachmeier. Grandmother and I'll care for you."

Corabell smiled and kissed Nola's cheek and bid the girls, "Stay away from the carriage traffic."

Abo found her waiting beneath a tall yellow pine. She leaned with her back to the trunk, her eyes closed, as she had the day she crossed the river. When she failed to speak and simply clasped his forearm, he knew something bothered her. Gerolf followed his brother and silently offered Corabell his arm for support.

Abo used the stillness to voice his concerns, "Soon the spring cattle will arrive from Texas and we'll return to fulltime work. I don't want you alone when the birthing begins."

"In my village, those big with child spend nights in the women's hut, so if the baby begins its journey, the husband and other family members may continue to sleep. Grandmothers care for the women, assisting in birth, nursing and childcare. Village girls and mothers stay during their moon time too, when they say we grow closer to the Creator. The women on this side of the river are far too loose. So much earth lies between our homes."

Abo gazed down at her, "Would you prefer to spend the nights at the Gottschalk house?" Corabell glanced up at him. Gerolf motioned to the dark gray clouds behind them in the north, "Perhaps another snowfall will slow the herd's progress."

Chapter Seventeen

Corabell

The sky lightened as Corabell ventured into the remains of last year's garden. The elements had dispersed the plant fragments and humus left from autumn. A mat of organic debris stretched past the wooden fencing. The damp air smelled of rich leaf decay, a pungent sharp scent. Corabell had the urge to rake, but the spreading light across the eastern sky made her turn to the cabin to make coffee. The dog followed behind her.

Beginning breakfast, Corabell scooped oatmeal into the pot with a pinch of salt. Covering it, she set it at the back of the fire while slabs of bacon blistered in the skillet. She combined the ingredients for corn cakes, removed the bacon and dribbled in the batter. She ate the first pancake as Gerolf stirred and Abo passed behind her.

Abo stood near the garden, pissing into the compost pile as his brother came and stood beside him. Corabell paused as a contraction pulled across her flesh, then dribbled more of the mix into the fat. She paused again before checking on the oatmeal.

At times, life without her clan and village made her feel detached, like a drifting leaf. The sentiment grew with her expanding belly and pushed through weak spots, amplifying petty quarrels with Gerolf or Abo. Corabell imagined the brothers incapable of grasping her sorrow and did not clarify herself, feeling words a shadow of her emotions.

Another contraction worked over her. Lacking the woman's herbs and comfort of the Grandmother's hands, without a pipe to dull her pain, Corabell ached for the women that would sing, rub her skin with oil and measure their own past pain against hers.

Gerolf unveiled the pan of baked apples from the previous day and brought them to the table. He passed Corabell, one hand on her belly, her eyes on the floor. "Frau Corabell, how do you feel?" Abo paused for her reply, pulling on his trousers. The brothers stood awaiting her answer, their faces expectant. Corabell gazed at them and smiled. She exhaled softly, "I think the baby'll come today."

The men looked at each other and Gerolf offered, "Shall I fetch Elke?" Corabell nodded but waved him to the table, bidding him eat breakfast first. She lifted the pot from the back and stirred the oatmeal before she ladled it into bowls.

Abo

Having tended pregnant cows and horses, the brothers knew birthing could be drawn out and tiresome. Gerolf agreed to alert the Gottschalks on the way to work, convey the reason for Abo's absence, and stay late if necessary. He patted Corabell on the shoulder before embracing her lightly, "I hope to see you tonight with a baby at your bosom." He tipped his head to his brother.

Abo considered walking with Corabell. He knew movement eased the strain the mother bore. Air and sun might fill her mind with the coming spring and the vegetables she hoped to plant. After her morning chores, Corabell donned her coat and joined Abo outside.

The dog trotted ahead, his tail up, checking behind him from time to time. Abo took Corabell's arm and walked her pace. Along the path, they passed scattered pinecones, a bird's nest and a large fish. Claiming the fish, the dog looked around for the source of such fortune.

Drawing closer to the Gottschalk home, the couple came around the back of the house and found the women, two boys and three sisters tending the garden. Rudy emerged from the hencoop with a shovel laden with straw and chicken dung. He inhaled deeply. Chickens ambled in and out of the shelter he secured open with a large tree branch. Rudy shouted a greeting and returned inside.

Rory rolled the wheelbarrow to the space designated by the women, dumping the refuse in a pile. Uta spread the straw and manure with a shovel, tossing the waste to more remote corners. Freda worked back and forth across the fenced rectangle, creating rows by turning the soil under itself.

Most work halted when they heard Rudy's salute to the couple. They left their tools and tasks and gathered at the fence, where Corabell and Abo waited. Freda leaned her hoe against a post, as Elke descended the back steps, "Girls, mind your aunt while I'm away!" Elke adjusted the satchel across her torso, "Oh I'm happy to see you! Gerolf passed with the news. I've gotten distracted. I'm glad you've been walking, come let's get back to the cabin. Nola! We're leaving!"

The grandmother took Corabell's free arm while Nola leapt down the porch stairs and trailed behind. The slow sporadic pace induced Elke to urge Nola, "Go ahead, dear. Restore the fire and put the kettle on."

Arriving at Center Street, they paused and turned onto the path that took them past the cabin, not yet wide enough for three adults. Abo strode in the sodden brown grass, not loosening his grip on Corabell's arm. She moaned softly as she slumped forward, not able to continue. In the distance, he saw Nola had fed the cabin fire. A steady stream of smoke rose from the chimney. Corabell groaned and a gush of liquid hit the ground at her feet.

The sun was high in the sky by the time they reached the door. Nola had found the beans Corabell soaked overnight and set them to boil. The scent of food wafted through the windows.

Corabell

Abo took the buckets and left Corabell in Elke's care. Another constricting wave overtook her. She spread her feet and squatted down on her heels as she had seen them do in the women's hut. The tightening dug across her belly. Elke asked, "Nola, kettle's simmering? Found the linens? Good girl." Elke set her cloth bag of essentials near the fire. Corabell pushed herself up when the wave relented, unlaced her corset and unbuttoned her dress.

"Mint tea, Miss Corabell." Nola set the cup near her on the table.

"Mm, thank you." She took a sip before another surge forced her to bend across the table, moaning lightly. Fluid and blood dribbled onto the stones beneath her.

Elke urged her, "To bed. Come." Corabell looked at her neatly made bed with its fresh, unblemished sheets and shook her head no. She threw one leg across the table, and scooted onto the surface, bringing her other foot up with her boots still on.

Nola slackened the laces of Corabell's boots while Elke lifted her skirts and felt her rounded belly, noting the beginning of another contraction. Corabell moaned loudly and then asserted, "Elke, I must move, it's making my back throb." She dropped over the side of the table, squatting, as the squeezing encircled her lower body. Closing her eyes, she moaned.

"Throw me a dry cloth and toss the others in the pot." Elke covered the puddle on the floor and drew off Corabell's dress, leaving her in a shift and thick woolen socks. Elke directed Nola, "Two hot cloths. Use the tongs, there by the hearth." Nola picked an edge from the roiling, steaming water. Holding it, she allowed the steam to escape before daring to touch it with her fingertips. Elke took the cloth, rang out the water and draped it over the slip covering Corabell's round belly. Corabell sighed, the warmth easing some tension.

While another tightening wave worked across her, Corabell focused on inner forces and squatted, shutting her eyes. As it eased, she rested, cheek and chest on the table, buttocks and belly hanging momentarily suspended. Elke told her, "We should place a cloth between your legs to ease the skin back, and avoid tearing." Abo opened the door, two pails of water in tow. He poured the water into the barrel, eyeing his wife who smiled fleetingly, temple pressed to the table's surface.

"My back aches terribly, while my feet and backside freeze."

"Come closer to the hearth, you can rest on this." Elke took a rag rug, and flung it open on the floor in front of the fire. Corabell gazed at the space and nodded. She moved with splayed legs, one hand holding the warm cloth, the other holding the shift up around her thighs. Unsure how to settle once she stood on the rug, a wave hit, forcing her to hands and knees. She turned, one side facing the fire. The contraction pulled slowly over her belly and downwards. The hearth's warmth dulled some of the powerful ache.

When the grip weakened, Elke asked, "How're you faring?"

Corabell frowned, silent. Abo approached and drew several stray hairs away from her face. She jerked away and faced him, "Look at me now. Look at me, here! You! You should've told me to go back to my people and the widows." She turned away from him.

Elke extracted a bottle from the cloth bag, and pulled off the cork. She offered it to Corabell, cautioning, "Careful, it's strong medicine." Lifting the glass, Corabell took three large swallows. Opening her mouth, the liquid flamed as it descended. Abo turned the bottle up and took a large swallow as well. "Ya, things are moving along nicely," Elke reassured the blond husband, patting his shoulder and he left the cabin.

Elke called, "Nola? A fresh cloth." She lifted the shift, and reapplied a fresh compress to the expanding folds, "Tell me when you feel the urge to push." Corabell nodded and drank the tea Nola offered. Another contraction began and tightened hard as an iron drum. Corabell groaned and threw her weight backwards squatting as blood streamed down her thighs. The wave tightened further and

Corabell fought to breathe. Seeking air, she found panic and sought Elke with wary eyes.

"It'll pass. Don't worry and don't fight. Find a position that feels better." Corabell settled again on hands and knees. She gave Elke a half smile. "I'm going to work some ointment into the opening where the baby'll pass." Nola handed her the tin of salve.

"Nola, bed pot?" Nola swept it under her as Corabell rocked back, releasing her bowels. A gush of clear fluid dripped into the bowl.

Elke asked, "What do you feel?"

"Different. Full."

With one hand, Corabell felt the baby's head lodged between her vaginal walls. Another contraction fell and she eased backwards on hands and splayed knees, bearing down.

Elke placed a hot towel over the thinning band of flesh covering the baby's skull, urging, "Gentle, gentle." Working a dollop of grease around the opening, another contraction sent the baby butting against the yielding lip.

Corabell grunted. "Mm hm," Elke replied. Nola fished another cloth from the boiling water. Corabell moaned. Elke eased the skin ribbon aside as Corabell's effort and a contraction pushed the head through the narrow space into waiting hands. Holding either sides of the face, "I've got your baby," Elke assured her, "You're almost done."

Nola fanned another steaming towel through the air. When the steam eased, she wrung it and brought it to Elke, who knelt beside Corabell's knees.

Several breaths later, Corabell pushed through another contraction, bearing the head to the floor. Shoulders slithered through the constricted space carrying the torso along in the surge. Elke noticed Nola beside her and motioned the girl back to the boiling pot, taking the fresh cloth from her hands.

Working a cloth over the tender features Elke wiped the transparent goo and cheesy-white film from the nose, eyes and mouth. The arms and legs splayed outward, unfamiliar with the change in confinement. Corabell shifted and turned to greet her baby as Elke rubbed the flesh. The baby's scrotum hung like a small plum between the chubby legs. Wiping, Elke turned the skin pink from shades of mottled blue.

Corabell took a foot in hand and Nola grinned while she waved a fresh cloth through the air. The baby opened his eyes and mouth. Nola brought a fresh hot towel, and Elke placed it over Corabell's tissues. Cutting the veiny cord inches from the babe, Elke tightened and knotted a silk thread, cinching in the stub. She wound the baby in a dry towel and set him in Corabell's open arms. Closing her eyes, Corabell held the dear bundle as Abo opened the door.

He knelt on the stone floor admiring his sleepy son briefly, before Corabell frowned, moaned and sought Elke who shook her head, "It's not over quite yet. You still need to pass the afterbirth, but the hard part's done." Abo withdrew and Elke draped Corabell's shoulders with the woolen shawl.

Later, Nola set the table and served soup. Elke assisted Corabell into bed with padding beneath her leaking tissues. When the two women prepared to leave, Elke counseled Corabell how to nurse the child and warned her, "Many women give a child to a wet nurse for failing to suckle properly." For Elke, Corabell practiced the correct nursing technique and then showed the faulty method that would surely result in cracked nipples.

Elke sought Abo, "Herr Abo. No activity. None. Not until the bleeding ends. You may thank me when mother and son are healthy and healed in the month to come. If you carry water for your wife she'll heal faster, and if her milk fails to come in by the third day, you must send for me."

Corabell dozed with the baby in the crook of one arm, listening to Abo chop wood. Gerolf arrived in the dimness of evening. The brothers ate soup, speaking in hushed voices. When Corabell woke, she found the child at her side, the brothers sitting at the hearth and called, "Gerolf, come see the baby."

Abo approached, "Don't trouble yourself, go back to sleep." He took the warm bundle gingerly, holding the infant like a large hen. At the fireside, Abo showed his brother his new son.

When the infant began to fuss, he brought the bundle back to Corabell and kissed her forehead. She bared her breast allowing the child to suckle. The baby took the breast readily, but tired easily and nursed in spurts. Corabell felt a sudden wetness through the swaddled layers and realized he needed fresh linens. "Abo can you fill the kettle? I need to bathe and change our new one."

Beneath her, she felt the cool wetness of blood. Worrying it had seeped into the mattress; Corabell stood and threw the woolen blanket back to reveal the bloodied cloths. She folded them and tossed them into a corner, replacing them with fresh layers. Unwinding the child, his limbs moved in the air and he cried as

Corabell sang. Once clean, dry and tightly bundled, he drifted to sleep in the wooden cradle.

Corabell stepped awkwardly to the hearth. Between her legs, everything felt frayed, numb in places and sore. The wet slip clung to her backside and thighs, and she stood trying to decide what to do first. The men turned and fell silent at the sight of her.

Abo sprang up. He grabbed a cloth hanging from the line in front of the hearth, spread it over the bench and took Corabell's hand, leading her there. Gerolf took the buckets and set out for the well. Throwing Corabell's shawl over her bare shoulders, Abo brought the soap and poured hot water into the basin.

"Ahh thank you," she whispered. Abo pulled the bench closer to the hearth, kneeled and began washing her foot and ankle where blood had dried in rivulets. The water grew red with blood and soap scum. Abo threw the water out the door and poured several more inches from the simmering kettle and Corabell murmured approvingly at the transient heat.

As Abo washed, he shared what Gerolf had learned from the boss. The cattle had passed Sedalia, Missouri. By any reckoning, they would be near Streator, Illinois, averaging a distance of fifteen miles a day. The foreman needed three butchers working regular hours on Monday.

Abo began washing with two hands, his stiff erection visible through the trousers. Corabell listened for Gerolf. When she failed to hear his steps, she took Abo's heavy penis in her hands and worked him back and forth with the salve that smelled of vines.

Chapter Eighteen

Corabell

In the morning darkness, Corabell searched for her corset. The tight leather over her abdomen eased the cramps while the top laces held the weight of her swollen bust. Stoking the fire, she added logs, put on the kettle and picked up the baby. Settling on the bench, she wished for more comfortable furniture and for the child to drain some breast fluid.

Nursing evoked a tingling sensation that spread rapidly upward, bringing the first milk into her breasts and making them rock hard under pressure. Liquid sprayed freely through each nipple. The infant choked on the forceful stream that blew through the thin shift onto the floor, where the dog lapped at it. Corabell brought the coughing baby to one shoulder. Acute thirst compelled her to rise and pour herself water.

Settling once more, Grandmother's song came to mind. Corabell rocked on the bench to the tune she hummed. Giving the child the breast again, he sucked freely, easing the fullness before stiffening to move his bowels and drift back to sleep.

Corabell wore her leggings with deerskin breeches on top to secure the cotton pads while she continued to bleed. Feeling quite sure Dietrich would frown at the attire, she gave thanks that he lived some distance away. What to wear to Sunday service was not something she was ready to consider. Abo suggested she could miss several weekends to allow for a full recovery.

As Elke had instructed, Abo brought water and filled the barrel by the hearth whenever he was present. Gerolf toted buckets as well, though he thought of it less often.

Spring planting preoccupied Corabell, though snows had occurred as late as the last week in April. While cool weather delayed the sowing of seed, Corabell gazed at her baby boy and bathed, wrapped and nursed him.

When she could no longer deny the season's change, Corabell began work in the garden. She kept the cradle nearby to hear the child when he fussed. The dog circled, smelling the small one in the wooden bed.

In the animal shelter, Corabell scraped dung from the shelving and floor, shoveling the waste to the open door. Tempting the sow out of her accustomed corner with wheels of dried apple, Corabell shoveled out the muck. Once out of the shelter, the swine basked in the sun. Shovel by shovel, Corabell brought out the droppings, spreading them in the garden and to its farthest ends.

When fussing turned to crying and the dog rose to sit beside the low bed, Corabell jabbed the spade in the earth and scooped up the baby. Wailing, his face flushed deep pink. He recognized his mother had rescued him and rooted for milk. Her solid bosom bore substantial weight since the last feeding. Corabell leaned against the open door frame and offered the child the fuller side. As her milk let down, the other breast spurted and soaked the gown. She gave thanks for the ample supply.

Producing milk, waking in the night to the crying baby and performing daily chores left Corabell drained. Hunger assailed her when it had previously crept up quietly.

Abo

Abo woke reluctantly in the morning after rousing in the dark hours to the wailing infant and Corabell's keen attempts to quiet him. Burying his head in the bedding, he hoped to drown out the persistent cries. On fortunate though fewer nights, Corabell rose before the babe and fed him silently before returning him to the cradle. If Gerolf woke, he might begin a soft lullaby in the foreign tongue, until his voice became breathy and slow, eventually breaking off as sleep resumed. Gerolf frequently slept through the worst of the baby's outrages. He often woke first, restored the fire and began preparing morning coffee.

May began and Gerolf accommodated the sleep disruption by retiring earlier. Abo's eyes wore dark shadows. During work breaks, he dozed outside leaning against the slaughterhouse wall.

Demand for beef grew and the butchers worked fast to meet the foreman's daily quota. Extra cowhands assisted in preparation for butchering; they killed the animals quickly and hung them to bleed.

Lassoed at the neck, the cowboy brought the animal down, tying it on the ground with rope. With a heavy blow across the brow, the workhand usually knocked the creature unconscious. A deep slash through the throat began the bleeding process. Not a day passed when a bull reluctant to take his last breath, required several men to take its life.

The shout for help startled Abo. He woke, facing the pale May sun, his back against the sidewall. Turning to the outside pens, he jogged through the aisles of stalls holding the day's cattle allotment. Muddy from urine and dung, Abo's boots sunk in the mire.

The voice came again, urgent. He ran faster, knowing the tone of a man in trouble. The younger cowboy, Ardus stood in the pen. Conroy lay still in the muck, hat gone. Pale hair stretched across his eyes and nose. An open mouth exposed his teeth.

"Grab Conroy!"

Abo recognized the smell of fear. Clearing the top fence rail, he hit the sludge solidly. The boot's splat riveted the eyes of the thick-necked bull. Ardus stood by, lasso in hand. Abo dove to the old cowman. Heaving the body from the mud, creamy white contents from the flattened forehead spilled into the slop. Abo dragged Conroy to the fence. Deftly skirting Ardus, the bull charged forward, lowering its horns.

At the pen fence, those reaching for the muddied man felt the impact of the massive head butt, heard the sudden splitting of skin, popping of bone and exclamation, "Uhh! Mein Gott!" Abo landed hard in the adjacent stall. Men ran to his aid.

Gerolf

"Gerolf! Gerolf! Your brother's down!"

Gerolf appeared, sprinting, thoughts tumbling through his head. Eyes wide, scanning the pens before vaulting the rail, he fell at his brother's side.

Abo lay, eyes open and wary. Face contorting in a grimace with each wheezing inhalation, he explored the sunken contour of his torso with both hands.

Abo's upper thigh pumped out blood before Gerolf knew to tie it off. He swept a rag from his apron under the bloody groin and pulled, jostling the torn limb.

"Verdammnis, Brudder!" Abo flailed, knocking Gerolf into the mud.

"Jesus!" The red stain moved across the canvas trousers and up to the waist. "Be still!" Gerolf bellowed.

Abo's face grew as pale as the whites of his eyes. Blinking repeatedly, foamy red spittle formed on his lips and he whispered, "Care for mein Frau."

"Nate!" Gerolf screamed, "The wagon!" and knotted the rag above the gushing wound. In back of the building, the hired men tossed pork barrels from the wagon onto the May grass. Abo's blood seeped through the trouser fabric and joined the red pool from the morning kill.

The men carried Abo as he howled and then fell silent and limp. Blood ran from his seat and ankle. They set Abo on the table across from Conroy, boots thick with muck hung off the edge. Gerolf stood, hands tucked beneath his brother's armpits as the foreman strode in to assess the workers.

The top of Conroy's skull pooled with blood in the cavity where the animal had stomped. The straight nose remained unscathed, though the mouth hung open, exposing his tongue. The foreman took a crumpled kerchief, shook it and released it over Conroy's flattened forehead. Moving beside Abo, the dented chest rose and fell, the remaining life wheezing in and out, "Ach. Bachmeier. Go! Take the wagon; haul him home to the wife."

Gerolf motioned for Ardus to grab the legs and they carried the body out to where Nate sat ready on the carriage bench, reins in hand. Laying Abo on the planks behind the seat, Gerolf leapt in and took his brother's blond head in his lap. Nate urged the horses to action. The wooden wheels hit several bumps. Gerolf tightened his hold on his brother, releasing one hand to grip the wagon side. He bowed low, sobbing.

Corabell

Corabell turned to watch the approaching wagon. Standing with feet in the earth, the shift hitched up to dirty knees and the baby in the sling across her bosom, her eyes took in Nate's expression and the way he gazed across the garden. Gerolf's dark head in the back caused her breath to freeze. Her stomach fell. She drew closer to the wagon as she wished it away.

Nate pulled the reins on the horse, the cart in line with the door. The man jumped from the bench and strode to the back. Gerolf rose, carrying Abo's upper body. Nate took both legs, leaving a slick of thick warm blood on the wood. All air left her lungs at the sight of her husband and his limp limbs. Gerolf headed to the table, shoved it close to the hearth, knocking aside a pile of baby linens.

Corabell hovered near the door. One hand covered her mouth, the other guarded the bundle in the sling. Moving forward, she felt Abo's brow, picked up his cool hand and laid it on the table. The wet red stain drew her to the trousers and the torn area where the bull's horn met a vessel. She swept her earth-covered fingers through the warm thickening blood and drew them across her forehead. The men looked on silently.

Nate turned away. He found the water barrel and filled a cup. Corabell stood by her husband, one hand on his chest, "He breathes still." The wet inhalations came fast. She looked to one man and then the other. Both shook their heads no.

She knew otherwise. Throwing a blanket over the torso, Corabell tucked it below the wide shoulders, noting Abo's blue lips. Taking off the mud coated boots; she left them outside where Nate and Gerolf spoke in low voices. The baby stirred in the pouch. Corabell sat on the bench to one side of Abo and offered the child a breast. Moments after her milk let down, the other nipple opened in a spray.

Holding the child tightly, Corabell crept over Abo's head and lowered the full breast to his mouth. Like the infant, he rooted to her nipple. Corabell gasped at the strong hold he took as Gerolf entered the dim cabin light. He saw Corabell bent over his brother and uttered, "I'm going to fetch the pastor, Nate's going to summon Dietrich and Elke and then return the horse and . . . buggy."

Words fell away. Gerolf watched his brother suckling at his wife's teat. Abo's cheeks pulled inwards, swallowing rhythmically. Gerolf's jaw dropped and he turned to Nate, who came to stand by his side.

Corabell's eyes assaulted the men, "He will not leave me." With clenched lips, Corabell shut her eyes and adjusted the awkward position over her two males.

Chapter Nineteen

Gerolf

Minister Schoenhofen and Elke rode on the bench. Gerolf sat alone in back, as Dietrich directed the horse to the cabin's door. No smoke came from the chimney; no baking scents lingered in the air. The sky darkened as the visitors dropped from the carriage and strode to the door.

Gerolf harbored an awkward anxiety about Abo's wife, having last seen his brother nursing at her teat. He leapt for the door, circumventing Dietrich whose hand reached for the latch. Bending his head in deference, Gerolf excused himself, begging a moment to ensure Corabell knew guests awaited.

Hurrying into the dark interior, his toe struck the bench and he pitched forward, "Versifft!" Abo's pale feet extended from the end of the table. Dim light illuminated the white skin of the face. He saw little else, though he heard the child nursing and smelled the soiled cloth. Gerolf skirted the table and stirred the gray-coated embers, finding the glowing coals, which he blew on and fed kindling to, until a blaze lit the hearth.

The light flickered onto the table where Corabell lay, the corset loose around her waist with the rolled down shift, the baby content between the parents. Her cheek pressed against the pearly skin of Abo's armpit. One loose hand draped across Abo's chest, her tapered fingers at ease. Gerolf hated to wake her and bring her back to the awful truth.

Dietrich entered and stood inside the door, his eyes adjusting to the depth of darkness. Gerolf loosened the shawl from his brother and swung it over Corabell as the minister strode forward and kicked the bench end into the table. The surface lurched, the man groaned and Corabell woke with a sharp breath intake. The baby struggled to maintain a hold on the breast while the mother swept him up, attempting to cover herself with the shawl. She moved quickly into the shadows, returning to the window light to search for buttonholes and rungs in her bodice.

Gerolf could not gauge her state of mind. He turned to the guests, "Please, my brother's here."

The chaplain swept a hand over Abo in the sign of the cross and began a German supplication. Elke and Dietrich stood by while Gerolf hung back. Setting two more logs on the fire, he lingered at his brother's feet.

Corabell washed the baby in the darkness, across the room, humming softly to the child. She carried the soiled water in the bedpan behind the visitors and returned, not regarding those that stood near the body. Silently making her way between visitors, she jerked the table away from the hearth.

Corabell
Filling the kettle with water, she placed it on the fire. The dry blood across her brow itched. Loose hair strands fell at her cheeks and her swollen gray eyes smarted. She took flour and worked in a hunk of lard and salt for biscuits, then took the candle to the steps down into the cellar.

Carrying a basket, Corabell reemerged. Tears wet her wide cheeks and fell into the hot grease where onions softened. She coated potato slices in fat, arranged carrots and sausage in the skillet, then added water and quickly secured the lid. The three standing prayed, while Gerolf paced and the scent of cooking food began to permeate the cabin.

With prayers complete, Dietrich turned to Gerolf and spoke in German. Corabell looked up, her eyes shifting between the men.

She sprang up, shaking her head. "No! You'll not take him!" Corabell clenched the trousers, meeting Dietrich and the minister with feral eyes, "No! You won't!" When no one uttered a word in opposition, Corabell withdrew, "Take him in the morning . . . after I've washed him."

Dietrich tipped his head. Corabell watched the creases at the edge of his eyes deepen while he asked, "May we lift the body from the table to dine?"

"But the floor's so cold," she objected. Gerolf nodded, his own tears falling as he held his brother's weight. Dietrich took the legs and they set him on the stones aside the door.

Corabell checked the biscuits and removed them. Dunking a cloth into a boiling pot, she picked it out with a fork and dropped it onto the blood soaked table.

Corabell served dinner as Elke set hot biscuits on a plate. The minister said a brief prayer and thanked Corabell for the meal. She fumbled with a biscuit and drank, not meeting his eyes.

Elke recounted, "The first day you ate at my table, you were hungry, a thin waif. Your eyes grew at the food on your plate. You couldn't hide your joy. Though you've no appetite; you must eat for your child and milk."

Corabell faced Elke with wet cheeks. She sighed deeply, wiped her eyes and chewed the food mechanically. Only the biscuit and the water went down easily.

Dietrich agreed to deliver Abo's body to the church cemetery before he was due at the slaughterhouse office. Minister Schoenhofen asked Gerolf, "Would you like to buy a casket, or have a funeral ceremony for your brother?" Gerolf gazed at him with dull eyes and the minister told him, "I'll announce the passing in Sunday service."

Gerolf's eyebrow rose and he nodded, "Thank you. Some words honoring my brother will suffice." The visitors left after the meal.

When the cadence of the horse and the creaking carriage faded, Corabell sighed and fed the baby who had been fretting. Gerolf found the bottle of spirits. "To Abo, my brother." He held the flask high and then brought it to his lips.

Accepting the vessel Gerolf offered her, she told him, "My kinfolk call this firewater." Corabell swallowed, then turned to pick up the dishes and begin the wash. The brown dog sniffed Abo's body and licked his face. Corabell shooed him away. On the bench, Gerolf stared into the flames.

Later, Corabell took another swallow from the bottle. She stood, mouth open, feeling the burning fluid descend. Stepping into the shadows to pick up her husband's head and shoulders, Corabell dragged him to the fire where she could see. She closed her eyes and smelled his ear and hairline. The familiar scent had fled. Broken ribs formed irregular jagged peaks under purple, bruised flesh and she set her hand lightly on the torso. "Gerolf, tell me how it happened."

Gerolf spoke to the flames, "I came fast when I heard the scream, 'Your brother's down!' I feared trouble. Abo lay in the muddy cattle pen. The bull stepped on the cattle hand's skull. Abo tried to assist. They said the creature threw Abo as he dragged Conroy from the pen. Ardus, I was told tried to divert the bull."

Corabell turned back to the pearly chilled flesh. Setting a hot cloth on the skin of Abo's chest, she unbound the trousers at the waist and pulled them to the groin. Turning to Gerolf, she told him, "I'm going to unbind the leg." He nodded, eyes watching the fire.

The fabric had stiffened in the round puncture hole. Using her knife, Corabell cut a hole around the perforation and tugged off the trousers. Blood from the wound stained Abo's abdomen and genitals deep red. She draped a warm wet cloth over the pale thigh and groin. Lathering, Corabell worked soap over the torso he had lowered to her when he needed her. She smelled his underarms before cleansing them, but there too his scent had gone. The slap startled Gerolf. He looked over at Corabell who spoke softly, "You leave me here. How could you? My people have gone." She beat Abo's cheeks with her palms.

Gerolf

The baby stirred. With tilting ears, the dog lifted his head and Gerolf felt he needed to intervene. He fished a fresh towel from the simmering pot. When the steam subsided, he wrung it, knelt at his brother's side and rinsed soap away.

Corabell drew back. She wiped her tears and lifted the cloth. Warmth and water had softened the blood and it coated her hands as she stroked the flesh of her husband's abdomen, penis and scrotum. She filled the chamber pot with cold water and rinsed her hands, then cleaned Abo's groin carefully before taking the darkened penis in her mouth.

Gerolf froze and stared, had she lost her wits? If she had, what would he do with her? Corabell peered up, met his eyes and muttered out the side of her mouth, "He'll come back to me. He will." The statement so sure, Gerolf almost believed it. The fire spat and the dog sighed and laid his head over a paw.

Corabell

Crying began to interfere with her ability to breath. The penis grew warmer and the change felt briefly encouraging. After some time, when she saw no pending erection, despite hands cupping the cooling balls, despair overwhelmed her along with a mounting wave of shame. She settled her head in Abo's blond groin and sobbed.

Later, when she could fathom something more than grief, she recognized the chilled body held no welcome for tears. She recoiled, rubbed her eyes and sat.

The thought arose a spell later. Gerolf needed to work in the morning. She gazed at the dark brother who slumped, leaning against the table leg on the far side of the body. The half-full bottle of liquor sat near one hand and his glazed eyes were bloodshot and swollen. Hair had fallen forward across his cheeks. Corabell whispered, "Go to bed. I'll finish washing and make you coffee in the morning." Gerolf looked at her and slowly stood. Trudging with a short gait, he left the cabin. She heard him outside pissing at the compost pile. Returning, he climbed the ladder to the sleeping platform.

The songs came to her. She hummed them before she began to sing the native words, softly so Gerolf would sleep. The notes caused tears to fall anew, but the melody made it bearable. Corabell worked cleaning every corner of her husband's skin, nails and hair. Tying a plait low at his neck, she prayed the Great Spirit would find him acceptable. Clothing him, she wound him tightly in their bed sheet and secured it with small, precise stitches.

Rousing the dog, they walked to the well and she bathed, taking her time, washing her hair and letting the cold water turn her skin frigid and hard. For several tolerable moments, Corabell felt entirely different, fresh, alive and cold.

Walking to the cabin naked in the early morning chill of late May, she wore only her boots. Corabell donned a slip, the russet skirt she had recently cut from the bodice and her corset that held her breasts high. Her wet hair dampened the fabric as she began making morning coffee.

The baby stirred and fussed and she picked him up before he cried. She took the child outside and nursed him, a cloth at her other breast to sop up the excess milk. The dog followed her out the door. In her arms, the child passed gas and moved his bowels. Feeling the warmth of the soiled cloth against her forearm, she thought of the laundry pile and wondered whether there were biscuits left from the previous evening.

Inside the cabin, the water boiled and Corabell pulled the kettle aside the direct heat. She made coffee, set oatmeal to cook and left to check for eggs. With a handful of cracked corn for the chickens and several more for the pig, she opened the coop, so the birds could forage.

Without Abo, her role in the cabin felt precarious. Corabell searched for an instance when a woman lived with a man who was not her husband, father or brother, but could not think of such an arrangement. Her father had left her and her mother in the village. They had belonged with her grandmother and her kin. Corabell imagined Abo would prefer she remain in the cabin, rather than take the trail the tribe used, following them west. Without his presence, her purpose seemed vague.

The thought of leaving made her chest heavy. Elke had been good to her. Gerolf she would miss. Who would tend the garden and care for the animals? Who would cook and wash for the other brother?

The particulars made her head pound and she poured coffee, mixed in honey and attended to her hair. Gerolf slept and the sun had fully risen. She cut slices of bacon for the skillet, checked the oatmeal and threw a cloth in the water for a shave. Cleaning the baby, she bundled and placed him in the sling. Still Gerolf did not stir. Corabell imagined she heard wagon wheels and peered out the side window but Dietrich had not yet appeared.

When she could wait no longer, the oatmeal had cooked, the eggs and bacon were ready and the coffee grew cold waiting, she hailed Gerolf. There was no response. She called him again, "Gerolf Bachmeier!" Briefly worried the firewater had killed him, Corabell took a cloth from the simmering pot with a fork, let it drip and flung it high onto the sleeping platform.

It landed with a splatter and Gerolf exclaimed, "Ugh. Versifft!" His face peered over the side of the platform, eyes puffy and dark hair on end.

Corabell set her hand on one hip, "Do you NOT have to work this day? Breakfast grows cold waiting for you!"

"Yes, yes. Yes." He took the ladder rungs slowly down, still dressed in the clothing and boots of the previous day. Corabell took the cloth from his shoulder and tossed it back in the pot, poured him black coffee and passed the honey jar.

Gerolf sat slumped on the bench facing the hearth, Abo's bound feet on the floor by his side. Corabell served bacon and eggs, scooped a cup of oatmeal into a bowl and poured maple syrup around the edge. Eggs were enough food for her; they slid easily down the throat. She slipped the rest onto Gerolf's plate.

He looked over at her and she shrugged, "I can't swallow anything more." The coffee urged her to the outhouse, but before leaving, she set a hot cloth on Gerolf's wild head. Returning, Corabell saw the cloud of dust, heard Dietrich's wagon wheels approaching and hurried back.

Dietrich declined coffee, but asked Gerolf to carry one end of the body to the wagon. Retaking the bench and the reins, he noted, "The gravedigger'll bury the body this morning, behind the church in the cemetery." With a hand pressed to her mouth, Corabell nodded, "Thank you, Sir," and the man flicked the horse reins.

A wave of fatigue crept through her. She gave the pig the remnants of breakfast. Gerolf moved slowly. Corabell wet another cloth for his face, thinking he would shave and change clothing, but he simply sat, tightening bootlaces and stuffing the half-soiled shirt deeper into his trousers. Corabell watched him, "Tame your hair at least, or I'll lose both brothers." He heard her, she could tell; he smiled absently.

When he made no effort to do as instructed, Corabell took her brush, stood behind him and brushed his hair back into a leather tie. He did not consult his mirror, but took a stick to clean his teeth as he waved farewell.

Corabell considered Dietrich's statement. Soon Abo would be buried in the church's cemetery. Beneath the earth, the Great Spirit might not find him. The white man buried their dead like other animals, under a blanket of soil where no creature would disturb the remains, not as the native folk whose dead faced the sky, or balanced in a fork of a tree where many would see and remember them. Corabell's head drubbed and stomach swam and she prayed, breathing into cupped palms to release the prayer to the air and spirits.

Chapter Twenty

Corabell

Fearing she would fall asleep if she sat, Corabell busied herself. She washed the breakfast dishes, set beans to soak, rinsed and washed the baby linens and discarded the soiled water. The sun shone high in the sky when she walked into the garden, a bucket of dishwater in either hand. Gently dousing the seedlings, she walked down the rows of burgeoning plants. The heat of the day beat on her and she felt thirsty, weak. Carrying the loss of Abo, a solid weight on her chest, she sought the coolness of the stone floor. After drinking several cups of water, Corabell fell onto the bed they had shared. Lightheaded still, she opened her bodice for the baby to suckle.

As the sun worked its way into the western sky, Corabell woke with ravenous hunger. Submersed in a bowl of water the beans unfurled. She emptied them into the kettle with a cut of bacon, maple syrup and two coarsely chopped onions. Stepping down into the cellar with a flaming candle in hand, she saw the apples wore wrinkled skins. For cooking it would not matter. Gathering raisins and black walnuts but lacking butter, she opted to use pork fat to make an oatmeal crust.

Corabell cracked the tough walnut shells on the table with a hammer, separating the nut from the woody parts. Abo used the hammer last when he put together the wardrobe. He had worked diligently, taking it apart various times after discovering measuring errors. Tears flowed over her cheeks. He had taken her milk in his last act, but still left her.

Gerolf opened the door, his clothing soaked in blood. Corabell raised a hand and wiped her cheeks. Unshaven, hair swept behind both ears, the tress she had made in the morning was gone. One hand found his head, his expression changing. "I brought no meat for dinner."

"There's food in the cellar still." Corabell shook her head, "You'll have dinner . . . if you wash." He nodded and the baby on the bed let out a loud yowl.

Corabell settled on the cold stones, back against the mattress to nurse the child. She lowered him into the sling before serving herself beans. Salt from the bacon permeated the soft legumes. The onion sheaves tasted sweet in contrast. Corabell caught the hint of cornbread in the air. Taking the heavy skillet from the fire, she set it on a cloth on the table. Toting two buckets of water Gerolf appeared steadying the water before pouring into the barrel Abo had left aside the hearth.

Finally, he sat and Corabell served dinner. So many unanswered questions flew through her mind. Gerolf had been the talkative brother. The silence wore on her. He ate steadily, having a second bowl before Corabell summoned the energy. "Gerolf," she said, catching his gaze. "What am I to do?"

He looked at her and tossed his hand. His voice a whisper he asked, "What've you considered?"

Corabell brought the apple crisp to the table and set it on a folded towel. Her hand clutched her forehead as she brought the sling and babe into her lap and sat opposite him. "I'll follow my people west. The soldiers at the fort should know where they've gone."

Gerolf's eyebrow rose and his jaw clenched. "No. My brother told me I was to care for you."

Corabell lowered the hand from her forehead, "Oh?" But I'm not sure I can live here without him. He was the reason I came across the river. I took a chance. I didn't know whether he had a woman. I was lucky, perhaps, but now I can return to my people, where I belong." Corabell covered her lips and sought his eyes, "You blame me for this?"

Gerolf did not meet her gaze, but served himself a large helping of baked apples and spoke slowly, "You changed my brother. Every Sunday he set out across the river, meeting people who might know your village. Then you appeared. He wanted you, meager or round. You made him happy." He looked at her then, "Please eat with me." Corabell served herself dessert. Neither of them had answers and in that moment, it was enough.

"I'll carry the child," Gerolf offered when the baby let out a yelp. Corabell lowered him into the sling.

"How?" She gazed at Gerolf with narrowed eyes.

"In my arms, the English way," he extended the limbs.

Corabell frowned, "That's not safe." She adjusted the strap and pulled the shawl around her shoulders, taking his arm. When Gerolf made no comment, she told him, "When you've your own children you may haul them anyway you like." Corabell wore the brown dress, adjusted to accommodate nursing. With Abo, she had been comfortable in the parish pew, now she questioned why she was going there.

The sun lit up the morning sky between clouds. The wind rushed past, steady and soothing, though Corabell felt twisted. They walked on, approaching the church from the narrow path with prairie grass on both sides. Sun on the turf gave off a sweet scent Corabell knew well and the perfume played against the shreds of her heart. Her tears began to stream and fall from her jaw. Not wanting to make Gerolf late for the service, Corabell nudged him forward, "Leave me here and go on."

Gerolf embraced her, "No one expects you to be without grief. You might find comfort in sharing your heartache." Corabell glanced up at him through her tears.

Before beginning service, the minister stood silently then spread his palms, "I announce this morning the death of a young parishioner who wed here not so long ago. Abo Bachmeier died from an accident at the slaughterhouse. I ask for your prayers for his son and widow, Corabell Bachmeier."

Fatigue moved over Corabell and lulled the pain of loss. During the final hymn, she heard only Gerolf's voice carry. The absence of Abo pummeled her anew. She sat, bowed her head and sobbed into her hands.

As the congregation filed out, Eva embraced the weeping widow, rocking her gently in her arms. Several well-wishers placed their hands on Corabell's head and shoulder, but their concern did nothing to dispel the weight of the shadow.

Outside Catharina Heck, the minister's widowed young sister, stood at Gerolf's shoulder while people pressed his hand offering condolences. Scanning the dress she wore, Corabell mused only a wife would stand so close to a man.

Corabell sought out the cemetery. Several men engulfed her on the path. The workers from the slaughterhouse introduced themselves, extending their hands in greetings while trying to meet her eyes. Their accents were as thick as her husband's had been.

She imagined the site for the dead would be empty and she would send a prayer to her spouse. At the gate, Corabell saw a group gathered at the newly dug grave and moved away.

Instead, Corabell found a cottonwood tree on the path home and stepped around it, away from the mingling families of the Sunday assembly. Making herself comfortable at the base, she leaned against the trunk and withdrew the fretting child from the pouch confines. She covered herself with the shawl and placed the baby at the right breast, which throbbed, stretched thin with milk. A second letdown filled the left breast to overflowing and she covered the nipple to sop up the excess milk. The baby emptied the right side quickly and Corabell moved him to the left, hoping to diffuse the taut pressure. He began lolling into a stupor, mouth slightly open, milk dripping from one cheek.

Someone approached on the path. The stride was quick and furtive, the cries akin to a blanketed, enraged cat. From between the knee-high grass, she spied Nate's square shoulders and tan face, but the path wound around a rain pool and the sounds grew fainter before they resumed.

The man breathed quickly. The lines across his forehead eased when he caught sight of her. Nate whispered loudly approaching hastily, "I looked fo' ya at de cabin. I's been hopin' ta find ya." He bobbed from side to side, soothing something within his coat. Corabell frowned. "Dis one's alive," his voice dipped into murmurs. "Alas, de mama's gone or drowned. Still, dis chile needs feeding."

"Yes, surely."

Nate knelt, opening the frock coat. The bulge across the belly squirmed and protested. He unbuttoned his shirt quickly. The deep honey colored skin tone brought memories of Mettawa's village to her, with sharp pangs of grief.

The baby was naked and nearly black. Corabell leaned forward, taking a cloth from her satchel. She set the writhing infant on her skirt and secured a diaper between the kicking legs.

Nate stated, "She's a strong girl. Lackin' her ma, she's had mostly water in de last days." Corabell put the infant to her left breast and the child latched on, taking in the nipple and surrounding flesh with a strong pull. She leaned back as the baby relieved the pressure of her engorged breast.

Under the influence of warm milk, the small one quieted and sucked fervently as the babe on the other breast had never done. "She's very hungry. What're you going to do with an orphaned slave child?" He had considered it; she could see from the way he avoided her eyes.

"I've aided other mamas, but few. It's fa' too dangerous. Babies cry. Only so much tonic ya can give dem ta hasten sleep. Ya lose the small ones, dhat way." Nate settled beside her elbow, back against the tree, leaning his head against the trunk and confided, "Sides, I don't know no other nursing ma ta bring a babe ta."

Had he fully thought about her suddenly having two babies, one quite darker than the first? How, for example, would she attend service?

Corabell questioned Nate. He answered quickly. "Dhese Christian people, would dey condemn ya fo' caring fo' an infant ya found?" She turned, met his eyes and smiled faintly. "By and by," Nate said, "I'll find a relation who'll care fo' de chile. Presently, I'd be grateful if ya'd treat dis baby as yar own."

Corabell looked down at the girl child at her breast and nodded, "Yes. Yes, of course."

Gerolf

Seeking Corabell, Gerolf wandered past Eva's girls. Rudy and Rory nodded to him. Nola seized his forearm, "Is the baby still waking at night? Does Corabell have adequate milk? How soon until she remarries?"

The last question caught him in the throat and he assured her, "As her brother-in-law, I'll see to her care." Nola gazed up into his face silently. The two rambled down the pathway where Corabell's voice joined another in conversation. They stepped around the tree, finding Corabell and Nate sitting against the base of a mature cottonwood.

The standing pair halted abruptly and surveyed the contentment of the two sitting together. "I must go; excuse me. My sisters are calling." Nola released Gerolf's arm while he nodded to Nate, who stood and bowed.

Corabell handed the child to Nate and rose. Upon standing, she turned away and pulled her shift closed. Gerolf's eyes widened. He regarded the two with one eyebrow high on his forehead. Nate nodded to the path. Gerolf and Corabell followed while he held the child within his coat, in the crook of one arm. Reaching an open area, Nate offered Corabell his other arm. He spoke in a low voice to Gerolf as they trod through the spring grass.

Corabell

The babies preferred the comfort of her moving body to the wooden cradle where they both fit. Given enough time crying they found comfort in each other's warmth. Nate passed by every Friday evening with nourishment for the nursing mother; a cut of cheese, a pint of cream, a small smoked turkey. Though regularly invited, he never stayed for dinner.

The turkey caused Gerolf to pace the floor. Corabell served dinner and urged him to sit. He said nothing, and continued patrolling the stones. Finally, he turned stating, "Corabell. My brother told me to care for you. I was a fool to think of marriage to Eva, a grieving widow, but she filled my heart. I fantasized about winning her over. Her girls like me. I would've given her more. When you arrived, you took my brother's heart. I saw him change. He was happier, more content and the Widow Heck simply seeks a spouse."

Corabell turned the beans over in her bowl and broke the round of cornbread down the middle, releasing a current of steam, "The Widow Heck's children are older than Eva's; it may be harder for you there, but she has a shapely form. Her hair reminds me of Abo's. Women say she's wealthy. I don't know if she'd be happy here, it's a bit plain for her. I believe she has servants." Gerolf gazed at her, one eyebrow steadily aloft and Corabell continued, "But, it'd be wrong to ignore Nola. She'll not be too young in a few years and the girl's so fond of you."

"But would you have me, Corabell?"

She shook her head, "Your brother weighs on me. I ache when I think of him and I think about him all the time. I hear him saying my name. I miss his smell, hair, moods and ways. No husband needs a wife that yearns for another." She looked up to see whether he understood. Nodding, his eyes held her rejection.

Chapter Twenty-One

Corabell

In June garden produce flavored most meals. Corabell added green onions to morning eggs. She served Gerolf baby lima beans with bacon and onion bulbs when he arrived home and dinner needed more time on the fire.

In the evenings, Corabell sat by the hearth and stitched baby frocks. The animals and children demanded her attention. Though she still gave in to grief, the barking dog, an infant's cry and the hens pecking at the window glass infringed on her acute heartache. Laundry needed washing and hanging. Fresh clothing drying in the sun brought satisfaction, but when the babies learned to smile and giggle, she laughed with them.

On a Friday evening in late July, Corabell knelt on the floor, pressed her lips over the belly of the baby girl and blew. The child chortled, turned over and crawled into Nate's lap. He sat leaning against the wall, as Corabell resumed making dinner. He asked her, "Why de chilren still have no names?"

Corabell scowled and planted a hand on one hip, "I've no husband. Without one, there can be no naming ceremony. But Abo wanted to call the boy Otto and I'm calling the girl child Plum."

Gerolf arrived from the well carrying two buckets of water and emptied them into the barrel. He threw his legs across the bench and sat while Corabell served soup. "Stay and have dinner with us," she suggested. Nate surprised her with a nod.

He had brought with him two jugs, one of hard cider and another of molasses. Nate pulled the cork from the cider and poured it three ways. He stretched his cup upward in a toast to the cook and Gerolf joined him.

Corabell smiled, the mound of rinsed greens took up most of the sideboard, but a few minutes in a hot skillet would turn the pile into three hearty portions. When the potatoes with rosemary, young red peppers and onions acquired a crisp brown edge, Corabell took the skillet from the heat. She served the spinach and sausage and the men served themselves potatoes. Gerolf broke the round of cornbread down the middle.

On the blanket, the babies began to fuss. Otto found his fist and Corabell picked up Plum and nursed her. Nate refilled their cups. When the child dozed,

Corabell slid from the bench and whispered, "Nate you should've brought your fiddle." She laid the baby belly-down on the blanket. The child belched a bubble of milk from her deeply puckered lips and sucked again at an imaginary breast.

Nate served himself another heaping spoonful of potatoes and nodded. Corabell gazed at Gerolf, "I've not heard you sing since Abo's death, except for church. I'm with musical men and hear only the wind through the house cracks."

Gerolf's eyebrow shot up and he pointed the tines of his fork at her, "There's not a crack in these walls."

Nate raised his cup. Gerolf and Corabell followed his toast, "Ta Abo Bachmeier, who plastered de walls. Tol' me he was gonna do it."

Corabell turned away. Abo Bachmeier, the man-spirit existed beyond the words of his name and any salute. In bed, he still warmed her side. Daily, she heard his voice say her name.

Corabell sat with the men in silence. Nate polished his plate with a slice of potato, laid down his fork and took a pouch of tobacco from his coat. He pulled a pipe from his trouser pocket and filled the bowl, stoked the mixture of red dogwood, bearberry and tobacco and released a plume of thick white smoke. Gazing over at Corabell he squinted, "Das de smoke trouble ya?"

"No, it smells of my home."

Nate smiled, "I traded fo' it some time ago afore de village left."

Nate looked about the place and spotted the wardrobe. The wooden rose carving sat leaning on the top, unsecured. Nate lifted his pipe and pointed to the piece of ornamentation, "Abo had troubled makin' dem rose petals."

Corabell commented, "You know, Gerolf's made the rest of this furniture. Before he moved in, Abo and I'd stand eating with our plates on the table."

Nate looked about the small interior, "Well ya lack fo' a rockin' chair, or two. One fo' de babies, de second for company, ya know?" Nate shifted uncomfortably on the wooden bench. "Gerolf," Nate gazed at the man who sat straight-backed in front of him, "Even slave women have rockers." Gerolf narrowed his eyes but Nate ignored the look, "I made my wife a rockin' chair, years ago. She rocked many babies in de chair; one must've been mine. She'd rock 'til de baby slept and her eyes'd shut and she'd keep rockin', findin' peace in de motion. A blest thing, a rockin' chair is. By and by, when ya've more chilren, ya'll need a rockin' chair."

The icy cast to Gerolf's face softened. He looked to Corabell, "Would you like a rocking chair?"

She smiled, "I would."

Nate thanked them for her hospitality, adding, "I don' see my family but being here does me good." He unfolded his lower limbs from beneath the table and touched the babies' heads before he stepped into the evening air.

Chapter Twenty-Two

Gerolf

In August, Gerolf passed time every Sunday with Henry's father, Patrick O'Shay, a skilled carpenter and woodworker. By the month's end, he brought the rocking chair home. Designed to fit Corabell's body, he had taken many measurements, the length of an arm, the distance between the heel and bend of a knee, the span from the rear to the crown of the head. He carved the seat lightly making a slight dip to cup the backside.

Corabell had been skeptical about the need for measurements, looking at him with wary eyes as he draped the tape measure against her shin. She allowed him to measure the distance between her seated behind and the part in her hair but refused any measurement around the hips, giving no explanation, saying only, "No."

Corabell

Gerolf carried the chair through the door on a Sunday evening and set it where a shaft of light ran across the stones. Taking the pails from the side of the hearth, he set out for the well. Corabell retrieved biscuits from the heat, stirred the soup and strode to the seat.

Small and simple, it was unadorned. Gathering up Plum who whined, Corabell unbuttoned her slip and nursed her, kicking off the floor and letting the chair sweep her backwards. As they rocked, their foreheads smoothed and their eyes softened. On the floor, Otto sucked his arm.

When Gerolf opened the door, Corabell startled. Her arms shot up as her foot met the floor. Plum lost the nipple and emptied a swallow-full of warm milk down her chin. Shifting and fretting, the baby patted Corabell's breast.

Gerolf

Gerolf smiled, setting down the pails, "Do you like it? It's not finished, I want to carve something into the back." Corabell rearranged Plum and kicked herself back. She smiled as she rocked and her contentment did not fade. He was not sure what it meant, but it pleased him.

Corabell commented with closed eyes, "I may never labor again."

"I'll serve my own soup."

Corabell waved to the sideboard, "We've biscuits and greens too." Gerolf served himself but left the plate on the table. Gazing at the pair, he lingered nearby.

Corabell opened her eyes and lay Plum on the quilt. Placing a hand on Gerolf's chest, Corabell met his gaze, while her other hand went to her heart. "The chair pleases me. I've had nothing grander."

Dropping her head, Gerolf saw her sadness and embraced her tightly. Her milk-damp clothing emitted a slight cheesy fragrance. He twisted away, hoping Corabell would not discern the attentive bulge in his trousers. The frown on her brow told him she noticed the evasive move. Another loss marked her features. Aware he could hurt her, it pleased him that he mattered so.

Corabell

She recognized something had changed between her and the younger brother. When he offered his arm to walk to church, she sensed the closeness of his hip. Grieving for Abo, she missed the former Gerolf who sang whenever the mood took him.

"Good Morning!" The Widow Heck hailed them as they approached the church steps. Gerolf tipped his hat while Corabell glared up at him, "You can accompany one widow to her pew before you speak with another."

He smiled, "It'd be my pleasure." Contrary to what Corabell imagined he would do, Gerolf held his seat next to her. His presence dissuaded other men from offering pleasantries. For that, she was grateful.

Following the service, Amsel distracted Gerolf, "Bachmeier, I hear you're working carpentry now. I've a proposal. A rocking chair for my bride, to give at Christmas this year." Corabell nodded to Gerolf and left him to attend to the two children.

Church members were keen to gaze upon the dark-skinned baby. The children touched her skin, marveling at the rosy sides of her feet and hands. Corabell told herself the community would grow accustomed to Plum and hoped their intrusive curiosity would wear off.

She sat with her shawl covering the nursing child, on a bench under a speading white oak tree. Otto perched beside her and giggled with Romy. The youngest sister swept Otto up and carried him away, calling to her mother, "Mama, watch me make Otto laugh."

Gerolf

Nola intercepted Gerolf as his gaze moved over the margins of the churchyard. She threaded a slender arm through his and walked alongside peppering him with questions.

He caught sight of Corabell on the bench with Plum across one shoulder. Striding closer with Nola pecking at an ear, he bid her good day. She allowed him to disengage his arm, though her head hung heavily. Corabell kissed the girl lightly, reached for Gerolf's arm and they strode off on the trodden path that passed the cabin.

Walking quietly, some time elapsed before Corabell asked, "When do you plan to marry, Gerolf?"

He heard the question. His heart pounded loudly. He felt conspicuously large next to her. The thought came haltingly from his mouth, an idea he had considered many times, "You were my brother's wife. Could you ever be my mine?"

Corabell clenched his arm and peered up at him, "Widow Heck and Eva both had husbands. You still desired them." Gerolf smiled, nodded and glanced down. She jabbed her elbow in his ribs and his wide beam faded.

"What would my brother want? Would it anger him? I'm sure it would. He's cold in the grave. "Care for mein Frau," he told me."

"What else did he say?"

His dark eyes met hers and he didn't answer but asked, "Wouldn't I be caring for you, if I was also your spouse?"

"Yes."

That word meant so much. Had she actually agreed? He did not pursue the matter, but reveled in her acquiescence, letting his feet take him home. They lived together. He hesitated to change the bond that seemed to work well for both of them.

Corabell

The garden was at its height of production. Elke had given her specific directions on how to pickle excess vegetables. In preparation, Corabell had washed all the vessels and lids and set them on the sideboard.

At her insistence, Gerolf procured two gallons of vinegar and a pound of salt. Corabell intended to begin preserving asparagus. The tenderest of vegetables, they would lose it in an early frost. Green beans, cucumbers, onions and peppers awaited attention. Having pulled up eight cabbage heads and hung them by the roots upside down in the root cellar, she left the others in the garden to fatten. Some vegetables would be fine in the soil until late autumn; those could wait.

Inside the cabin, dill, chive, chamomile and fennel hung in clumps wrapped in twine, drying from the ceiling beams. Corabell dried goose greens for the chickens in the winter months; several dozen bunches hung aside the herbs. Ears of sweet corn in different hues hung pointing downwards from a beam Corabell could only reach when standing on the table. She would pound some corn into meal, a portion would feed the animals and a fraction would keep for sowing in next year's garden. Three medium sized pumpkins waited to be cut into thin slabs for drying, before the sun's rays grew too weak. Sweet peas lay in a wide shallow basket on the side counter. Most hard-shell beans still hung in their husks toughening in the garden.

Four months had passed since the death of Abo when a sudden knock made the dog howl and lope across the front of the house. The babies looked up from their bellies on the floor. Corabell gestured to the door and rolled her eyes at Gerolf, at the tub where she worked. He took the dog by the neck scruff and opened the door to Minister Schoenhofen standing, hat in hand.

"Come in, Sir. I'm sorry, we've finished dinner." Corabell craned her neck to see who stood in the doorway.

The white haired man entered and waved his hat, as he spoke. "Oh no, my visit is purely within the boundaries of work, not truly a social call."

Gerolf raised an eyebrow, gazed at Corabell, who continued working and queried, "Who is it you'd like an audience with?"

Corabell failed to believe he would possibly seek her company. However, since Gerolf asked the question, she conceived at once that she was in trouble. Perchance slave catchers were scouring for the baby, or soldiers had arrived to escort her to the far side of the river. She frowned and watched Gerolf as she quickly dried her hands.

The brother's dark eyes bore no hint of his thoughts. Though the babies seemed content to kick about on the quilt on the floor, Corabell picked them up, set them in her lap and took a seat on the bench facing the minister, who strolled back and forth in front of the hearth.

It seemed the older man felt stymied and knew not where to begin, adding to Corabell's angst. She began tapping one foot, making the babies bounce and their round cheeks jiggle.

Gerolf paced behind Corabell. She heard his footfalls and his turns. Several moments passed in stillness before the pastor recognized the tension in the cabin.

"It's really a simple matter." He quit strolling, gazed down at the hat in his hand and spoke without meeting their eyes, "It's a formality really, one that concerns the parish. As you may know my younger sister, the Widow Heck, seeks a spouse, as do others of the congregation. Men who've been in the parish for years, who'd likely stay in the area also seek marriage partners.

The issue's vexing and runs affront of tradition, which gives you Corabell, the bereaved spouse, a year to decide the best course for your future. Because it's been such a short time since Abo's death, the situation is uncomfortable, yet I represent a code of ethics that prevails over the timespan given to mourning and declaration of marriage bans. As the head of the congregation, I must insist on standards. You're young, susceptible to passion. Feelings perhaps you didn't know you had, for each other." Corabell frowned and turned from the face of the clergyman to the features of Gerolf behind her.

Gerolf froze mid-stride and interrupted the senior man, "Sir, may I say?" His eyes went to Corabell who faced him. "My sister-in-law and I are but brother and sister to one another."

"Ah yes," the pastor inspected the hat in his hand. "If you were to share your intentions to marry, say become engaged or promised to a lady at some time in the near future, that would quell the gossip that flies about the two of you.

"Truly, it's the way things appear, rather than the actual substance of your bond. You're both young and vital and attractive by the grace of God. Suitors male and female question the wisdom of allowing you to continue living together unwed.

"People are a curious lot. What they seek, I believe is some clarification on the matter of your relationship."

Gerolf declared, "Sir, my dying brother asked me to care for his wife."

"That may be. Let me assure you, there're other men who'd gladly give their hand to Corabell. They're but staunch laborers at the slaughterhouse, not as highly qualified as yourself. Surely, you'd feel your commitment to your brother met if you were to see your sister-in-law at service and if she and the child resided in the vicinity."

Gerolf nodded slowly, his face expressionless, the tie in his hair gone and the locks at his brow aloft.

The guest ran his fingers idly along the brim of the dark hat, his back to the flames. "At the very least, it would please the parish if one of you would divulge your intentions. I believe that would appease the rumors that whisper about the sinful nature of your cohabitation."

Corabell adjusted her hold on the children, "Sir, this cabin's been my home since Abo fixed the roof shingles and I scrubbed the leaves and mouse dirt from the stones. I cultivated the garden and now the harvest's due. I'm stocking the root cellar and laying in provisions for winter. Now I must make a home with another?"

She swallowed and her voice rose. "Yes, I was married to Abo. Yet his brother's been a constant presence in my life since that day and even before, when I lodged in the home of the Gottschalk family. He made the bench I sit on, the sideboard I work on and the rocking chair to ease my legs. He and his brother made the root cellar, the outhouse and the garden fence. I cannot imagine my life without this man . . ." Corabell clenched her lips. The babies grew anxious, sensing her ferocity. Plum let out a wail.

Gerolf took the child, who quieted in his arms. Corabell continued, "I lie in bed at night and desire no man. I had a man and I left my people for him. He was my life. When he died, I thought I'd return to my kin . . . And now . . . If it must be and I may choose . . . I'd have Gerolf for my spouse."

She glanced at the man holding the baby girl as she said his name and her eyes returned to the minister, "Yet he sought the Widow Gottschalk and when she took the farmer, his heart tore. The women flatter him with their attention . . . and you would press him into marriage? Widow Heck, a pretty woman with greater years; Nola still a child; and me grieving for Abo only months in the grave, it seems no one's ready to be his."

"I hoped not to press at all. You see, I saw more in you than you know. I admit I thought you'd already given yourselves to each other and I would've happily made you lawfully wed. Now I hear otherwise and see that it's so. Perhaps the congregation requires a sermon on chastity and idle tongues.

"I see that I've brought you some aggravation. Please pardon me. Can you perhaps, appreciate the concerns of the church members as well?"

Gerolf sighed and shifted Plum to one side before bowing in front of Corabell. A half-smile lit his face, "Corabell, come be my wife. We live and breathe." Gerolf's hand went to his chest, "We'll mourn together. I'll not press you. When you're ready to be my wife in the flesh, you'll come to me. By law, we'll be one. Will you have me?" He fixed his dark eyes on her.

She frowned, "You've thought what this'll mean for you?" From the swift reply, she knew he had. Corabell stared and nodded.

Gerolf turned to the minister who ambled near the hearth clutching his hat. "Sir, you came here seeking some clarification of our intentions. We'll wed. You may make us lawfully bound." Corabell stood, baby at her hip, suddenly aware of the rapid change in matters.

"Oh, we've no wine. May I offer you water?" The minister waved a hand and pulled off his black overcoat. From a pocket, he pulled the stole and tossed it across his shoulders. Lifting his palms, he beckoned to the young couple holding babies. Gerolf and Corabell drew nearer and the minister began reciting the words he knew so well.

Corabell had heard them before, but had been too nervous to comprehend their meaning. Now it seemed the most natural act. Who else could tend a babe like Gerolf? She smiled as the cleric spoke.

Corabell stated her promise, as did Gerolf. The pastor ended the ceremony and pronounced them husband and wife. He had other calls to make before the sky grew dark. They bid him farewell. He set his hat on his head and walked in the direction of Center Street.

Allowing her eyes to drift slowly over Gerolf's dark features, Corabell told him, "You've a most pleasing face. I thought you did but I couldn't allow myself to see its beauty." A familiar sadness found her. She slipped Otto into the sling, stepped in front of the basin of fresh asparagus spears and set to filling the clean jars.

Gerolf's expression changed. He leapt up the ladder to the sleeping platform where Corabell heard him rustling. He returned quickly to stand across from the basin and asked, "May I have your hand?" Corabell withdrew her left hand, exposing the heavy silver band still adorning her finger. He frowned. "Your other hand?" Corabell shook the water from her right hand and held it out. Gerolf gently pushed the silver filigree ring on her longest wet finger. She brought her hand up and admired the craftsmanship, beaming.

Chapter Twenty-Three

Gerolf

On Sunday before service, Minister Schoenhofen stood before the seated congregation and announced, "Gerolf and Corabell Bachmeier have wed under my authority. I caution parishioners to curtail their imaginations. The couple married under duress of social pressures conceived by idle minds."

Sighs and whispers from the younger folk sent the atmosphere inside the church to new depths. The first hymn lacked several standard voices.

At the conclusion of service, older members congratulated the pair. Dietrich and Elke gave them their blessing, as did most of the Gottschalk family. Two workers from the slaughterhouse paid their respects. Gerolf noted them; an immigrant with graying hair and a younger fellow he recognized. He could not imagine Corabell content with either. Young Nola did not present herself, though Romy and Uta followed their grandmother's polite gestures. The Widow Heck avoided socializing.

Corabell

Months ago when Nate handed the naked and ravenous baby to Corabell, she had appeared the same age as Otto. Growing acquainted with the child, Corabell's impression changed. The little girl crawled, found her hands readily, sucked her thumb and patted the breast as she nursed.

At the end of September, Plum began learning to walk while Otto sat independently, but still had no interest in moving about the floor. Plum pulled herself to standing while Otto watched. The increased activity diminished her padding and swelled her appetite. At dinner, she chewed corn bread, brought peas and beans to her mouth and tasted small bits of meat. Otto's sole interested remained breast milk.

While the baby boy rode on her hip, Plum wanted out of the confining sling. She stood and dipped her knees bouncing, holding the bench for support. When Corabell sang, Plum accompanied her, crooning. In the morning, the brown baby stepped from the cradle, leaving Otto sitting, holding the sides of the swaying wooden bed.

Accomplishing work became harder. Gerolf constructed a pen that Corabell carried outside when she worked in the garden. Confining Plum with sufficient spoons, cloths and bowls to manipulate held her for a time. After that, she had surely thrown her utensils out and might be hanging from the railing, griping. At other times, Corabell carried her on her back and set Otto in the pen. If she sang, she might be able to work until noon, especially if she interested the baby girl in picking carrots or radishes.

In late September, as the summer heat lingered, Corabell showed the Plum the difference between the red beet stalks and small weeds that sprang up randomly. The little one knelt in the earth, extracting the wild plants for a time until Otto howled from the pen. Corabell hoisted Plum on her hip and went to check on him.

Plum gave up nursing when she began to walk. She drank water with two hands from a pewter cup and when Gerolf brought milk home, she drank that as well.

Gerolf made her a swing. Securing two eyebolts through an overhead beam, he draped rope through each. For the seat, he used a piece of pliable pig's hide. Among Abo's tools, Corabell found an awl and punched holes in the skin, securing rope with thick thread to each end.

She feared the child was too young for such a mobile toy when she toppled on the stone floor. Yet by the end of the first week, the little girl hung with her forearms over the pig's hide, gripping the leather. Twisting side to side as Corabell sang, Plum made her own versions of tunes.

At dinnertime, she sat on Gerolf's thigh. He chided her if she was too messy. Nate brought dairy products when he learned the child had weaned herself from the breast. He urged Corabell to rub salve into her skin and restrain her tight curls in braids.

Corabell prodded Nate about a shoemaker. Plum could not walk barefoot for much longer. The soles of her own native boots had holes and Corabell had taken to wearing a pair of Elke's old clogs. She confided that she had long wanted a pair of native mukluks. Nate nodded as she described the boot she imagined, but Gerolf objected, "I like those women's boots with the fancy laces. Maybe it's time we go to town."

"Careful dere, many people'll see de dark chile."

The couple and two small ones accompanied Elke and Dietrich to town on a Saturday afternoon in October. Little Plum went barefoot. Corabell quickly found a pair of acceptable boots for herself, with five eyelets across the front, five hooks up the ankle and one last eyelet at the top.

Plum did not want shoes. Corabell tried to persuade her. The child grew irritated and thrashed at the candy stick the saleswoman offered. When her cries grew louder and the clerk caught a flying foot, Corabell asked Gerolf to buy the least expensive pair. Shifting her head away from the child Corabell advised, "Gerolf, shoes with flexible soles, large enough to last the winter." Shoppers paused and watched, wagging their heads. Soothing Plum on the store's front porch, Corabell rocked the little girl in her arms, obscuring her from those passing in the street.

Plum finally settled, giving in to the swaying motion. Asleep against one shoulder, Corabell breathed a sigh of relief. The child's silence after such a battle seemed a gift.

Re-entering the store, Corabell found Gerolf and Otto browsing the soaps. Gerolf chose two different bars for shaving.

"A bar for my hair?" Corabell requested softly.

Gerolf nodded and he and Otto selected a cake scented with rose, another of citrus and one with bits of bergamot and rosemary.

"Anything more?"

"Diapering linens," Corabell whispered, pointing to the fabric, "A few yards'll do." Soon after, they headed to the alley where Dietrich had left the wagon. Corabell attempted to place Plum on her belly in the carriage cart. When she balked, Corabell took her again in her arms.

Otto appeared content to remain with Gerolf and the two wandered down the street exploring the windows of other shops. They reappeared from a public house with a stein of cool cider. Returning the stein to the shop, Gerolf re-emerged toting a sizeable barrel under his free arm when Elke and Dietrich appeared carrying their purchases.

At home, Plum shrieked and fought off any attempt to lie in bed. She rejected water and sipped only the diluted, alcoholic cider. Falling asleep at last, Corabell eased the child onto her mattress. Night wore on and Corabell shed her clothing and lay down next to the baby.

Before the rooster crowed, the little girl stirred. She shook her head gently from side to side. Then her swinging limbs turned violent and battered the bed, kicking wildly as if running. Abruptly, Plum sat and screamed, waking herself and Gerolf, who lay above on the sleeping platform. The brother cursed. The little one slumped and cried mournfully.

Lying beside her on the mattress, Corabell felt the heat from the child's body. She took off the small gown and directed her words to the balcony above, "Go back to sleep. Plum's ill." Gerolf replied gruffly and turned over. Corabell rose and poured more cider for Plum, who emptied the cup. Groggy, the child fell into a light sleep that enabled Corabell to start the fire, make coffee and nurse Otto.

A Sunday morning, Corabell wondered whether to take Plum to church service. The journey would further aggravate her, but she enjoyed the weekly company. The chance to socialize, Corabell considered she might learn something from Elke to stifle the fever. Willow tea, the only remedy she knew, required walking to the riverbank to cut off shards of bark.

Clouds blanketed the morning sky and wind loosened debris from the ground. She decided to stay home. Gerolf could inquire into remedies for fever and perhaps bring home the tree bark.

Corabell began to cook and Gerolf came down the ladder in his underwear. He gazed at Plum asleep on the bed and murmured, "The baby's sweat dampens the sheet where she lies. Her fever rages."

Gerolf pulled the hair back from his face, poured coffee and spooned in maple syrup. Since the minister performed their marriage rite, he had become more casual about his attire. Corabell made no comment about the scant clothing, her eyes wandering over him.

Gerolf

When Corabell conveyed her doubt about attending church, Gerolf agreed. "I'll take Otto with me. The less he's around Plum the less likely he'll fall ill."

By the set of her jaw, he knew Corabell loathed the idea. Frowning and turning away from the hearth where morning eggs fried she asked, "What'll you do if he gets hungry?"

Gerolf allowed an eyebrow to rise as he swallowed a sip of coffee, "He's unlikely to starve in that amount of time, but I could bring a corn muffin for him to chew."

"And if his pants need changing?"

Gerolf lifted both eyebrows and smirked. "Perhaps Nola'll help with that."

Corabell smiled faintly and packed her satchel for him, including extra linens and the hardened muffins from yesterday's dinner. She embraced them, "Send my greetings to everyone and please tell Elke that baby Plum's ill."

Corabell

The baby lay half-awake, attentive enough to moan. On her back with parted lips, her features contorted when she swallowed. Corabell took her to the window. A trail of spit rolled from Plum's cheek and fell dark upon the stone floor. Opening the child's mouth in the light, she saw bright red patches lined her mouth. The base of her tongue and throat oozed blood. Corabell inhaled sharply, clenched the child to her breast and carried her outside.

She must be mistaken. Corabell held back escalating horror. Sitting on the threshold with the door flung open, Plum rested on her thighs while Corabell inspected her skin. Neck, arms and torso appeared normal; her muscular legs, fine. She peered between the full baby lips into the small mouth more carefully. Red areas ran together across the upper palate. Corabell inspected Plum's nose, trying to see inside it unsuccessfully, then lifted the lid of an eye. What should have been white shone solid red.

Her heart hammered and her hands shook. Not wanting to see more, she held Plum tightly to her chest and walked while she wept until the little girl wriggled against the tense embrace. Corabell adjusted the child, carrying her as she had when younger, over one shoulder to feel the quick baby breaths against her neck.

Corabell walked through the garden trying to recall the rhythm of Grandmother's healing song. The tunes that came were chants for the dead. She dared not hum them, for fear they would purge any chance of recuperation. Praying to the Great Spirit, Corabell asked for guidance. Soon her tears dried. She swayed gently in the rocker with Plum against one shoulder, holding her bottom. The puffy baby lips parted slightly and blood oozed from her mouth.

They dozed. Corabell felt warmth and wetness on her hands. Thinking the baby had peed; Corabell opened her eyes and gazed at her blood-covered hands. She sang then, because she knew of nothing else. The songs of the dead and the tune Plum had crooned soared out.

Corabell quieted to the sounds of approaching voices. Before she could think of what to do, they opened the cabin door and stood before her, staring in grades of disbelief and alarm. Elke bid them, "Go home, everyone!"

Gerolf stood with Otto in his arms. The child reached out for her and Gerolf stepped back with the boy. The action caused Otto to complain, provoking Corabell's milk to flood the front of the brown frock.

She stood. Plum lay silent, the rhythm of the warm breath on her neck, gone. Elke commented, "We'll need a suitable sheet for the child."

"In the wardrobe." Elke spread the cloth on the floor and Corabell laid the small body tenderly on it. "Elke, red patches stretched down her throat, oozing blood." Corabell bent and kissed the child's forehead. The fabric of her dress stuck to her, where the baby's blood had seeped through, joining the flood of milk.

"Black Pox! You must go and wash yourself. Now! Go! Go now, before you feed the boy. Go wash! Take soap! Wash everything. Everything! Wash your hair. Leave all your clothing outside!"

Corabell jerked back from the body, certain she had never seen Elke so forceful. Striding to the well, Corabell looked back and saw Gerolf holding Otto. Waiting, distracting the unhappy boy, swinging him side to side, Gerolf kept an eye on her.

Corabell let the pail down into the well and pulled up the bucket. Lathering, she recalled how Plum fought off shoes. Corabell worried Elke would forbid her from washing Plum's body, but the weight of her heavy breasts demanded she feed Otto. Rinsing, she lathered a second time. Dropping the bucket into the well again, she rinsed and wound a towel around herself, stepped into the clogs and hurried past the blood soaked garments. Perhaps Elke would let her wash them. She feared the woman meant to burn the clothes, her oldest frock.

Corabell entered the cabin to see Elke had stoked the fire and was in the process of boiling or burning the sheets and all the linens and clothing Plum might have contacted or recently worn. The woman allowed her to dress and to nurse Otto. Gerolf loitered at the doorway.

Gerolf

Elke approached him, "Gerolf, you must dig a deep hole for the body. The minister won't bury a poxed black baby in the church graveyard. Even if he agreed, the church members wouldn't allow it." Gerolf nodded, sought out the shovel and roamed outside looking for a suitable site.

Then it occurred to him, it might be better to bury the body under the cabin. No one would inquire about the fresh grave and there would be no evidence to entice the passing slave catchers. He returned to the open front door.

Corabell watched him as she sat on the bench, Otto nursing in her arms, "What is it?" Gerolf stood with one hand fixed in his hair, the shovel aloft his shoulder.

He spoke in a low voice, "Maybe I should bury the girl-child beneath the floor. People'll question; they'll want to know where she is. If the slave catchers pass looking for her, no fresh grave'll give away the truth, she was here."

Failing to hear the notion, Elke rambled, "Perhaps the child's gone to the Almighty, who'll care for her, for all eternity. We mustn't mention pox, you understand why and Corabell, it behooves you to stay home another Sunday before returning to service, just in case. You've been with the pox. Girl, do you understand?"

Corabell met her eyes and nodded, "Gerolf suggests burying the baby under the house . . . there'll be no fresh grave if the slave men come this way."

Corabell moved Otto to the other breast. Elke glanced at Gerolf. With her arms spread over the expanse of hard rock under her feet, "Do you mean to go through the granite? We've not that much time!"

Gerolf's smile caused Elke to emit a short snarl. She thrust one hand to her hip, tilted her head and waited. "No. Frau Gottschalk, I'm proposing to dig a hole through the cellar floor."

Elke gazed at him, her eyes softening, "The longer the body lies here unburied, the greater our chances of catching this dreadful disease." She slapped her hands, "The hole, please!"

Chapter Twenty-Four

Corabell

Corabell lit the root cellar with candles along every wall and Gerolf began to dig. Though the hole needed to be deep, it did not have to be wide. Baby Plum was small. Gerolf dug a pit wide enough to stand and work. When he could see nothing, Corabell melted candles onto sticks she impaled in the sides of the earthen cavity.

When Gerolf's head disappeared from view, he asked Corabell to inquire about the depth. Elke carried out the basin of boiled linens to hang on the line, "Gerolf's height? Nein, deeper still."

Later, Gerolf stepped into the daylight and beat the soil from his clothing. Elke pointed to Corabell's discarded attire, "Gerolf! Bury the bloody shift and frock." He scooped the fabric up with the shovel and brought it inside.

"My dress! No, don't burn my dress! Please, Elke. My grandmother traded for that cloth."

"She'd like to bury it," Gerolf informed her, his eyebrow rising, looking to the older woman.

Elke eyed Corabell and smoothed a strand of hair from her forehead, "Ya, fine. I'll boil it then. In the pot with it, Gerolf. But bury that shift." Gerolf lowered the brown fabric into the boiling pot and caught up the bloody cotton with a cooking fork.

Tears impairing her sight, Corabell knelt beside Plum and pulled up the sheet edge.

"Leave her!" Elke frowned, "You've a living child, still."

"I haven't washed her . . . I can't bind her?" Corabell wiped her nose.

"And risk death? Leave the baby." A small warm pool collected beneath the still dark child.

Elke kept her distance. Gerolf dismantled Plum's swing and slid the pigskin under the seeping form. Lifting the body with the swing's ropes, he and Corabell carried the small one into the pantry and lowered her into the candle-lit depths.

"Bury this sheet, too!" Elke called out.

Gerolf released the ropes into the hole and loosened the bloodstained shift from the cooking fork. The fabric fluttered catching fire on a flame in the wall, briefly illuminating the grave. Returning to the main room, he wound the blood soaked sheet in the metal tines. Corabell fought to curb her sobs and dropped in a large sprig of sage, beside her, Gerolf slid in the bundled cotton. Tears dampened the earth they pushed back into the pit and then tamped down.

Corabell emerged from the pantry, face, neck and hands black with earth. Gerolf closed the hatch in the cellar floor and pulled the storeroom door shut.

Elke bid them, "Disrobe!" Corabell pulled off her slip and stood nude. Elke sank the garment into a roiling pot as Corabell shielded her breasts.

"Where're you going?" Elke questioned.

"To cover myself." Corabell turned away from Gerolf and strode across the floor.

"No! Stay here." Corabell froze, turned around and saw Gerolf eyeing her.

"Must you gape at me?" Corabell blared. He abruptly took the empty water buckets and threw the door shut behind him.

"Are you not wed?" Elke inquired. Not waiting for a reply, she pulled in the metal bathtub, poured in scalding water and demanded, "You must wash with the hottest water you can bear."

"But Elke, just my face and hands, I've scrubbed . . ." Corabell countered.

Elke pierced her with an eye, interrupting, "Wash! Wash, you! It may mean your life and you've a child left to nurse, so wash!" With no energy to quarrel, Corabell stepped into the metal tub and sank into the shallow water that singed her skin.

"Wash your hair as well." Elke handed her a bar of soap. While Corabell washed, Elke threw a pot of boiling water over the bloody stain on the floor and then swept it over the stones. She brought Corabell a fresh kettle of near simmering water to rinse her hair. Feeling certain her skin would peel off, Corabell's hot tears met her blazing red flesh. Elke allowed her a towel.

Gerolf set the full buckets at the hearth as Elke demanded, "Yes, your turn. In the tub!" When he simply stood, one eyebrow tilted high, she clapped her hands, "Gerolf Bachmeier, I saw you naked every day at the well. Bitte, come." He grumbled, disrobed and Elke poured in more boiling water while Corabell donned a fresh slip and sat to comb her hair.

Elke stewed the earth and blood-soiled clothing in a kettle. As another pot bubbled, she bid Corabell watch her feet and threw the contents over the floor. The steaming water dispersed and sank into the smallest cracks of mortar and stone. Elke followed with another vessel of scorching water, dousing the cradle, rocking chair, benches, table and surrounding floor. Eventually she gave Gerolf a towel and allowed him to don fresh clothes.

The horse's gait outside the cabin hastened his dressing. Elke rushed to the window and spied Dietrich in the wagon. She grabbed her hat, "Pray for our souls!" She shut the door behind her. An instant later, she reopened the entry and poked her head in, "The child was gravely ill. The illness came suddenly, taking her in hours. This's what we'll say, no mention of pox. No mention! No mention at all." Elke pushed the door closed.

Gerolf

He sighed and buttoned his trouser fly, feeling some relief from Elke's presence. The woman was surely mad with the boiling and cleaning. Corabell took wailing Otto from the cradle and sat on her mattress, then reclined slowly backwards. She patted the area by her side, "Come lie a bit."

Gerolf settled easily on the bed as the aroma of pine moved about them. They gazed up at the beams in the ceiling before their eyes drifted to the open window, where the light dimmed. "Gerolf, Plum's cider cup, it's there on the ledge." Corabell looked at him, her voice flat.

He stared at the metal vessel, "Leave it. Stay away from it. Woman, we need nourishment. Make us supper and I'll pour you cider." Gerolf rose and made his way to the sideboard. Corabell roused herself and saw the kettle contained her boiling brown dress. She used the skillet instead, rinsing potatoes and tossing onions into a dollop of pork fat. Regaining her sense of time, Corabell commented to Gerolf the animals would be hungry. "I'll see to them. You make dinner."

Corabell

Corabell sought the cellar for a string of sausages. She knew the darkness, having hung a smoked turkey, placed pumpkins, mounded potatoes in soil and stored apples in barrels. The space felt more familiar with little Plum nestled in the ground. Humming a favorite song for the brown child, her tears ran anew. Without the white man's burial or a native send away, the young spirit might never find peace. She carried that tight fear in her belly and worried she had disappointed Nate.

Gerolf saw her tears, "I thought you'd leave when Nate gave you the baby. I thought he sought you for himself. I'm thankful you stayed. If you'd gone away, I'd have left too. This cabin was Abo's dream. But with you, it's become mine."

Gerolf walked slowly to the sideboard and recovered a bowl of recently picked radishes. Corabell stopped him, recalling the spirit of cleansing Elke had acquired, took the radishes and washed them with soap.

From a sprig overhead, she pulled a bunch of dry rosemary and sprinkled the withered leaves over the onions and potatoes in the skillet, then added sausages. The smell ran through the cabin and Otto protested on the floor. Gerolf rose and took the child on his knee. Corabell brought them a plate of dry corn biscuits.

Outside the door, the dog whined. When allowed in, he smelled the stones, the space on the floor where Plum's body had lain and sat keeping the occupants in sight. As they ate dinner, the dog slipped closer to the floor until he set his head over one paw, his eyebrows moving as he watched their faces.

Corabell combined the leftovers with oatmeal from the morning and gave the dog his dinner. With food and cider in her belly, she felt stodgy and weary. Gerolf rested, his head on a hand, surveying Corabell as she washed up and pulled the boiling frock from the fire. The dog licked the remnants of the baby's dinner from the floor stones. Otto amused himself by sucking on a wooden spoon while Gerolf held him the way he had Plum; on a knee, with his chest and belly for support.

He righted himself and told her, "I wish to make you happy Corabell. Perhaps you'll let me bring you some pleasure. I'd like to try and please you and this child needs milk. Perhaps when he's finished, I might hold you awhile."

Corabell turned with a half-smile, hearing his words and intentions. She took the baby and nursed him in the rocker as Gerolf moved into the darkness of the corner near her bed.

Having washed, changed the baby's diaper and set him in the cradle, she came upon Gerolf's discarded clothing. He slept nude on the mattress. Corabell tossed her shift on the floor as well, took the sheet and spread it in the air over Gerolf's form, then slid beneath it. She lay down beside him and let the darkness of Plum's death settle over her.

In the following nights, Gerolf took his bed on the platform above her head. In the evenings, he began work on the chair for Eva, using the measurements

Amsel had provided. Corabell did not remind him of the pleasure he thought to give her.

In October, cool days alternated with mild days of brilliant clarity. The trees shed their stained leaves as the loss of Plum and Abo fell hard on those who remained. Though Corabell was freer with one child to mind, nothing replaced the company of the little girl with bare feet in the garden or in the cabin where she hung on the pigskin seat, humming.

Corabell placed the remaining frocks in the back of the wardrobe so she did not see them as often. Nate no longer visited every Friday evening.

On days obscured by clouds, Corabell felt her heart scar acutely. To ward off the spirits that sang of bleakness, she took Abo's traps and set them in the low grass and scrub. She checked them daily. It gave her days rhythm that did not revolve around childcare, meals or washing. While out, she gathered willow bark, herbs and materials for weaving baskets.

Corabell doted on her baby. When gazing at him, she saw shades of his father. He had the wide face of the Bachmeier brothers and it seemed he would have their size. While Plum had been delicate and nimble, Otto was a solid inert brick. His dark straight hair and curvy upper lip seemed the only traits he had acquired from his mother and her kin.

The days grew shorter and with them, the heavy darkness within Corabell festered. It seemed an appropriate act to hibernate. She began napping when Otto lay down in the afternoon. Pulling the boy child close in the cold cabin, the two drifted to sleep while the embers fell to the hearth floor and the temperature around them dipped.

Gerolf

He found them in bed the day the last cattle had been slain and butchered and workers were only needed for half days until the spring thaw. They did not stir when he entered in heavy boots. The open door cast light over their still forms.

Loosening the scarf, he left his hat and stalked to their bodies. Only then did he recognize the suffering in the woman. The child she cradled was plump and long and she had grown slender, so slim the bone of one cheek jutted beneath her skin. Gazing at them, Gerolf stood and wondered whether she was ill.

The last time he had seen Corabell's faint smile was the night of Plum's death. He had offered to give her some pleasure but had been exhausted and slept.

Only some change would save her. He came to her side and touched her shoulder. Corabell opened her eyes. Gerolf urged her away from the baby and she placed the shawl across his back.

Sweeping a finger to his lips, Gerolf took off his boots. When he lifted off the soiled shirt, Corabell frowned. Coming closer, Gerolf kneeled and loosened her corset laces, spreading the leather sides wide apart so the laces ran through the holes. He discarded the support on the floor. Unfastening the buttons at her sternum, he lifted a breast in each chilled hand.

Corabell sat blinking, half-naked before him, staring up at his face. Gerolf lifted her skirt and ran both hands under the fabric, gripping the flesh of each buttock. She drew in a breath and opened her knees to meet the sides of the stained, filth-covered trousers. Urging her forward to the side of the mattress, he whispered, "I can't wait for you to come to me; you need what I can bring you or you'll waste away. Will you have me? I'll not force you."

"Yes, yes I'll have you," her voice was low, without a smile. He moved his hands to the insides of her legs, opening them further as he gazed at her hair and thighs. Corabell unbuttoned his trouser fly.

The canvas material slipped to his knees, revealing an erection beneath his woolen underwear. Corabell slid both hands beneath the pliable warm fabric, bringing the rigid flesh to the chilled air.

He spoke in a murmur, tossing back a strand of hair, "You'll help me Corabell. I've never been with a woman. You must show me what's best." Corabell cupped his scrotum. Moistening her own tissues with spit, she bid him come closer.

"Closer, Gerolf, closer still, come to me, come." Corabell grabbed an arm and pulled him and he entered the warmth of her body. She groaned softly and held his torso. He withdrew and slipped away, but she held his penis and placed it at her entrance, bidding him, "Come this way, again." He slipped back inside her as she exhaled. He watched her features as he made a space inside her for himself.

She opened for him and it changed her countenance. He had never heard flesh beat upon flesh as their bodies collided, nor had he ever heard Corabell moan so.

A sudden withdrawal and Corabell's body lay open for him, her pink tissues exposed. She reached for him. Looking down, he saw his penis covered in a sheath of blood. He gasped, "Corabell, you bleed. You're bleeding, what's this? I'm hurting you."

"No. Well, yes... and it's fine. Come here. We're not finished." Corabell took his penis in hand and her touch made him agreeable.

Corabell

Corabell waited for her husband and lover, remembering his scent and seeking his caresses. When arriving home, she greeted him, catching up her skirts and exposing a leg or glimpse of buttocks.

She grew acutely aware of Widow Heck gazing at her spouse while striding to the Sunday morning pew. Even the clear doe-eyes of Nola bothered her when they lingered over Gerolf.

Corabell could not hold her annoyance long. She shared her irritation on the walks home. When Gerolf pleaded innocence and told her he desired only her, it did not appease her. Only a lingering kiss against a leafless maple tree and the sensation of his hard desire could renew her affection.

Chapter Twenty-Five

Gerolf

Having weighed the matter for a lengthy while, Gerolf visited the construction company that employed the O'Shay men. Henry had joined his father's work crew when his wife, Emily persuaded him sawmill work was far too hazardous. To father her children, she needed a breathing spouse.

Informed of Abraham Lincoln's intent to begin the Illinois-Michigan Canal, the contractor and homebuilder F.C. Sherman began hiring men with construction skills. With twenty-six bridges, four aqueducts and fifteen locks, the plan estimated a cost of thirteen million dollars. Digging would begin the summer of 1836, though they needed worker housing before then. The canal would use a native portage route to connect the Great Lakes to the Mississippi River, through the Illinois River at the town of Peru.

Gerolf began employment when Henry and Patrick O'Shay vouched for his talents and work ethic. He arranged to work partial days in the winter months, transitioning to full-time construction labor with spring's arrival.

Gerolf allayed Corabell's irritation over the news of the second position telling her, "My clothing won't be as foul and my income'll be greater through the bitter cold months. Otto needs warm winter clothing and you a pair of mukluk boots."

Corabell frowned, "We'll lose the regular supply of pork!"

Gerolf gazed at her, "Not until spring, but I won't let you go hungry. Abo and I came to this country for the slaughterhouse apprenticeships." Gerolf looked away and shook his head, "The vices there're too many to relate. Every day we shovel animal debris—skulls, horns, bones, hooves, layers of fat, shit and blood into the river. The boss requires it. But I think Abo hated the place more than I do.

"He never spoke about butchering." Corabell interjected.

Gerolf raised an eyebrow and nodded, "In summer the stink catches in my nose and's all I smell." Corabell nodded. "The wolves dine on the refuse in winter months; I've seen the pack on the far riverbank."

In preparation for the birth of the Lord Christ Jesus, Corabell wove baskets for the Gottschalk families while Gerolf put the final details on the rocking chair

Amsel would present to Eva. He toted the seat to church on a Sunday morning in early December and left it at the back.

From the second week in December of 1835 and throughout the cold of winter, Gerolf finished morning work at the slaughterhouse, ate dinner at a public house and joined the team of Sherman carpenters. Using balloon-framing techniques to assemble buildings from precut pieces of wood, the construction crew raised sturdy houses quickly. Few had finished floors or adornment, but they were capable of weathering strong winds. Clapboards finished the exteriors, while lath and plaster completed interior walls.

Demand for homes kept them busy, though weather complied with no deadlines. If they were behind schedule, they worked into the night under the light of any moon, until they finished.

Strong winds made placing sideboards difficult and required more men. Days when fingers and toes froze and nails were too cold to handle, were times many dreamed of working in indoor workshops. Patrick O'Shay commented regularly and Henry rolled his eyes when his father told Gerolf, "If half my daughters were sons I'd have enough hands to open my own cabinet-maker shop."

Between pounding in nails, Henry informed Gerolf, "My sisters excel in other pursuits. Bridgette's convinced Pa she needs a freestanding shop, equipped with an oven within the town's confines. Transporting pies from the home oven to market on Saturday is too cumbersome. A site in town eliminates travel and increases production. Bridgette and the younger girls are bakers in a sweet shop near the north edge of town on Chicago Avenue."

Gerolf

Gerolf and Corabell celebrated Christmas of 1835 by attending service the evening of December 24th. Widow Heck erected a German style Christmas tree and decorated it with transparent red glass ornaments from across the sea. She hung cookies, heavy with cinnamon and nutmeg on ribbons from the branches and lit small candles in holders balanced on the outspread boughs.

Gerolf took Corabell's hand as they walked home. Baby Otto lay asleep over his shoulder, one smooth cheek flattened against his coat. The steady rustle of footsteps in the dead leaves gave away their presence. An owl hooted close by. Another bird responded. Gerolf felt Corabell stiffen and her steps faltered. She swept close to him whispering, "Someone's here."

They stood immobile and silent, while a dozen dark forms emerged from the deep shadows. Wraps fell from heads and shoulders to the earth. Bound in fabric and obscured under layers, those passing were clearly human. Men or women, it appeared impossible to say. Dark skin blended into the night and they simply disappeared. Nate led the group. The man bowed his head in a greeting. Corabell sighed and squeezed Gerolf's hand, "There're no small ones traveling with them."

Gerolf shook his head, "Maybe underneath all that garb."

Returning to the cabin, Otto slept without fussing when Gerolf lowered him into the cradle. While stoking the fire, Gerolf glimpsed Corabell undressing. She moved in the shadows, away from the firelight. Though she bathed naked at the well, around him she disrobed in darkness. He wondered if she would ever lose the desire to hide from his eyes, though more often, he mused whether she preferred him to his brother.

Corabell

Corabell had not put words to it, for fear the spoken sounds would reach Abo and provoke him. The first sighting occurred the evening Gerolf slackened her corset and asked her to accept him. In her peripheral vision, it stood attentive beside the hearth unblinking, staring at the bed, its white face immobile and stony. Drawing closer the blue eyes remained passive. The cool proximity evoked gooseflesh. Pressing her forehead against Gerolf's chest, Corabell felt the warmth of his hands and wished the phantom away.

Though she glimpsed the figure moving along margins of the mattress, a remnant of her dead man, Corabell resolved to deny it any fear. Pleasure was vengeance for his desertion. The silent spirit watched impassively while she made Gerolf eager. Imagining Abo envious made her bold, though the ghost gave no suggestion of sentiment.

On occasions like that evening, when it seemed they would not couple, the presence turned away, waiting and standing, a sentry at a distance. They lay intertwined and drained from the events of the day, the pewter cup on the windowsill, just within sight. Slowly they floated into sleep.

Before the final days of December, the various arms of the Gottschalk family and close relations met to celebrate Christmas and the New Year. Corabell glowed with anticipation of the gathering. An entire year had passed since Eva had left her girls for the farming man. The daughters pined for her.

The day began unseasonably warm. Sun and a bright blue sky invited the children to run outdoors. Corabell sat with Konrad's wife Beatriz and her twins for a long spell on the front porch. The babies sported fat pink cheeks, still passing a lot of time at their mother's bosom. Beatriz' ample buttocks had narrowed considerably since her pregnancy, yet she complained of woman's issues to any female of suitable age who might listen.

Nola

Nola could not bear to hear her aunt speak of the condition again. Knowing Aunt Beatriz had carried, delivered, fed and tended two babies at once was hard enough. It seemed simply unfair that her innards failed to stay within. Nola could think of nothing worse. She kept her distance.

Eva and Amsel arrived in the wagon with the children between them. Eva dressed the eldest in a dress Romy had worn years ago, gathering up the hem and taking in the seams. Amsel helped his family out near the front porch and urged the horse on to the barn and pasture.

Nola fell in with her mother's steps. An arm around her shoulder drew her near and Eva kissed her forehead, while holding the hand of the boy, who managed the stairs. On the porch, the older girl wore polished boots with shiny black buttons. Golden curls appeared out the back of the small bonnet. She curtsied to the women, bidding them, "How do you do?" before unlatching the front door and scanning the inside for children.

Corabell

Corabell raised her eyebrows and smiled, "Oh, you're looking well." Eva's brown eyes shone. Her cheeks had flushed from the ride. She kissed the women and admired the babies Beatriz held before the small blond boy tugged her arm and led her inside.

Freda stepped out to the front porch and wondered, "Do you think it's warm enough to eat dinner out here?" Dietrich strode past her and gazed at the sky. Bright, only the smallest whispers of clouds adorned the blue expanse high, high up.

"I'll pull the table out; I think it's likely to stay warm." Dietrich took the steps and vanished around the side of the house.

Inside, the younger women worked through various stages of recipes. Uta and Romy pushed cookie cutters into sheets of gingerbread dough that Fiza rolled thin. Nola returned to chopping potatoes while Freda's boys, Rudy and Rory made regular trips to feed the fire, ensuring the turkey continued to cook in the smoke house.

In the distance, Corabell saw a cloud of dust kicked into the air by horse's hooves and wheels of a fast forthcoming carriage. Halting to an abrupt jerk near the front porch, Henry O'Shay let Emily down from the bench. The young woman trotted up the stairs and whisked about the porch, kissing them all and wishing them the happiest of Christmases. She swept a baby into her arms and took the infant with her as Corabell heard her greet those inside.

Gerolf

Amsel wandered to the back of the house where Dietrich and Gerolf positioned the dinner table. He greeted the men, extending a hand as Dietrich inquired, "How's married life after a year?"

Amsel took the hat from his head and raked his fingers through the cut locks, "The woman's willful. She's not the easy female I understood her to be, nor quiet as the first."

Gerolf stepped back, his eyes met the ground, while Dietrich queried, "You forgot what it is to have a woman run a household; where you must leave your boots."

"Maybe, the children do her bidding, but're slow to do mine. She seeks a wooden floor; the sand's old fashioned. Why can't I fashion a pump within the house, so she need not freeze while toting water? She's a mind and brings me hellfire. Yet she shaves me well and I'd have no other. Yes, she pleases me in the end."

Dietrich nodded, "It's good to hear, she's dear to me. Seems you've put a smile on her face as well." Eva appeared at the doorway with little Henry on one hip, her bonnet off, dark hair turned into a twist. She beamed, greeting Dietrich with a kiss. He asked about her parents.

"They may visit later. They'd like to see the girls." The blond boy wriggled in her arms and Eva set him on the ground. Dietrich nodded, turned to Amsel and asked, "Dare we prepare for dinner outside?"

Gerolf bowed to Eva, left the men's company and wandered through the house recalling the nights of sleeping with his brother's warm back against his own. The customary woe found him. He asked, "Frau Gottschalk, how may I be of service?" She pointed to the empty water pails at the doorway and patted his arm. Gerolf left his coat over a chair and headed to the pump.

The wall of green leaves shielding the water source had withered and died. He recalled Corabell watching them, before Dietrich insisted they construct the blind. The impression of woman's eyes on his flesh had excited him. He had turned away from his brother, but Abo knew anyway and poked fun at him, though he was hard as well. Christmas without his older brother, such an idea had never entered his mind and the family in Germany had still not learned of the death.

"Gerolf! Come with me." Leaving the pails on the porch, he strode to Corabell. She took his hand and directed him to the far side of the barn where only the animals watched them. "Fiza's agreed to watch Otto for a bit. I thought of you." Circling his waist, Corabell drew him close and he allowed himself to be led. "I saw you naked twice before we married. Once at the pump, you and your brother came from work, covered in mire and blood. You shed your clothes. The other time you stood at the door in the rain, angry and bare. Gerolf? Corabell looked up at him and he watched how the arc in her upper lip moved as she spoke of illicit things. "Where're your thoughts? Gerolf . . ."

Corabell unbuttoned the linen shirt he wore and moved her hands across his chest. She stretched to her tiptoes, opened her mouth and lightly took the lump at his throat between her teeth. Fondling his erection, before raising herself onto the windowsill, Corabell lifted her skirts and guided him within her. He lingered in her, pleasing her and it eased the loss of his brother.

They lay together in the straw behind the stable for some time. When they overheard voices, Gerolf plucked the dry grass blades from the mass of braids low on Corabell's head and swatted the remnants clinging to her skirts. Walking behind her, he clasped her waist and Corabell turned to look over one shoulder, a smile spreading from the corners of her mouth across her cheeks.

He gazed at the curve from her waist to her bottom, "Corabell, you're a beautiful woman. I noticed when I first spotted you, leaning against the cottonwood, your eyes shut in repose. Had Abo not become acquainted with you first, I'd have sought your hand."

Her smile faded. Halfway to the house, he halted and drew her close, "Motherhood makes you shine. When do you think your woman cycle will return?"

"Gerolf? I . . . don't know," Corabell frowned. "When the baby's weaned, or sometime earlier. Without Plum, I've less milk. I've not had my cycle in ages; the last was far before Otto. It's been so long."

"Corabell, it'd satisfy me greatly, if you'd bear another child. My child." She had loosened his burdens and given him hope.

Corabell

Corabell watched Gerolf's intense dark eyes and tight jaw as his grip tensed at her corset and that desire for her gave the days new meaning. She told him, "I've always enjoyed gazing upon you." Still feeling him within her, Corabell savored his smell. He returned the embrace, dropping low to inhale the scent of her bare warm neck.

On the porch, Dietrich, Amsel and Nola turned their heads away from the display of affection. Only Amsel commented as Gerolf and Corabell ascended the stairs. "Marriage to your brother's wife agrees with you, Gerolf."

Corabell froze, a hand flew to her chest, though Gerolf shook his head, disregarding the comment and strode indoors. Corabell turned slowly, met Amsel's gaze with an icy frown and pronounced her words firmly and slowly, "Sir, you choose the rudest combination of words!"

Amsel tipped his hat and bowed, "My aim wasn't to offend; merely to observe." Corabell turned on her heel, leaving the men to position the benches as Nola looked on.

Soon after, Thomas Flaherty arrived on foot, a beer barrel balanced on one shoulder, a crate on the other. He nodded to Beatriz who sat on the front porch, a child in each arm. Curiosity loosened her tongue. "Mr. Flaherty, you're young and healthy, yet still unwed," she observed and boldly inquired, "Can you not find a lass that suits your taste?"

Thomas dipped his head, "Happy New Year, Frau Corabell," and met Beatriz' gaze, "Ah, Mrs. Gottschalk. Alas, but you've married and wit' two young'uns in yer arms as well. Dhere is no one else for me." He took the stairs while Corabell grinned and opened the door for him. Upon entering the house, Romy and Amsel's daughter, Hanna, greeted the man bearing a substantial load, by seizing his legs.

Elke smiled at Thomas, who stood pinned at the ankles, "A Merry Christmas Thomas! Romy!" Elke clapped her hands. "You've far better manners. Show them. NOW!" Romy quickly unhanded the man's ankle and Hanna followed her example as Konrad and Gerolf drew him into conversation about his latest brewing endeavor.

Beneath the table, Otto lay on his back with Amsel's boy at his side. Her hands coated in flour and fat, Willa worked on biscuit dough. Elke caught Corabell as she turned away, "Would you mind bringing up the cider, Corabell? Dietrich brought it from the trading post. I think it's chilling in the cellar."

"No . . . yes, surely."

Elke thrust a candle in her direction, "Thank you, my dear." Shielding the flame, Corabell made her way down the dark steps, as the scent of damp earth engulfed her. She stood briefly, her eyes accommodating to the darkness.

Winter found Elke well prepared. Corabell gazed at the quantity of earthenware vessels lining the walls. She spotted the ivory jug, hiked it to her hip and climbed the stairs.

Those in the house heard the rumbling cadence of horses before they saw them. From the front porch, Beatriz's cries sounded through the interior, "Konrad!" "Dietrich!"

Corabell set the jug on the table and beckoned Otto out from under the table as Fiza stared at her frowning, her mouth gaping. The young woman hustled to join her mother on the front porch, where other guests gathered and waited as three men on horses galloped towards the house. Corabell, with Otto on her hip, watched among the women and children.

It took several moments for the horsemen to arrive in a dust cloud. They did not dismount. The largest called out, "Seekin' tha homeowner!"

"That would be me, Dietrich Gottschalk. I own this parcel and home." Gerolf descended the steps in two leaps and stood by Konrad's shoulder, on the yellow front lawn with Dietrich.

A slight pale man directed his horse forward. A black hat pressed over his skull. The reins of the horse in one hand, a horsewhip in the other, he spat into the dried flowers beside the steps before he spoke.

The pale rider's words were so thick with accent when they fell from his lips, neither Dietrich nor Konrad grasped their meaning. They looked at each other with empty eyes until Thomas drew out from the porch crowd and explained the stranger's meaning.

"Dhey're seekin' a slave woman. He says she was wit' child when she took off. She must' a been aided, otherwise she would notta gotten so far. Dhere's word she come by dhis way."

In unison, the Gottschalk men shrugged and spread their arms, palms to the sky, shaking their heads in negation.

The pale man spat again and directed the horse to the front porch where the women stood. The two broad men covered in grime hung back.

Thomas related, "Dhe man wants to know if anyone's seen dhe slave woman. Dhere's a reward for 'er capture, twenty dollars for anyone with information dhat leads to 'er." As he made the words plain, the slight man took in the faces of the women, gazing at Eva, then Emily. Sweeping over other figures, he spotted Corabell standing with her child on one hip. He eyed her from head to toe, urging the horse closer until Corabell smelled the currents of air the creature exhaled. Raising the whip, he set it against her cheek.

"Yeh, got an injun Ma o' an injun Pa?"

When she remained silent, he tapped her cheek with the whip end. Corabell nodded, watching the slender lips of the white hairless face. "Yeh kin bess cease assistin' de slave fowk. Ye hear me? I'll 'ave y'all strung up, ever' last one y'all."

Corabell understood. It was not complex. She drew words up from the back of her throat, summoning a defiant tone, "Merry Christmas to you, Sir" and swung an arm up, swatting the whip away. The pallid man stared, cleared the phlegm from his throat and spat a gob of brown, puss-colored tobacco beside her foot.

Gerolf ascended the porch steps in two strides, strode down the planks and stepped in front of her. Corabell's nose wrinkled as the man grinned widely, his mouth open. The sun exposed gummy areas devoid of teeth and rows of darkly stained molars.

The man craned his neck past Gerolf's frame to Corabell, who peered out from behind. Pointing the whip at her, he whacked it against the wooden deck. Dinner guests flinched and the youngest children dashed indoors. The pale rider pulled his horse sideways, spun around and gestured to one of his partners.

The bulky figure approached Dietrich atop the mount. Road filth coated everything from the beaten hat to the horse that bore his weight. From inside the coat he pulled a freshly printed paper bulletin and handed it to Dietrich. The white-faced leader nodded to the men and they fell in behind him as he urged the horse away, back to the road.

Gerolf found Corabell and hastily pulled her around to face him, "What possessed you to speak?"

"The man addressed me. He held a whip to my face!"

"Why act so foolishly? Striking his hand? Why mention the holiday? Do you mean to tangle with this character?"

"Defending myself! If you'd been here, nothing of the sort would've occurred."

"Is my presence vital to keep you from harm?"

Dinner guests moved past her and Corabell spoke softly, "You're absent from me most of the day. If harm finds me, I'll surely have to thwart it myself." Corabell gazed up at him. She reached to pull him close hoping to soothe him. He did not move willingly, his body taut. When Otto stretched an arm out to him, Gerolf took the boy. Corabell brought her husband's hand to her lips, "Husband, don't be angry with me." He did not answer, but took her by the shoulder past Beatriz who remained in the rocking chair.

Dietrich read only the headline aloud, "Twenty Dollars Reward." He handed the paper bill to Konrad and walked slowly up the stairs.

Corabell hoped to take her time with the printed words. Reading was a slow, precarious process. When the flier finally arrived in her hands, she took it back to the front porch where Beatriz might correct the difficult words. With no shame in her poor ability to decipher the sounds, Corabell delighted when the phrases made sense to her ears.

Though the holiday remained unseasonably warm, the riders cast a dark cloud over the festivities. Dietrich accepted a tall glass of Thomas Flaherty's beer. The younger girls began setting the table. Dietrich asked Rudy and Rory, "Boys, what's the report on the smoker?"

"The fire still smokes strongly; but we think the meat's cooked, Opa." Dietrich gestured to the smokehouse and followed the young men. It was past three o'clock and their empty bellies groaned.

Uta brought out a large basket of cornbread and Nola followed her, carrying a hot serving dish of roasted vegetables. The aromas of the holiday feast met the air. The men watched as Dietrich and the boys brought the turkeys to the table on slabs of wood. Elke bid the women bring out the remaining dishes, so they might say grace. Someone summoned Beatriz from her seat on the front porch. She trudged awkwardly to the table in the backyard, an infant in each arm.

Elke called to Fiza, "Girl, fetch the cradle, so your mother can eat dinner," and whispered loudly to Beatriz, "There's a remedy for what ails you, a device of sorts that keeps the insides hooked within." After setting the babies down, Beatriz made the sign of the cross over her face and breast and mumbled her thanks to God.

Chapter Twenty-Six

Corabell

Family and guests gathered. Dietrich said grace in the usual fashion. Around the table, people passed and served themselves and others from platters and tureens. At one end, Konrad carved the turkeys. Fiza poured cider, Thomas refilled the men's steins and Uta served water to others.

Henry stood and raised his stein, "A toast to my wife Emily, who the Lord's blessed with child." Emily smiled and grew progressively pinker under the congratulations of those around the table. Amsel looked across the table at his wife and Eva shook her head.

Conversation about the horsemen arose later. Slow-witted Fiza asked the question that began the discussion about the black baby. Corabell answered her after finishing a mouthful of turkey and dressing. In those brief moments, she committed never to name the man who gave her the child and conjured a quick story.

"I came upon the baby in the woods, gathering acorns for the sow. The sounds were like animal cries. Coming closer, my heart pounded, it sounded more human. The child was naked, lying on a thin wet blanket. Ants crawled across her dark belly."

Corabell set her fork on the plate side, "Someone must've set her down. It was getting cold. I needed to get home. If I left, the child would've frozen, or a coyote eaten her. I thought no more and took her."

Corabell picked up the fork and gave herself a mouthful of red cabbage and a moment to reflect on the story she had fashioned. As she chewed, her gaze crossed the table to Gerolf. He cut dark turkey meat from the bone and did not meet her eyes. Silence fell over the table until Uta asked, "Corabell? How did the baby die?"

Corabell turned to her, "The day we went downtown with the Gottschalks, I sought shoes for Plum. She was walking, the ground growing cold. She hated trying on shoes. When the clerk tried to fit the leather on her foot she wailed and kicked." Corabell's eyes welled, "Plum never wore those shoes, she died with fever the next day, while I rocked her in the chair Gerolf made." How Plum crooned while she hung on the swing, brought Corabell's tears and they slipped down her cheeks.

"The child must've been a slave. She's black, most surely, she was a slave. Perhaps abandoned, or simply left behind. Yet these men seek the mother. You never saw the mother?" Konrad inquired loudly.

Corabell looked over at him, wiped her eyes and frowned, "If I'd seen the mother I'd not have taken the child. She was cold, hungry... bugs crawled on her. I couldn't leave her in the woods."

Konrad swallowed and set his stein down, "Think on that Corabell. You know the penalty for aiding a runaway slave? A year in prison and a thousand dollar fine on the head of the house."

Corabell stabbed her fork in a hunk of pork and faced Konrad, "Runaway? A baby! Alone, cold." Konrad's face remained stony.

"Father, ants crawled on her belly!" Fiza stared at her stepfather, her jaw slack. He shook his head, turning his face to the plate.

Corabell looked to Gerolf, who spoke over his fork to Konrad, "The slave catchers seek a woman. The reward's for her. You happily inform us of the risk of caring for the baby, but proposed nothing when she breathed." Gerolf held Konrad in a steady gaze and the eldest Gottschalk son held his tongue.

Corabell nodded. She should have sought the willow bark and made tea for Plum. Perchance it would have broken the fever and maybe she would be alive still. Guilty, Corabell knew she had given freely only what she easily could.

Nola, Uta and Romy rose and curtsied in unison welcoming the elegantly clad Oberweiss grandparents, while Eva and Amsel exchanged greetings with them. The girls took their previous places at the table, where they lingered over the remains of the meal. The older couple, having previously dined, allowed themselves to be included at the table.

Mother Oberweiss observed, "Eva my dearest, marriage to Amsel has transformed you; you seemed relaxed, even content." The remark caused Eva to blush. She looked to Amsel and gave him a small nod. The farmer stood, cleared his voice and announced, "A toast to my wife, Eva, who's been blessed to bear another child." He projected his pewter cup to the blue sky and declared, "Prost!"

Dietrich

Dietrich looked to his wife and saw the reflection of his own remorse in her face. Elke caught his eyes and gave him a small smile. The thin old man extricated his long legs from beneath the bench and table, cup in hand. He had not finished dinner, but he felt an urgency to address a situation he had accepted a long year ago. A family concern then, it seemed right to attend to the matter again as a group.

He stood at the head of the table, "A year ago I didn't approve of my grandchildren living with their mother and her intended husband, Amsel. An entire year has passed with the three girls under my roof. They're a year older and more mature and settled in their ways. I'm confident they'll continue their studies independent of my guidance; they're curious and intelligent and'll one day make their parents and family proud. Should they wish to abide in another household, I'd give that some consideration."

Dietrich raised his cup and urged, "Let's toast to Rurik's three girls: Nola, Uta and Romy." All those at the table, save for the smallest, lifted their glasses and echoed, "To Nola, Uta and Romy!" Eva smiled and rose to embrace Dietrich before he reclaimed his seat.

The girls sought each other with serious expressions and whispered across the table. Mrs. Oberweiss spun a pearl from the strand she wore around her neck and spilled her concerns, "My Nola, my gifted granddaughter eats dinner naturally, aware of only the most elemental rules of etiquette. She's still not sixteen, though she might be twelve by her slight figure and brown hair she wears long and unkempt."

"None of Elke's urging or her mother's insistence can persuade her to pin it up, except on Sundays when she feels it betters her soul to comply with her elder's petitions," Dietrich enlightened her.

Mr. Oberweiss sipped beer and nibbled on the tastiest parts of the meal, having bits of turkey, roast vegetables and sampling the red cabbage. He heard one word in three, though more of the conversation came in peculiarities of gesture and decorum. With definite feeling for his granddaughter, he commented loudly, "Dietrich, I have to say, I worry for Nola. She's approaching maturity without the guidance of Rurik. I suggest you allow her to accompany us to the city and remain in our household for a time, where she'll meet the families and figureheads of town."

Dietrich welcomed the proposal from his contemporary. He nodded to the man as he expressed in full volume that it sounded like a wise idea. Nola frowned into her plate. She turned the bone of a turkey leg repeatedly until Grandmother Oberweiss swatted her hand.

Corabell
Franz began tuning his fiddle on the porch. Nola sat across the table, a stricken look on her face and Corabell extended a hand, palm up to the girl. Nola took it as tears welled in her eyes and Franz began the first tune.

Wiping her eyes, Nola gathered the empty plates and took them into the house. Corabell let the violin's notes soothe her. She wondered if Beatriz felt conflicted about bearing children with her second husband. Clearly not, Corabell corrected herself, Beatriz' major concern was plainly the bulging tissue emanating from between her legs.

Corabell knew the problem. A village woman had nursed her fourth child until he could walk and then left for the women's hut. Her husband would not touch her. The Grandmothers gave her little relief and when the mother confided she wished to die, one of the old ones made her a deadly tea. Which of the Grandmothers it was, no one would say, not even to Chief Mettawa.

Konrad noted, "The sky darkens in the distance. A cold front approaches. With some luck, we should've time to eat dessert before the winds come." Emily carried apple-cranberry, apple crumb and a rum-raisin pie from Bridgette's sweet shop carefully to the table.

Calm fell on them as they used forks to take up the remains of crumbs. Romy set her chin on the table and smiled. When she shifted her cheek to lie squarely on the table and her brown eyes blinked slowly, Elke clapped her hands and bid them, "Girls! Come, give us your Christmas carols." Romy lifted her head, alert at once and went to stand on the porch.

The three sisters stood side by side. Eva watched them from the bench, beaming. They looked to Elke for direction and began, "Good Christian Men, Rejoice," as she dropped her hand. Nola tapped her foot to keep time. Their voices rose in regular rhythm and after three verses they ended with, "Christ was born to save! Christ was born to save!" The second song, "Lo, How a Rose E'er Blooming" they sang together. Short, with two stanzas, they hummed it a second time.

The two younger girls sang, "Oh Tannebaum" in English while Nola sang in German. At the end of the foreign lyrics, a broad smile crept over Nola's features. They began, "The holly and the ivy, when they are both full grown, Of all the trees that are in the wood, the holly bears the crown," and ended with a curtsy in unison as cousin Franz began, "Greensleeves." The dark cloud mass in the north lumbered overhead and the wind whipped strongly.

Elke

Dietrich asked the Oberweiss couple to linger so they might discuss details involving Nola. Eva remained as well. Nola watched the elders, catching snippets of conversation.

Elke preferred Nola live with them and attend the regular Sunday service in German. Mrs. Oberweiss assured her the German tutor would spend an hour with Nola daily, building on language skills. She would instruct Nola on etiquette and social talents and the girl would apply them in the town's social sphere. It seemed decided; Nola would pass the winter at least, in the Oberweiss household.

When Uta and Romy learned their sister would live in town, in their grandparent's home with servants, a cook and a driver, they exchanged perplexed faces. Having shared the same bed most of their lives, the news took some shine from their holiday.

Corabell

Corabell gave baskets and hand salve to the women of the family and thick mittens to Dietrich. Emily had baked cranberry-apple pies for everyone. She gave Thomas one as well.

Thomas distributed bottles of whisky from a wooden crate and Konrad remarked, "You'll be a godsend when I've sold the land and bought a pub."

Beatriz narrowed her eyes at her husband, "Sell the land? I'll not hear of it! We won that site after squatting for years. No more thought to that." Konrad turned from his wife, thanking Thomas for the bottle.

Uta and Romy distributed gingerbread men and Elke gave scented pouches to the women. Fiza assisted Freda in dispersing bottles of rosemary shampoo. Willa handed out loaves of fruitcake soaked in brandy, secured in wooden boxes. Dietrich had tried to make wine and made vinegar instead. Elke had sunken herbs in the vinegar and gave the bottles to the guests.

Before Otto fell asleep, Corabell and Gerolf bid all farewell and Merry Christmas. The temperature outside had dropped sharply. The dog greeted them as they approached Center Street. Inside the cold cabin, Corabell lit a flame as Gerolf brought in kindling and logs of substantial diameter. Otto did not wake to nurse and Corabell laid him in the cradle.

Gerolf whispered, "I want to fill you with a child."

"Sometimes I feel Abo watches us. I'm not sure he'd want me to bear your children. I'm not certain he'd forgive me." She immediately regretted her frankness.

Gerolf turned away, "There'll always be my brother between us. He doesn't breathe, crap, belch or labor. Worms eat his flesh as it rots and he has no need of you." His words softened, "As I do, as Otto does. Turn to us, Corabell." Gerolf poured water to wash his face and hands. He took a stick from the mantle and cleaned his teeth as he stood in front of the fire.

Corabell murmured, "Come to bed and I'll show the phantom how much I want you. Come. Come here!" Gerolf moved slowly to the bed where Corabell sat on the edge. He stood and let her unbutton his fly and take his trousers down. She stroked the length of him with one hand and cupped his balls with the other. He moved into her gently and Corabell did not open her eyes to check for the spirit's presence.

Chapter Twenty-Seven

Corabell

Otto gripped the cradle sides and tipped from side to side. Corabell felt grateful he was not yet able to climb out. She knitted a cap of the softest wool and the child wore it daily in the chilly cabin. His blue eyes grew darker until they became gray. His appetite matured and changed the contents of his diaper. When he learned to coordinate the alternating movement of his limbs, the dog and door drew him closer. If the entry was open or ajar, the child and the dog were there, gazing out.

Gerolf left for work in the morning darkness and returned after nightfall. Short days urged Corabell outside. She scouted for basket making materials and attended the traps she set regularly. Otto sat heavily on her hip, adding to the weight of her deerskin coat. Carrying him, she soon felt sweat running beneath her clothing.

On harshly cold days when the wind funneled through any cracks in the chinks and daubing of the cabin walls, Gerolf stayed home. He worked constructing a sled for Corabell to pull Otto through the snow and ice.

On an afternoon so cold ice thickened across the interior window glass, Corabell left Otto with Gerolf and set out to check the bird traps. She bundled heavily, covering the curves of her form and left the kettle on for tea.

It had snowed. The frozen ground rested beneath a white blanket. Sunrays stretching from the western sky blinded her and she walked toward the river and woods, not recognizing the tracks on the ground. The dog ran ahead.

She heard the men and smelled the smoke before she saw them. Their voices slurred with alcohol, they sat around a blazing fire. Corabell halted. They saw her and rose from the orbit of warmth. The small pale man she knew; he had rested the horsewhip against her cheek. He stood, fidgeting with the familiar length of leather, then tipped his head to the men, who turned from the flames and trudged in her direction.

The fabric of their filthy coats strained across their heavy torsos. The closer one approached fast and Corabell saw his ears were as purple as his nose. She imagined the parts would soon turn black and fall off. The horses waited their breath white in the tree limbs.

Corabell stepped backwards hastily, adrenaline sparking her limbs as she turned and fled. Like dogs, her flight enticed them. The closer man accelerated. His breathing labored in the air and he threw himself at her encumbered form, capturing her feet. Lifting himself, he grabbed her collar and brought her up, pulling her to the fire by the nape of her coat, backwards through the snow. At their camp, he dumped her.

The small pallid man spat a wad of tobacco and mucus into the snow beside her and lowered the whip to her head. "Leh me see yer face." Panting, Corabell pulled her scarf down under her chin. His eyes scanned her features. He swiped the cap from her crown and threw it in the flames. Settling the whip across her cheek, "Yer da injun, 'alfbreed. Seems we' acquainted. Wha chyoo know 'bout dhis?" He tapped the trampled snow with his boot and lifted a hinged wooden lid.

"I don't know anything about it."

The white hunter dropped the trapdoor. "I dhink ya doo. Murray, take off' er fleece. Leh see wha' she got in dhar." Corabell fought to keep her coat on and the undersized man raised the horsewhip and brought it down over her head.

The sting reverberated through her skull. A stream of warm wetness turned cold rolling through her hair. "Be still gir' or I beat ya' bloody! Done it many' a time." Poking at her coat, he shouted, "Open dhis!" Corabell's hands shook. She fumbled to undo her outer layer and soon revealed the large woolen sweater she had made for Abo.

The boss-man shook his head, spit and brought the horsewhip across the sweater, "I'm needin' a bit a pleasin' in dis frikin norden col', a frikin darkie nighmare. Ya ginna pleazur me gir' or I beat ya' hear? Opin yer mout! Or I whomp yeh."

With small white hands, the man unbuttoned his coat and pulled out his penis while the men snickered from their seats around the fire. Corabell lifted her hands to receive the tiny organ in the frigid air.

Touching the pasty skin, the man leapt back, "Frikin beetch! Frikin col' 'ands! Yeh pud de hans down! Yeh moov de 'ands, I flog yeh." Twirling the whip in a forceful x-shape, the leather raked her clothing. The pale penis hardened; he noted the change and lashed her again, creating a full erection. The others watched the white boss approach Corabell, his penis standing in the cold air. Corabell opened her mouth.

The child-sized hands seized Corabell by the ears and hauled her up to his groin, forcing himself down her throat. The stench of male groin filled her nose. She choked and struggled to breathe. His excitement grew and he pummeled her. She vomited. Thrusting through the rush of hot fluid, he drove harder and then abruptly let go.

Corabell bit down. Her teeth broke through the taut skin. Bearing through, she ripped her head to one side as she found her feet and fled.

The cold air hit her face and Corabell swallowed. Behind her, screams resonated over the frozen ground. She willed herself to move faster, hearing a man's panting breath behind her. He threw himself at her ankles and Corabell pitched forward. With his weight against her back, he held her face in the snow. The cold melted against her skin as she struggled to inhale. Flailing, she kicking her limbs. He tore at the layers of leather, wool and thickly woven cotton.

Gasping, the second man stopped alongside. "Move over, I'll cut through that, make the injun naked." The man grunted and slid off her back and a pointed sharpness moved from her neck to her buttocks.

Clothing peeled away as icy air pinched skin. Cold clumsy hands groped her backside. The men plied apart her legs. Frigid air met her warmth and a boot planted her face further into the frozen snow. Her back prickled and burned.

The weight above shifted and Corabell threw herself up against the bulk. The figure stumbled sideways, trousers unbuttoned, gaping open. Scrambled on her hands and knees, she screamed.

They sprang heaving themselves on skin that flashed beneath tiers of flapping fabrics. She cried out again and again. Panic spiraled beyond control. Her urine sprayed through the air. The grunting one flattened her face in the ice, though her legs flew, catching a body briefly. Hands caught her legs and forced them apart and she wriggled. Bitter air cut at her flesh. Then she heard the dog growl.

The man yelped, let go and fell against her. At her shoulder, the other swore. A pistol blasted and the dog exhaled. The fishy scent of canine fear met the air. The man over her grunted and leaned away. Corabell clambered up, fleeing. A second bullet fired. Horrified for the dog, with no feeling in her legs or feet, she threw herself forward. Her eyes ached. Squinting, wind iced her sight.

Center Street close, the cabin not far, he felled her. A flaccid penis met her thigh and he rubbed himself over her and grew hard, probing for an entry. Recoiling, hands prodded until he found the opening. Corabell raised her head and screamed. The man cuffed her head. Resuming his position, his hands held her unfurled flesh and he swore.

She heard the crack and felt the blow. The impact thrust her into the hard earth, taking her breath. Under the oppressive weight, she sucked for air. Gerolf's voice sounded, but the words had no meaning. As the burden moved, Corabell dragged herself out. Hot blood ran warm on her skin, quickly turning cold.

Tears streamed down Gerolf's face as he pulled the ax from the skull, wiped the blood off in the snow and swung it over one shoulder. "Oh, Gerolf."

He beckoned, threw a free arm across her shoulder and stepped away from the body. "Come home. Now!" Corabell fell into his fast stride, shaking. His warmth made her skin burn. They hurried, tears falling.

Otto sat within the entrance, peering into the shallow light, cheeks reddened by cold air. Gerolf grabbed the boy and held him as though he were a new babe, before setting him near the hearth's glow. Bringing Corabell the shawl, he stoked the fire, put on several large logs and paced about the cabin.

Corabell perched on the warm rocks of the fireplace. Sensation returned, bringing pain with it. Her head and throat ached and her skin scorched. Tears ran, stinging her face.

To make willow bark tea, she took a chunk from a canister on the mantle and tossed it in the kettle. Seizing the bedpan, she vomited. Raking through the contents, she withdrew a stubby object. "I bit off his manhood." The ragged raspy whisper sounded tones deeper than her voice.

Gerolf turned and stared at her and then at the disgorged organ. "Corabell, mien Gott. You did that? I wish I owned a pistol."

"I'd rather've killed him . . . it's all I could do. Think he'll come for me?" She looked into Gerolf's face, gauging his reaction. Tilting his head, he picked up the child and strode in large fast circles, patting the boy's back.

"How can he return home? He'll never explain that. He'll require doctoring, no? Surely, he bled. Perhaps he'll bleed to death. No, I doubt it. Yes, mien Gott, I fear we'll see him again. I'll not leave you alone until I buy a pistol and you can shoot."

Gerolf set the child on the mattress and sought the bottle of Christmas spirits. Swallowing several large mouthfuls, he handed the bottle to Corabell. "There were three," she whispered, "now there're two: one missing an organ, one with a dog bite." She took a swallow and winced as the liquid descended, searing her raw tissues.

Gerolf smiled grimly and drew closer, laying a hand gently on her head. Without her cap and scarf, her hair had escaped from her long braid. She mouthed hoarsely, "He forced himself down my throat, beat me with the horsewhip, burned my cap and planted my face in the ice."

Gerolf stooped to face her, "Open your mouth." He took a candle to the side of her head and peered into her throat, "It's too dark." With her cheek in his palm, he gently kissed her burnt skin. "I heard your cries. I saw his hands on you."

"The big man, who cut my clothes . . . the dog bit him. I heard the cry. Did you hear the shot?"

"Yes. But what did they do here?" Gerolf ran his hand over her darkened brow, cheekbone and jaw.

"He whipped me, hit me and shoved my face into the ground. I couldn't breathe or feel my skin."

Gerolf shook his head, "I want to hold you."

Corabell gazed up at him, her face reddish-purple, "I don't have a place that doesn't hurt."

"Later then, when you've healed a bit. Bathe and drink your tea. Otto and I'll make supper."

Beside the hearth, Corabell removed her tattered, tangled clothes. Repairing the leather coat would take time, but it seemed possible. The cut was almost straight down the back. Her corset might be repaired as well. The stitches of Abo's sweater unraveled. What remained of the front stunk of vomit. She recalled the drowning sensation when the pale one beat down her throat against the flood of puke.

Corabell shuddered, bundled the sweater and threw it into the heat. The dress might be sewn, though the seam would require careful work to hide. She drew her shift over her head, the fabric cut and filthy with urine, blood and grime. Corabell gathered it into a ball and tossed it in the fire. The flames leapt into it. Her woolen leggings followed. She stood naked beneath her blue shawl, poured boiling water into the bowl and wet a cloth. Gerolf brought her the rosemary soap, poured her tea and refilled the kettle.

She wrung out a cloth and placed it on her face. The wet warmth stung. Her head bumpy and bruised, her hair was matted with blood. Corabell sighed. Summoning the energy to wash, she dropped the shawl and revealed her back with the incision along the spine.

"Let me do that for you."

Corabell gave him the cloth. Gerolf swabbed the blood down her back and kissed the bend of her shoulder. "I'm sorry Corabell I wasn't there sooner. I'd've put the ax through all their skulls. The body's outdoors, where the wolves and coyotes'll find it and tear through the flesh—a suitable end. Our dog lies without a burial, as well." Corabell nodded silently.

Cleaner, though sore and sleepy from the alcohol and hot tea, Corabell lay down. Finding a position on the mattress for her tender skull was difficult. When she found that place, she pulled the woolen blanket to her chin. Grateful for the comfort of home, her bed and Gerolf, she drifted to sleep.

Corabell felt Gerolf slide between the covers, but could not budge. Her head and throat throbbed. She knew more tea would ease the soreness and reluctantly eased herself from the warmth. Without the dog, there was no warm body beside the hearth at such an hour.

She might have eventually forgiven what they did to her, but shooting the dog went beyond pardon. Corabell sat on the bench with a mug of tea and let tears drip onto the old table.

Chapter Twenty-Eight

Corabell

In the morning, the bruises had begun to bloom. Corabell cooked, carefully sipping coffee. Gerolf bid her, "Dress and ready yourself; you'll spend the morning with the Gottschalks. I'll purchase a pistol at the trading post and collect you on the way home. It's way too cold for carpentry."

Corabell stepped back and whispered, "My throat pains me. My head aches. I need to mend my coat. Truly, I prefer staying home."

Gerolf frowned, "Wear Abo's coat if you must, but ready yourself and the child."

"I'm ashamed and staying here."

Gerolf lay his steady eyes on her, "I'll take you whether you're ready or not." He turned away and shaved, gazing into the small hand mirror. Corabell conceded when he growled, "Ach! Hasten, NOW!" and stomped a foot. She slid into Abo's coat, the sleeves reaching her knees.

Outside, the day was as frigid as the previous one. Breathing caused the lungs to ache. The wind bit like razors countering her raw throat. Corabell covered her face and mouth, taking Gerolf's arm. Feeling oddly potent beneath the oversized garment, she trod on its length, walking with so many tender bumps and bruises.

At the end of the lane, they passed a hairy leg partially bound in a fragment of fabric. Around it, animals had left prints in the snow. Other pieces of clothing lay discarded about the frozen ground where carriage wheels had passed. Frozen blood mixed with snow and road dirt. Gerolf did not allow Corabell to pause, or break the rhythm of her stride. He told her, "On the way home we'll look for the dog."

He knocked on the front door and as Freda answered, he bowed his head, "Corabell's been attacked by the slave hunters. If they pass this way it'd be best to hide her in the root cellar or attic." Freda could not raise her eyebrows higher. Her gaze went to Corabell.

Freda took Corabell by the arm and directed her inside. "You're wearing a man's coat. You're meant to be in disguise?" Corabell unwound the blue shawl exposing bruises, swollen eyelids and lips. The skin of her forehead and cheeks, in deeper hues of purple-red, appeared scorched by the cold. Responding to Freda's question, the whispery-raspy hoarseness of her voice caused the woman to step back.

"They slit my coat. I had nothing warmer to wear. Gerolf demanded I wear Abo's." Corabell set her bag on the floor as she wrangled with the woolen garment, bringing Otto into the house light. She hung the long cloak at the doorway and slung the shawl back over her shoulders.

Freda frowned and motioned to come, "I'll make you some tea. I was just washing the morning dishes. The children're tending to morning chores and Elke's in the barn, but should return soon. Dietrich left for the slaughterhouse not long ago."

Corabell nodded. Slipping cautiously into the rocker, she closed her eyes while holding Otto and gently shifted to and fro across the creaking floorboards.

When Elke glimpsed her face, she bid Corabell remove herself to the bedroom. "You should be resting in bed. The girls'll care for Otto."

Corabell hesitated, "I brought work to do."

"Fine, but you must work in the bedroom." Corabell got up from the warmth of the hearth and handed her the child. Unsure if Elke objected to the sight of her and dependent on the hospitality, Corabell took the bag with tools and her coat.

"Which bedroom may I use?" she mouthed.

"Take mine, please."

The goose down comforter billowed high above the mattress of straw. Corabell hesitated when she saw the neatly made bed. Walking behind, Elke bid her, "Keep on your shift and leggings." As she disrobed, Elke glimpsed the gash down her spine, "Oh, your back, but what of your voice?"

"Injured my throat."

"Other areas?"

"Beaten, slapped, whipped . . . and they shot my dog."

Elke exhaled, "Dear heart," and drew Corabell gently to her. Tears dampened Elke's dress as Corabell listened to her beating heart. The saltiness stung the burnt skin of her cheeks and Corabell wiped them away. She had spent her sobs grieving for the dog.

"Get between the feather bed and comforter; you'll be warm soon enough."

A dusky poultry smell emanated from inside the cocoon of feathers sheathed in cotton. Her breath vapor rolled over the covers. In the softness of feathers and down, Corabell found a comfortable position for her skull with ease. Slowly her body warmth heated the surrounding area and she rested, cold air settling on her swollen, bruised face.

Closing her eyes, thankful for the help with Otto, Corabell drifted. The morning trek through the polar frost had invigorated her muscles; the warm nest of feathers lulled her again.

Elke

In the adjoining room, Elke told the girls no one was to disturb Corabell. Returning later to treat the wounds, the regular breath beneath the covers told her Corabell slept. Elke turned and pulled the door closed. Sleep was the best medicine for healing flesh wounds. Wrongs to the spirit took longer to mend.

Corabell

When Corabell woke, she dared not enter the house without Elke's permission. She used the bedpan, dressed and began considering how to repair the deerskin coat. If she worked carefully, the garment might even fit her better. Previously, it had fallen straight from her shoulders. Now cut open, she might fashion a coat with a waist. Laying the hide on the floor, Corabell stared at it, gauging how much to remove to ensure the sides were symmetric.

Elke

She rapped lightly on the door and entered. Scanning the sliced coat on the floor, her hand flew to cover her mouth, "I'd rather not relate what the thugs sought. It's better the girls remain innocent."

"Surely they'll see I was beaten."

"Beaten yes. Nothing more vile?"

Corabell tilted her head, "I didn't surrender my womanhood." Elke nodded, clenched her lips and opened the door to the main room of the house. Corabell followed her to the table near the hearth.

Whispering hello to the younger ones, Corabell added, "Thank you for caring for Otto." Rory held the boy balanced, belly down across his knees at that moment, as he lay warming in his coat, to one side of the fire.

Corabell

Uta sat on a chair beside her cousin, creating something blue with two knitting needles. Bigger and blonder than her older sister Nola, Uta spoke to no one in particular, "The instructions said this was easy, they lied. I've worked for weeks. I will finish, even if I must take out rows of stitches." A frown drew the ridges of her eyebrows together. "I truly despise knitting."

Romy occupied one end of the long table. Her hands worked, buried beneath a mound of flour. Romy looked up immediately as Corabell came in, her eyes following as she drew close to the fire and warmth of the room. Corabell set her tools between the ends of the table and attempted to smile at the youngest sister. The swollen tissues of her lips and face prevented much movement of facial muscles.

Romy stared frowning, "Mrs. Bachmeier, what happened to you?"

Corabell glanced at her, "Remember the slave catchers? I came upon them and they beat me."

"The man with the horsewhip?"

Corabell nodded, "Himself." Romy gazed into her bowl and her eyes pooled with tears. She sniffled. Uta paused in her stitches. Her eyes took in the changes of Corabell's face and speech and she stared, speechless. On the floor, Rory rose to his elbows, his expression stiffening when he noted her injuries.

Corabell had not thought about the impact she might have on the young people. She doubted Gerolf had considered it either. It was Elke's first concern.

Elke gazed at Corabell while stirring the contents of the pot hanging over the fire. "Making biscuits?" Corabell asked the youngest sister.

Her voice was so raspy and brittle that Romy looked at her, "Did he mar your throat as well? Corabell nodded and turned her attention to the slice down the back of her coat.

Uta took a seat opposite her, frowning when she saw the coat's condition, "They cut your coat." Corabell nodded and Rory shook his head.

"Corabell's safe now," Elke volunteered.

Romy brushed a tear away, creating a streak of white flour across one cheek. She retorted, "But no, Corabell's not safe at home alone with baby Otto. Your dog didn't protect you?"

Corabell wondered whether Elke would prefer that she lie. "He defended me well, biting one attacking the other." She recalled the quick exhalation when the bullet hit and how the second bullet fired as she ran. Corabell glanced at Romy and whispered, "He was a good dog."

"Was? They killed him?" Corabell nodded, knowing Elke did not approve. Rory shook his head again, while Otto hung from his shoulder. Romy had ceased to work on the biscuits she prepared for lunch. Elke strode past and knocked on the bowl.

For some time, the three attended to separate tasks and then Uta gazed up from her knitting and asked, "Miss Corabell? Will you come again tomorrow?"

Corabell took the scissors, sat on the bench and replied in her loudest whisper, "I've got laundry that needs washing and Gerolf intends to purchase a pistol from the trading post." Both girls, Rory, Elke and Freda riveted their eyes to her.

Uta dropped the project in her lap, "Gerolf thinks they'll come back?" Corabell nodded and seeing it was an insufficient reply, added, "He fears one in particular'll come back." The four women and young Rory listened for what would follow but Corabell did not explain in deference to Elke.

Only Romy had the curiosity and gumption to inquire, "Why?"

"I hurt him badly." Rory hid his smirk from his grandmother.

"Ha!" Romy grinned. A sly smirk crept across Uta's wide cheeks as she bent over her knitting. They soon changed the subject of their intermittent banter to how Nola fared living in the household of the Oberweiss grandparents.

Elke

Elke strove to live according to teachings of Christ Jesus: To him that smites you on one cheek offer also the other. She concealed her vast pleasure in learning Corabell had pained her tormenters, by adding a log to the flames and whisking into the cellar for a bottle of woman's elixir.

To make the restorative tonic she had gathered and dried a bushel each of nettle leaves, oak straw, horsetail and alfalfa leaves. Using the cauldron her mother had used for making soap, she prepared a stew of the vegetable matter outside in the fire pit. As dusk approached, she left the pot to cool. In the morning, she strained and squeezed the organic material free of the liquid. The vegetation went to the compost heap. She poured the mineral-rich liquid into a pot, which she brought inside to use as the base for the elixir. To it, she added dried raspberry leaves and dried fruits for color and taste, as well as red clover for its ability to cleanse the blood.

Schwarze Johannisbeere black currants were foreign to the land. Her mother had given her the plant when Elke was newly married, impressing her with the small berry's ability to maintain health throughout the cold long winters of the Midwest.

Elke added the dried berries to the potion for their rich source of nutrients and ability to retard spoilage. She steeped the fluid over the fire and when the tea acquired a dark red hue, she set the pot outside to cool. In the morning, when time permitted, she strained and squeezed the vegetable matter from the concoction. Once more, she brought the liquid to simmer. To make the remedy palatable she added sugar. Romy and Uta sampled the hot sweet mixture and gave their taste opinions before Elke felt satisfied, poured the remedy into clean bottles and corked and stored them.

Corabell

Corabell knew of Elke's tonics. She had received one when pregnant with Otto. This however, looked much more appealing than the oily syrup she had taken nightly in the past.

To heal her throat, Elke instructed her to make a salve with equal parts of vinegar and honey. The thick liquid needed sipping at regular intervals for several days to aid in recovery of the soft throat tissues. She handed Corabell a spoon, pushed the stoneware crock of mix her way and emphasized that she need start taking it immediately. Corabell swallowed a spoonful.

Gerolf

The smell of cooking dough greeted the men as they walked the route to the Gottschalk home. Dietrich opposed the pistol purchase but could not dissuade Gerolf, who failed to inform his mentor he had cracked a man's skull with an ax.

Gerolf could not fathom how Dietrich thought Corabell alone could repel such vile rats. Having discussed the matter at length, they had come to no consensus. "The village elected a constable, Orsemus Morrison. He's taken on two deputies. You should report the crime to them."

Gerolf wagged his head and clamped his jaw. Dietrich would not deviate from his pacifist beliefs. The senior man would simply permit the vermin to victimize his wife.

"In the future, I'd prefer you seek refuge in the church. I fear involvement with these pointed characters'll put my own family in peril." Gerolf held his tongue.

Arriving at the home where dinner was ready, people assembled and hungry, Elke insisted Corabell and Gerolf stay. Dietrich gazed at Corabell's face, then sought her hand, "I'm sorry you fell victim to the godless slave catching rabble. Let's pray for our enemies." Grasping Uta's arm, he bid everyone gather so they could pray. Corabell found Gerolf's fingers and followed Uta's gestures.

Corabell

Chief Mettawa seldom, if ever, promoted revenge when white men killed his kin or burned village homes, but Corabell doubted he ever prayed for the enemy. She bent her head respectfully, though she wished her foes only the most severe of endings.

From the corner of her eye, she spied Gerolf's posture. Head erect and eyes wide, he lacked the attitude of someone in commune with the Great Spirit. She squeezed his hand sharply. Gerolf closed his eyes, though he continued to hold his head. She felt it was concession enough. A grown man should act as such; the wife and children had no such luxury.

At the table, the group grew quiet as they ate sausage, onions, beans and pickled eggs. Romy brought a tray of biscuits around to all. Lightly cooked, they retained flour dust. Inside the crusty outer shell lay a center of fatty moist ground wheat. While hot, they pleased the mouth and nose with satisfying rich moisture. Later in the meal, when polishing a plate with a biscuit wedge, they were less appealing. The chilled fatty dampness tasted greasy and the crust solidified resisting the tooth.

Gerolf rose stiffly, "Thank you, Herr Dietrich and Frau Elke, for your hospitality during this time of peril." Elke frowned and patted Gerolf's shoulder, though Dietrich nodded and took the rocker in front of the fire.

Elke reminded Corabell, "Take the tonic daily and perhaps twice a day if you feel a malady coming on. Don't forget, equal parts vinegar and honey for the throat." The girls came to the door and waved farewell. Elke placed her hand on Gerolf's cheek and gazed into his eyes before letting them go.

When they were out of hearing range, Corabell turned to Gerolf, "And your purchase?" He silently took her hand and brought it into the pocket of his overcoat. She felt the outline of a firearm and gazed up at his features.

"I'd be happier if Dietrich saw my perspective on defending oneself."

"What would he have me do? Lay there and surrender?"

Gerolf pulled her closer and tilted his face downwards, "He seems to think it's preferable to shooting a man. Can't tell if he takes little value in women, or can't move from religious teachings, or both. He told me not to seek shelter in his home. Church, he believes, is a more suitable place for asylum."

Corabell let the meaning of the words sink beneath her skin where they burned. She found it hard to accept Elke would harbor the same feelings, yet the grandmother had wanted to keep her from the children. "Elke's been a mother to me."

"Elke's not the head of the family. Her desires have no weight."

Corabell kept silent until they approached the grounds where Gerolf struck the slave man down and reminded him, "We must look for the dog's body."

Gerolf sighed heavily, swinging his arms through the frigid air, "Where do you suppose that'd be? And what if it's not in one piece?" Corabell met his eyes and turned to scan the ground.

Prints, blood, bits of fabric and frozen flesh remained from the previous day. Corabell followed the dog paw depressions, as Gerolf trailed behind. She walked west on Center Street to the river, eventually arriving at the site where she had landed, belly down under the weight of the man's body. Drips of frozen blood speckled the snow. Farther along, boot prints went west while the dog prints turned north. She followed the trail of paws. Gerolf caught up with her, seized her arm and spoke in hushed tones, "I thought you said they killed the dog!"

"I heard two shots. The first hit him. I heard his breath escape." Gerolf pulled her closer. The woolen cap covered his ears but she saw the frozen hairs in his nose. His skin was paler in the cold.

"Corabell, though I've the gun in my trousers, I've never fired it, nor does it have cartridges in the barrel. If the dog lives, he'll come home, soon. When ready. Come. The baby's with us, let's be on our way." He pulled her arm lightly. Corabell gazed back at the paw prints. She allowed Gerolf to guide her away while a flicker of hope swirled about her heart.

They arrived to a cold cabin. A film of ice coated the water in the barrel near the sideboard. Neither took off their boots or coats. Corabell raked the coals, searching for a red-hot ember she could induce to burn. Gerolf brought in several split logs and laid them at her feet. In time, Corabell coaxed embers into flame with more wood and put the kettle on for tea. Otto wiggled beneath the heavy man's coat and Corabell shed the garment.

Gerolf sat down and placed the weapon and ammunition on the table in front of him. He slid a cartridge into the slot at the back, took several others in hand and headed to the door. "Wait for me!" Corabell urged. Gerolf strode away, silent.

Outside, she heard a single blast and Gerolf exclaim. The second shot sounded farther away. Washing potatoes, she dunked them in the kettle to boil. Grabbing Abo's coat from the hook, Corabell set Otto within the sling over one hip.

Gerolf held the pistol, his arms straight out in front of him. He fired a third cartridge and a shaggy barked hickory tree on the lane to the west shed a piece of its outer mantel. "Oh, you hit the tree!" Gerolf looked at her, his dark eyes distant. He shook his head.

"It's a powerful piece, with a very heavy kick. I'm afraid it'll be difficult for you to hit a target. I should've purchased a rifle."

"Surely, a rifle wouldn't be easy . . ." Corabell replied.

"No, but it would've been more useful. I hesitate to let you try. Brace your arms in front of your body," Gerolf demonstrated, "and expect to feel the pistol kick back toward you." He showed her how to stand, planting her feet solidly in the snow and offered the gun to Corabell who pushed the long coat sleeves up her arms. "Point the muzzle at a far tree and when you're ready, pull the trigger while holding the weapon steady."

Corabell stood in the pose, fixing the target in the distance. Her bare hands shook on the cold metal. Readjusting her grip, she retook the position. "Corabell. Hear me. You'll not have all this time. You'll see the brute and you'll shoot," Gerolf sighed and stalked back and forth.

"Oh, I'm shaking Gerolf . . . I'm not even afraid . . . I'm not sure I can do this." Corabell lowered the weapon.

"You must know the feel of it, so you're aware of what'll happen. After the bullet exits the muzzle, it'll rock back swiftly. Expect that to happen."

Corabell stood once more in the stance Gerolf recommended, held her breath and steadied the pistol. Fixing the end on the hickory tree, she pulled the trigger.

The blast rang in her ears. The weapon heaved in her hands, hitting her squarely on the forehead. She fell back, dazed.

Otto screamed and beat within the coat. "Versift!" Gerolf swore, took the pistol and placed a palm across her forehead. "Corabell, mein Gott, Oh, that's it. You may kill yourself and the boy. Come, how do you feel? Give me the child."

He unbuttoned the coat and took screaming Otto, who sought him out with waving arms. The child comforted in his hands and he slid the boy within his layers.

Corabell sat on the ground. She blinked and raised a hand to her head where a mound formed above the bridge of her nose, "Oh."

"Willow bark tea, for the headache you'll have. Come, come away, you did fine." Gerolf extended a hand. Corabell took it and set a wad of snow along her brow where the weapon had struck.

That evening, Gerolf constructed a barricade for the door that lacked a key, lock or doorknob. A wooden plank, greater than the width of the entry, fell within troughs aligning on both sides and running along the door's middle. The windows of the cabin would also require securing, but the sky had darkened and Gerolf had not decided on those details.

Chapter Twenty-Nine

Gerolf

Resolving to secure the cabin, Gerolf built shutters for the windows on subsequent days when frigid conditions prevented outdoor construction with the Sherman work crew. Completing most labor within the cabin, Gerolf hung them outside. Each panel folded flat against the cabin's wall when open. When closed, the shutter received four iron pins that penetrated through its edges and the thick cabin walls.

Inside, two horizontal planks barred each window and accepted the heavy pins. The iron pin tip projected through the plank and received a hefty bolt. When secure, the shutters, interior planks, pins and bolts held the windows impassable. Once closed, the interior received no light. Corabell placed candles around the cabin though nothing substituted for the sun's radiance.

Corabell

Corabell lay in bed listening, wondering whether she had dreamt the bark. The dog had grown accustomed to resting his hind end on the threshold stoop, his front legs on the ground. She rose from the bed's warmth, lifted the beam and pushed the door outwards against the animal's mass, happily letting him in.

He nudged her arm encouraging her caresses. Scents of pine and smoke came off the long cold fur. Following her to the fire's warmth, the dog sat and Corabell scanned him for wounds. The animal's body seemed free of injury and nothing on the torso appeared tender. Corabell examined his face and noticed the left ear in an awkward fold. Straightening it, a hole penetrated the supple flesh. The beast shook his head gently. Corabell nuzzled his brow, embracing the white-bibbed neck welcoming him home.

Taking her affection, the dog brushed past her to sniff the deflated tissue stub lying on the warm stones in front of the fire. Lifting the fragment in his teeth, he settled with his forelegs stretched out before him, dropped the flesh on the stones near his paws and shredded the tissue into shear strips before swallowing it. When Corabell slid back between the sheets, her heart glowed though her bruises spread in shades of purple, green and blue.

Gerolf

Every morning, Gerolf passed the fence-enclosed pen where Abo had landed. He told his brother he was sorry, it should have been him. Family in Germany had no notion of the accident. He had still not written. As days passed, Gerolf considered what good the letter would serve. Lutherans did not pray for their dead; it did them no good. Each soul built a pact with its maker and the petitions of others to the almighty could not intercede.

Whether due to the absolute darkness of the cabin, or the season itself, Corabell rose later while the shutters kept the fear of the slave hunter and his man out.

Gerolf noted the change in his wife and thought it curious. He preferred having her in bed in the morning, where he could unwrap her slowly as he felt for her warmest areas, arousing her and causing her to anticipate his next thrust. Then she would help him shave before making breakfast. She kissed him passionately before he left. In former days, she would have insisted on bathing nude with cold well water. The new routine meant he arrived later to the half-day of swine slaughter. When weather permitted carpentry, he returned in darkness to dinner waiting in the dim cabin confines.

Corabell

Corabell mended, taking the willow bark tea daily as well as Elke's tonic. Bruises faded and the back scar peeled and grew less pink. Cold dark months wore on. In moments when she felt safe within the cottage, the dog and pistol close, she wondered about the brute she had deformed. What could a man do with half his organ? How would it affect his nature? Corabell predicted the clipped organ would change the man's behavior if he had some capacity for shame.

After weeks of living with the shutters in place, Corabell's eyes grew accustomed to the dim interior. The first glance of brilliant white snow through the open door blinded her. She took Otto out daily though she was wary of sounds, alert for footprints, bent twigs and the smoke of other fires.

Corabell tended the animals in the shelter and planned the spring garden. Gerolf bid her stay near the cabin, but she needed to set the traps afar, in places the birds dwelled. The dog tended to stay at her side though he eagerly ran for rabbits, returning with creatures limp in his mouth.

Slowly the whims of weather shifted towards springtime. The first warmish day at March's end caused the accumulated snow to turn mushy. By nightfall, the earth had absorbed the excess. Air smells changed. The wind carrying the slight fishy lake odor drew Corabell outside. Turning over last fall's dry plant stalks, she worked them underneath the top layer of leaves and humus.

Returning to the dark cabin felt wrong. Corabell urged, "Gerolf, we must open the shutters and let in the sun and breeze. It's been long enough without the light."

He said nothing at first, but finally countered, "If you have another turn with the pistol I agree to uncover the windows."

"Yes and I won't get hit in the head."

On the gray, chilly morning memories of warmer, brighter days occupied her mind. She would try the pistol again; whether she hit anything did not matter. The shutters would fold against the cabin sides and she would welcome in the light and breeze.

Gerolf urged her to stand squarely, shifting her weight slightly forward as she stretched the gun out in her hands. He cautioned her again about the recoil.

Corabell imagined spring without the scent of the garden coming through the windows and knew she could shoot the man with half a penis if he came for her. Whether she hit him was another affair. She avoided pondering that scenario.

Gerolf held Otto. Corabell pulled the trigger without hesitation. The blast rang, her straight arms swung up. The muscles around her locked joints ached. As the explosion eased, Corabell beamed at Gerolf. She would take the shutters off that day, even if Gerolf insisted she wear the loaded pistol.

Gerolf

Gerolf stood near the open door and buckled the holster strap to her waist. In the shaft of morning light, he noted the leather laces of the mended corset strained across her width. Surely, Corabell had been thinner. He remembered a slender body. She saw his expression and asked, "Where're your thoughts?"

His eyes drifted to her corset and he laid a hand against her abdomen, "You've a belly now. Quick, take off your dress."

"A belly? You'll be late for work."

Gerolf shook his head and gestured with his hand, "No, I don't mean to have you. I want to see you in the light." Corabell loosened the laces of her corset. Tossing it on the table, she lifted the dress and shift over her head.

Her breasts had widened; he saw a round belly beneath them and smiled. Corabell ran a hand across her breast. "You think I'm with child?" He nodded. "Well let's not speak of it," Corabell cautioned.

His heartbeat pounded joy. Finally he would be a husband to the woman he chose. With no warning, he needed her. Cool hands sought her warmest flesh. Corabell backed onto the table holding breakfast dishes and moaned as he filled her. The boy on the bench asked, "Mama?"

"Your mama's fine. Be still."

Before leaving, Gerolf placed the pistol in the holster at her hip and forbid her from taking it off. She agreed easily, kissing him more then he desired.

Chapter Thirty

Corabell

Corabell washed herself and the boy, who had grown to her thigh in height. Straight dark hair fell over his forehead framing almond-shaped gray eyes. The pleasant regularity of features caused Corabell to imagine him a handsome young man with the height and width of his father's people. He had quickly outgrown the shoes bought for Plum. Elke replaced them with the smallest pair of clogs her spouse made long ago.

Otto lost the wooden shoes at regular intervals. Corabell found her son balancing on one foot in the slush, the shoe a pace behind him. Blessed with a peaceful spirit, he sprawled over the dog's back, gripping both sides of the animal's fur-bound neck. The dog stood and carried him around the cabin's interior, the boy grinning, one cheek flush against the dark fur. Otto preferred the comfort of the dog's belly to the wooden cradle, where he needed to bend his knees to fit. The animal found the boy's side at any opportunity.

That gray morning after the first tease of spring, Corabell stretched up, balancing on an overturned water pail and used the claw end of the hammer to pry the iron screw head loose. She gouged at the wood trying to ease the tool under the metal head. The dog growled from within the cabin and sprinted through the open door. Corabell turned and watched him vanish.

To the south, a horse trotted eastward pulling a buggy. Behind, two men on horses and a figure followed on foot. One wore a dark hat; he was the smallest in the group.

Fear rising in her belly, Corabell kept her eyes on them, telling herself they might not turn down the lane. She had not freed the screw when she grabbed the other metal pegs and ran them back through their holes.

The dog reached the travelers and barked, heckling the horses until they reared and snorted. Shots fired and the dog retreated low into the dry stalks of prairie grass. The men on horseback turned onto the footpath and proceeded toward the cabin. Corabell hoped they had not spotted her. She flattened herself against the exterior wall while moving to the door.

The door opened to the outside. Her blue, shawl-clad shoulders became more visible as she flung herself around the entry and dashed inside. Throwing the door beam through the slots, Corabell thrust the window planks up through the iron screws jutting inward. Then she gazed into the darkened interior for Otto.

The hearth gave faint light to the dimness inside. Otto sat with his back to the fire, eating breakfast biscuits on the bench at the table. His chin poked several inches above the surface and both arms stretched across the top. He watched her while he ate, mouth full of wheat and lard. She whispered, "Otto, bad men're coming this way."

The boy nodded and chewed. Corabell paced, listening to the cadence of approaching horses. She grabbed a cup, filled it with water and took a biscuit. "Otto, come here!" She whispered and walked on her toes to the pantry door. Otto's wooden shoes clip-clopped across the stone floor several times before Corabell swept the clogs from his feet. Opening the root cellar door, she stepped into complete darkness and descended a step. "Otto, you're safe here. You need to be quiet as a mouse until I open the door." She gave him the biscuit. "When I close the door, it'll be dark, very dark and the darkness is the safest place where the bad men won't find you."

"Mama? Dog with me?"

"No, Dog ran to the horses. Dog's outside with the bad men." She kissed his forehead, rose and stepped out, "I'll do my best to keep Dog safe." Corabell gazed at Otto staring up her in the darkness. Lying along the third step, a biscuit balanced on his belly. The water cup sat on the step above. Closing the cellar door on her boy, Corabell pulled the pantry door shut.

Three strikes on the door made her startle. Corabell recognized the voice: "Opin yer dohr. Ye gonna mehk us som fo' 'r empdee bellies. I's seen yer fire smokin'. Know yer in dhar. Opin!" It occurred to Corabell he might not know who she was. Sitting on the floor leaning against the thick wood of the entrance, nothing could make her lift the door beam.

Corabell told herself she was safe and adjusted the belt at her waist. Her gaze moved to the window by her side. Screws poked through the planks; one barely cleared the surface. None of the threaded irons held bolts.

Panic flooded her limbs. She scrambled on her knees, hands searching the floor to collect the bolts. Above her head, a pin slid through the plank. The next screws slipped out just as easily. The last came out after a sharp blow and the board and shutter fell, sending daylight through the wavy glass panel.

Corabell blinked. She looked up at the window and saw the face of the pale-skinned man in a black hat craning to see her through the rippled windowpane. She held her breath. He threw a fist up, "Opin yer door, afor I smash yer winda'!"

Corabell stood swallowing quickly. She rocked the pistol from the holster, pointing it at the window. Outside, the white face darkened in recognition and rage. He snarled, black teeth and slits for eyes through the glass.

She doubted he could squeeze through the window. When she fired, the pane would shatter and he would want in. Hearing Gerolf's instructions, Corabell readied her stance and pulled the trigger.

Glass flew. The pistol arched backwards as her arms vaulted up and she waited. Her pulse beat in her ears. A gust of air soared through the opening. The white man outside roared and swore. A voice commented, "Hey, Boss, ther're other homes that'll welcome our kind."

Ignoring the comment, the pale one swiped the hat to cover his fist and pounded loose large shards of glass, scattering them from the sill before heaving himself up onto the window ledge.

Loading another cartridge into the back of the gun, Corabell readied herself. The torso filled the windowsill and red eyes stared. Corabell compelled her knees to stillness, raised her arms and fired.

The figure barely flinched. Slowly, grimy hands sought the growing redness high on the left arm. Tossing the beaten hat on the floor, he hurled his legs through the opening. Clothing caught on the remaining jagged points and he wriggled from his coat, dropping to the floor.

Searching frantically for more cartridges, Corabell backed into the stones beside the hearth. Her hands shook. She fumbled with the back of the pistol. Holding her breath, she readied to shoot.

The voice sounded distant, but the squeal of the dog she knew, "Shoot again, I kill the dog!" The man inside jammed the hat atop his greasy strands and unbarred the door. Entering, the hulking blond one nodded, dragging a rope in each hand.

A cord dug into the dog's neck fur so tightly the animal's extended tongue hung loose and its hind end drooped, limp. A tall, dark-skinned woman staggered at the doorway, her bound hands extended in front as she stumbled on the stoop.

Corabell gazed at the dog, raised the gun to the bulky blond and shouted, "Loosen that rope!"

Paying no heed, the stout slave hunter pointed to the side of the hearth and the woman bent her knees, easing herself downward. Corabell watched her weakened animal struggle to inhale and feared he would die as she looked on. Gerolf's words directed her wide stance, "Slacken the cord!" Failing to attend, she fired.

The massive form dropped on the stone floor. Corabell reloaded the back of the pistol, her hands increasingly steady as rage poured through her blood. Striding forward, Corabell abruptly released the cable and yanked the line off. She grasped the animal by the neck fur and pulled, urging him to the open door. Abruptly she felt a grip on her ankle.

Pointing the gun at the grasping hand, Corabell pulled the trigger. Rocking up and back, the gun flung her off balance. Corabell hit the half-open door as the dog regained his ability to stand. She brought her foot across the departing furry rump and pulled the latch shut behind her. On the floor, blood ran along gullies of mortar. The body of the large blond man lay still.

Corabell swallowed hard. She scanned the interior and addressed the pale one, who sat bent over the table, "I may be willing to cook, if you agree to leave me in peace."

The man threw his head up and roared, eyes glazed. Gripping the wounded arm, he panted in pain. "Peace? Yeh dink I get any peace widou' me pecka'? I na good ta da wie woman, she na wan me. Da only pleasin' I's gittin' is from de blac ho'. She na care, she agotta do de deed, els she ded. Firs yeh mek me som victuals for me empdee belly, den we see bout de pleasin'."

The man stood and trod through the cabin, holding the long limb in front of him. He yanked his coat from the window and fought to don it. Grabbing Plum's pewter cup, he tipped the barrel. Water sloshed onto the stones and he filled the cup from the stream. Corabell watched, pointing the pistol at him, "I'll put a bullet through you, before I do any pleasing."

"Seen yeh shoot da pisto'. Ain' ovlie gifded I see. Don got me in de arm. Ben on de 'orse fo' deys, seem righ' nice, abit a ospitalitee."

"I killed your man. I'll kill you too."

"Injun woman, yeh flappin ye jaw. Yeh kil me han' Blon' Murray." The man gestured to bulky figure askew on the floor in a widening blood puddle. "Wus a gudt man, an' me empdee belly na happee. Jes getta de fixin', eh?"

"Good man? Not to me." The pale one retook the bench, dropped the cup heavily on the table and groaned as he positioned the wounded arm in his lap.

Corabell assessed the situation. Blood on the floor flowed through the cement shallows to the door. Soon blood would find a way outside. She remembered blood dripping from Plum and Abo, lying on the table where he had seeped. Enough blood. Corabell filled the pistol chamber, nestled the loaded weapon in her holster and surveyed the sideboard.

They had potatoes and a piece of bacon. She thought to make a dozen fresh biscuits, while beans boiled for the evening meal. She would check on Otto in the cellar and retrieve a jar of fruit preserves and applesauce. Corabell busied herself. The man asked for more water. Corabell poured water from the ladle rather than touch the pewter cup.

The scent of cooking dough soon emanated from the fireplace. The dark skinned woman accepted a cup of water and reclined against the warm stones to the side of the hearth. Watching Corabell, her eyelids drooped and closed. She slept. Wearing large men's boots, a long woolen sweater covered the thin dress fabric, a muffler circled her neck and a homespun cloth wound tightly around her dark head.

The body on the floor released its bowels and the stench of warm shit mingled with the aroma of food. The scent disturbed Corabell so, she tapped on the white man's shoulder, "Get that body out of the house, or you'll have nothing to eat. Try me. I'll throw everything in the flames."

Tilting his nose up, he inhaled deeply and slowly withdrew his legs from the bench, muttering, "Eh, blac escapee ged up, ded Blon' Murray stinkin' up de 'ouse." The woman straightened against the wall. She held out her bound wrists and he sliced the cord that bound her hands in perpetual prayer.

The pale one grabbed the armpits of the coat, the woman took the lower body and they hauled the mass over the threshold. It took three to hoist the heavy figure over the back of the horse. Corabell came out reluctantly when the man called for aid. Urine and dung spread to the knees of the trousers. Corabell refused to touch the soiled fabric, but lifted the ankles and the dark woman heaved the body over the saddle.

Covering the pool of blood on the floor with rags, Corabell washed her face and hands before resuming meal preparations. The man had no inclination for hygiene.

The travelers took their former positions and soon the warmth of the cottage induced them both to doze. Corabell opened the pantry door, lifted the cellar access and motioned with a finger pressed to her lips, to hush. Otto blinked. She picked him up and whispered in his ear, "Climb up to Pa's old sleeping place. Don't move or make a sound. The bad man's in the house."

Corabell passed quietly behind the slave hunter's back. Otto lifted his head to eye the man snoring sprawled over the table and the woman asleep on the ground. He shimmied up the ladder. When Corabell glanced at the woman on the floor, her eyes were open.

Bringing a basin, Corabell poured in hot water, cooling it with several ladles from the barrel. She handed the woman a bar of soap and towel and the dark one began to wash. Unlacing her boots, she washed her feet. Foamy scum soon accumulated and floated atop the soiled water. Corabell took the basin, discarded the liquid and poured fresh water. The woman nodded and Corabell returned to preparations.

The tall woman stood to lift the woolen sweater over her head, revealing a round belly protruding beneath her frock. Her warm form gave off whiffs of spent male. Slightly sweet, that scent combined with mildew and rot from the pale man, made Corabell grateful for the intermittent cold air that burst through the shattered windowpane.

Remembering Abo's woolen underwear, she searched the wardrobe and brought the clothing to the woman who received them with down cast eyes. Corabell reached out and brought the woman's chin high. Gazing at the full lips, the width of her face and the height of her forehead, she thought of Plum. Corabell asked, "You've children? Babies?"

"I ha' many chilren, na a one evva stay wit me, 'cept my girl."

"They took your babies?" The woman looked at her, her expression flat. Corabell shuddered and inquired, "Did you lose a baby girl on the road up north?" The woman's features widened and her frozen exterior softened. She searched Corabell's eyes.

Corabell felt suddenly worse. She could report nothing good; the baby lay dead and buried. Still, curiosity compelled her to know if the woman was Plum's mother. Corabell shook her head and withdrew, but the woman stared, "Somon fond my baby girl?"

Corabell took the biscuits from the heat and did not answer. She did not trust herself to lie. She rummaged through the wardrobe and found two small shifts she had sewn for the child. Placing the frocks near the woman, she told her, "A good man brought me a baby, while I nursed my boy. I cared for her 'till she ate from the table . . . She sickened in the fall. By the following evening she'd died. . . they said it was black pox that killed her. While she lived, she was a happy girl. I called her Plum."

The woman's eyes ran over the stitches of the cotton dresses, holding them aloft to gauge their size. Corabell bid her come and eat. Dividing the potatoes in two portions, she gave the pale man the larger section of bacon. Corabell passed the woman biscuits and opened the preserves and container of chunky applesauce. The woman began eating as the man breathed heavily at regular intervals.

Corabell could see no reason to wake him, other than the cooling temperature of food. The sleeping man lifted his head as the aroma from his plate drifted his way. He seized his fork. Each bite exposed rotting green and black tooth points. Corabell averted her eyes.

The captive woman had full, even white teeth. Her face and its features were symmetric and pleasing. Though her dark hands were much larger, her fingers were long like her own. Sitting on the bench at the table, the woman appeared twice her height. It occurred to Corabell Plum had been a small child. She whispered, "Your baby, was she tall like you?"

"Small she was, small as a mouse an' black as me. She slip ou' easy. Ma other uns was lighter, like dey masta, an bigga', caust dey fed me so. Was cuz her I run. 'Fraid she'd be too black fa' de masta, an' dey trow her in de pond."

Corabell's eyes broadened. The woman spoke in soft tones, but the man at the other end paid no heed. He asked, "Miss, han't yeh an mo' meat in yeh hom? Paps som jerky e'en?"

"I'll see what I can find." Corabell rose and as she left, her eyes swept the edge of the sleeping platform. Otto had recoiled. Hopefully he would stay there. From the cellar, she returned with a string of small sausages. The man's eyes grew when he saw the bounty.

"You're consuming my food for the days to come."

"Appears yeh ha sustenance enuf, fo' yersef an yer man. Lemme see dem sausageh. How long yeh ha' dese? Seem righ' hart." The man tugged the string away from Corabell with his good hand, bit into an end and chewed with an open mouth.

Indeed, the string of sausages had hung in the cellar for a long while. Made by Eva's girls, Corabell had been wary of them in the beginning. She had not summoned the courage to combine them in a dish of potatoes, nor thought to feed them to the pig.

The pale man chomped, the string hanging from his mouth and rose, the bloody left arm motionless at his side. Stepping out from the bench, onto the glass shards, he lingered at the window. Outside, the body lay face down across the horse, blood dripping from the upper half onto the ground. "Dam shame yeh kilt Blon' Murray, dam shame." The man swung the sausages in a tighter circle around his neck.

He grappled with the waist and fly of his trousers with one wrinkly child-size hand. Corabell gasped, lifted the pistol and drew back against the sideboard, behind the slave woman and table.

The man paid Corabell no heed. He disrobed until he stood wearing the coat, trousers at the ankles. The sausages hung like a necklace of brown dung across his shirt and narrow chest. "O injun woman, time we see about pleasin' de man in de hom. Sees 'ow yeh made da pecka', a mere wee cock, seems yeh owe me som pleasin'. Be needin' a bit moa yeh time, seems a me."

"Lay a hand on me and I'll make you bleed."

The rat-faced little man pulled the bench out from the table, pushed the coat fabric backwards and sat spreading his pale legs. He tugged the shirt back exposing his privates that set darkly on the bench surface. No penis appeared to Corabell's eyes.

Then the man ran dirty fingernails through his personal hair and flipped the edge of slack appendage back and forth. Abo's white skin flashed through Corabell's memory as she watched the shameless man. The phallus missed the wider head. What remained was misshapen and pink with scar tissue. Evidently, he still derived pleasure from it. Corabell fixed her eyes on the shortened shaft and did not move, though the slave woman did.

Corabell wondered what motivated the woman; surely staying alive was involved. The dark one knelt at the man's knees and took the half-penis in her mouth. He did not grab her ears or force himself upon her, but sat with the injured arm and allowed her to gratify him.

Corabell watched the two, surmising they were accustomed to the practice. Only when sated did he emit several grunts of pleasure. The woman rose. She scanned the table for her water vessel and drained the cup.

Slightly less vile with the trimmed organ, the hunter rose from the bench and hiked up the trousers. Tucking his shirt in with one hand, he drew the coat collar up and flattened the black hat down to his greasy dome. "'Nuf settin', blac escapee, gotta ged back on de 'orse. Cock chewin' injun woman, I'd be blest ta na' see yeh evah agin."

Corabell quickly offered the woman Abo's coat. With a head dip and small smile, the slave accepted it. The wool covered her round belly and hung nearly to her knees. Emptying the biscuits into a cloth, Corabell passed them to her outstretched hands.

The pale man swung open the door. Mounting his horse, he drew up alongside the burdened mare, took the reins and led her away. Blond Murray had bound the woman's hands and led her while he rode. The white one allowed her hands to swing.

Corabell watched from the broken window. The dark one caught up with the horses, the man's lifeless arms swaying freely with the mount's movement. Blood dripped from the fingers, leaving a scant red trail behind.

When Corabell climbed the ladder, she saw Otto had fallen asleep wound in the woolen blanket Gerolf had left. She jostled his shoulder and he woke.

Tired, worn and with tangled thoughts, Corabell wished Gerolf would come home. Knowing it would be dark before she would have his physical comfort, Corabell lost herself in chores.

Securing the front window with the shutter, she called the dog. He came to her, his tail tentative to whether he had dropped from favor. She embraced him, her tones assuring she preferred him alive, for her sake as well as Otto's.

Corabell fed the fire and checked the simmering beans. She added several onions, a ham bone and maple syrup. After stirring the contents, she sat with the dog in front of the fire while Otto rolled onto the beast's belly, pretending to be a pup.

Chapter Thirty-One

Corabell

Corabell could still feel Blond Murray's grasp, tight around her ankle. Without regard to her stance or thought to the target, she had turned and shot. Murray's remark to the pale boss, "Ther're other homes that'll welcome our kind," played again and again through her mind. Corabell considered what she knew of the Ten Commandments and concluded that in the eyes of the church she had done wrong. Gerolf opened the door and stomped into the quiet cabin, startling them all.

Gerolf

He knew something was amiss when he saw the three rise from the hearth. At least the cabin smelled of food. Scents of beans, onions and ham bones welcomed him. He left his coat and hat by the door, though he carried in an aura of cold fresh air.

They gravitated to him. Corabell flattened her cheek against his chest. Otto swung around his leg. The dog impeded his stride, panting and circling, whipping the boy's head with his tail. A more common welcome would have involved one of the three.

Gerolf patted Corabell on the back. Wading forward, weighed down with a boy and obstructed by the heavy dog, he had passed hungry ages ago. Washing his hands and face, he sat and took Otto on his knee.

Corabell brought two cups of water to the table and Otto spoke several words about bad men. Gerolf encouraged the child to speak as Corabell mixed ingredients for corn cakes.

"Mama said hide, Pa. Dark all around." The boy waved his arms, gray eyes steady on Gerolf. "Pa?" Mama said "Sh, quiet like mouse." The child pursed his lips and held a stout finger to them. "In dark, safe. Pa? Bad men." Gerolf nodded.

When Corabell brought over the first of the patties, he asked her to sit and speak. He scanned her face as she recalled the earlier events of the day—how the bullet had shattered the glass and the pale figure leapt through the empty pane. She described the woman, the meal, the shortened penis, the sexual favor, how Blond Murray released his bowels and that blood had dripped from the body atop the horse.

"I wish it all hadn't happened. I thought they'd wrong me as they did in the snow." Her hands moved across her small round belly.

Gerolf stood and leaned over the table. He took her cheeks in his palms and kissed her forehead and then her lips. Corabell kept her seat and unbuckled the belt that kept the pistol in place. "Do you believe they'll leave us alone now?"

Gerolf took a corn patty and sopped up the bean broth with it, "Hm. You did what you had to do."

He watched Corabell rise and hang the holster from the pin high over the mantel. "The pale one took Plum's cup and used it to drink. I filled it several times, but didn't touch it." Corabell sunk onto the bench again, bringing a full bowl of beans with her. She took a spoon in hand and held it over her bowl, her eyes meeting his, "I yearned for you."

Corabell

Her face turned to the table and her eyes filled with tears. Several drops fell into the beans and her chest heaved while she breathed. Corabell rose and Gerolf folded her against his chest. Soothing her by rocking, she drew her hands underneath his shirt. The smell, the male scent of wood and labor, calmed her. She wanted nothing more than to flee from the events of the day. Corabell stood and ran her hand up his neck, whispering, "Come to bed."

"The child."

"I'm the mother. I need you."

Gerolf positioned Otto on the bench, scooting it closer to the table. He looked at the boy, "Your mother needs me, we won't be long." Corabell took Gerolf's hand and he followed her to the dark corner where she mounted him and closed her eyes, shutting out the world.

Not long after, he pulled his underwear and trousers over his buttocks. He kissed her on the mouth and left her to resume eating supper with Otto.

Corabell emerged from the shadows, pulling the strings of her corset tight and swiping a strand of hair from her cheek. She sighed, hummed several notes of a native tune and retook her seat and spoon. Gerolf smiled at the change in her.

Corabell had not fully appreciated the dwindling stores of produce. Potatoes kept better covered with a layer of cool soil. She could not recall the size of the mound after harvest. The last container of applesauce sat empty on the sideboard, only vinegar covered the bottom in the final vat of pickled vegetables. Dusty brown apple wheels decorated the doorway lintel but they were fit only for the cooking pot, lacking most flavor. Only when the pale one asked for jerky did Corabell recognize all that remained of meat were the sausages made by Eva's girls.

By April's end when the weather alternated between mild and freezing and the skies remained gray, the lack of fresh vegetables moved Corabell into the garden to turn the soil. Otto collected rocks from the earth, mounding them along the garden fence. Searching for stones, the boy found several carrots, beets and potatoes. Hidden from last year's harvest, they swelled with extra time in the ground. At the table, they were prizes.

Corabell recalled spring in her village. Few families ever put up sufficient stores of produce to last the winter. Having such harvest bounty, people ate through their provisions until only dried berries remained. These they chewed when their empty bellies demanded fuel. Without produce and with sporadic meat, the native population ate the faintly sweet inner bark of the white pine tree and scavenged the woods for edible fungi, bulbs, tubers and roots that harbored starches.

Easter Sunday of 1836 fell early on April third. Temperatures shifted relentlessly, creating volatility in the air. Elke planned the holiday dinner. The meal would be rich in starches. Vegetables might be purchased from an enterprising soul who transported produce north from more southern states. Such fare would be expensive and bought up quickly. Markets in town sold fruits and vegetables in sugar syrups or beneath vinegars and oils. Corabell savored the remains of Elke's elixir, which harbored the essence of vegetation.

Gerolf

With the arrival of the new Texas herd, Gerolf gave up butchering at the slaughterhouse and began fulltime employment with F.C. Sherman Construction. Though relieved to be free of the bellowing and blood, he missed bringing home free beef, pork and sausage.

Construction gave him satisfaction butchering lacked. He carried no shame for his efforts. Though a fine cut of meat might be appreciated in a meal, a solidly built home stood for years. From Henry and Patrick O'Shay, Gerolf learned the details of building assembly.

On Easter Sunday, puffy cumulus clouds raced across the blue sky, obscuring the sunlight intermittently. The wind picked up fine chaff and debris, whipping the refuse into the faces and eyes of those walking to the Gottschalk home. Enduring the onslaught, women held each other's arms and walked with their eyes shielded beneath the brims of their hats.

Gerolf picked up Otto and strode with him on his shoulders. The boy crouched low, pressing his cheek to Gerolf's black hat, his eyes tightly shut. Corabell seized her husband's arm and allowed him to direct her steps.

Elke

The extended family and guests descended on the cabin from different directions. Keeping to the Catholic faith, Thomas Flaherty, the Oberweiss and O'Shay families attended St. Patrick's, a large wooden structure, on Adams Street. Most other callers traveled from the Lutheran parish.

Dietrich unhitched the buggy, took the horse into the pasture and stood at the hearth. He commented, "Oh Mutter, my head pounds fiercely in my skull."

"Sit, I'll steep you some willow bark tea." Elke pulled out the provisions for the meal. Dietrich took the chair before the fire and brightened when his grandchildren arrived on Beatriz' hips. She greeted Dietrich with a kiss on the cheek. He admired the babies and Elke relayed, "Poor Papa's head throbs."

When Dietrich had emptied the teacup, he kissed Elke's cheek, "Mutter, I'm going to lie down. Wake me if I've not risen by dinner."

At three o'clock, the family and friends had gathered. Konrad and Henry brought out the long benches from the barn and set up the table Dietrich usually pounded together. Elke covered it with a long swath of homespun fabric. The younger girls began setting down utensils, plates and glasses.

An hour later, the hungriest people began taking seats. Elke left the guests to check on her spouse. Imagining he would stir when she swung the creaking door, he did not wake. Elke touched his shoulder gently. When he failed to respond, she shook him as her heart broke. Wailing, she jostled his face side to side.

Emily found her mother standing over her father, who appeared to sleep. "Papa?" Dietrich laid still, his gray cheeks sunken below the bones of his face. Emily withdrew to her mother's side.

One hand across her mouth, the other over her heart, Elke sank to her knees in the silent room. Emily followed her, kneeling.

When Eva appeared in the doorway, she gasped and called, "Konrad!" He quickly appeared at her elbow and stalked silently to the foot of the bed, his eyes steady on his father's thin form.

"Come with me." Elke wiped her nose. The children followed her to the dining table where people sat in conversation. Eva attended to the knock on the door and welcomed the Oberweiss Grandparents and Nola.

Elke stood at the head of the dining table, grasping the back of a chair, "I'm grieved to tell you, I believe Papa's left us today. Easter Sunday. Please dine heartily. It's the day of resurrection, whether Dietrich enjoys it or not. Children, expecting mothers and all others need sustenance. Konrad will say grace."

Konrad nodded to his mother, spread his arms and bent his head, "Come Lord Jesus, be our guest and let Thy gifts to us be blessed."

Emily made sure all the prepared dishes made it to the table, where people passed them to one another. Thomas Flaherty poured the woman of the house a stein of hard cider. Her hunger gone, Elke excused herself, took the mug with her and returned to the unheated bedroom where her spouse lay.

Everyone passed some time at Dietrich's bedside. Some prayed on their knees, others stood with bowed heads. Several cried. Romy spoke with her grandfather. She paid no attention to the lack of reply, kissing his forehead and cheeks while Nola sang a hymn.

Minister Schoenhofen had previously agreed to visit. Elke sat with her unresponsive husband and waited for the pastor while she overheard the dinner table banter.

Corabell

Tales of Dietrich dominated the dinner conversation. "I was twelve or thirteen," Konrad recalled, "I wanted a pair of English boots so badly I burned the clogs I wore every day. It was winter. Dad gave me his pair and bought himself new ones. All winter I stumbled about in those big leather boats. The following autumn, father relented. He took me to have my feet sized and my first leather shoes crafted."

Franz swallowed and cleared his throat, "Thanks for my boots, Pa." Konrad nodded to his stepson.

Corabell set her fork on her plate side and recounted, "Dietrich questioned my background when I arrived from the far side of the river." The table hushed to hear her tale.

"You took a big chance, traveling to the slaughterhouse," Eva exclaimed.

Emily inquired, "What would you've done if Abo had been married?"

Corabell's face blanched when she saw they awaited her reply. Gerolf exclaimed, "I'd have asked her for her hand."

She smiled at him, "I'd never even seen you." Turning to the faces around the table, she continued, "I'd thought I'd join my village in the distant lands that would be their new home."

"Alone?" A young voice inquired.

Corabell shrugged, "I had the wolf-dog then. He accompanied me everywhere."

Nola's high voice rang out, "Miss Corabell would you've married Gerolf back then?"

She frowned, "I wasn't aware of him. It was Abo I came to see. Abo stood on the riverbank and hailed me . . . he kissed my hand and asked me to return." Corabell swallowed heavily and turned to cut Otto's meat.

Emily redirected the conversation, "Beatriz what was your first meeting with Papa like?"

Beatriz smiled, "To be truthful, I knew Dietrich wasn't happy his eldest son considered marrying me, a widow with young ones. He probably preferred Konrad wed a woman more his age. I was grateful Konrad consented to have me; Dietrich respected his son and has been good to me."

Nola's voice rose again over the clatter of the table, "But Auntie, who else could you've wed?"

Beatriz glanced at the girl and answered slowly, "There was a white-haired man with a grizzled beard, who sought a wife, his children were grown."

"Nola, dear, it's time you begin picking up plates. When you've finished with that, you may refill our glasses," Emily instructed her niece.

The front door shuddered under the force of a solid knock. Freda answered and received the minister's coat. She explained, "Minister Schoenhofen, my father's in need of prayers. He lies in bed stricken, with mother at his side." The reverend bowed to those at the table. "Would you like some tea? You've arrived in time for dessert, if you please."

"Thank you, Freda. I'll see to your parents, first."

Elke

When the cleric entered the bedroom, he found Elke folded against Dietrich on the bed, his wiry gray hair cradled at her breast. She stirred at the sound of feet on the floorboards and sat. The minister walked to the far side and put a palm on the forehead of the man who had been a parishioner since he acquired the post. Elke smiled faintly.

"I'm very sorry, your spouse has passed away. Shall we pray?" She dropped her hand over the cooling face, noticing indeed that Dietrich failed to breathe. Not responding, Elke settled her cheek against the bony face and the pastor left the room.

Minister Schoenhofen stood and faced the dinner guests. Their conversations dwindled as they noticed him. "It's a sad event to announce the head of the house has passed, on this the day of resurrection. May I lead you in prayer?"

Those at the table bent their heads as Elke joined them. With dinner long past and dessert continuing, people wandered in and out of the bedroom where Dietrich lay. Thomas Flaherty opened a fresh barrel of ale to toast the man who had befriended him. Uta and Fiza began washing dinner dishes.

Eva

Joining her eldest daughter drying dishes, Eva asked, "Nola my girl, we've so little time together, what're your days like living in town?"

Nola glanced at her sisters, looked at her mother and shook her head, "Opa's growing deaf. I fear his hearing's a hindrance in business. I've started taking notes for him at meetings. He misses important details. Last week, Grandmother bought a hearing-trumpet for him. We were trying it out when he walked in, but he wasn't angry."

Uta jostled her sister's arm, "What's a hearing-trumpet?"

Nola took the wet plate from her sister's hands, "We found it in a shop. It's shiny brass and telescopes out long. One end expands like a trumpet. You stick the small end in your ear and it lets you hear whispers.

But the more exciting thing; I sat taking notes for Opa. The State's selling land plots on the sides of the Illinois and Michigan Canal, to pay for its construction cost. Opa and his partners argue railroads're a better way to link the Illinois towns.

On railways or canals, they believe more settlers and businesses'll come out this way." Uta glanced at her sister and handed her another wet plate.

Amsel approached, "Frau, the children are sleeping, let me help you into the carriage before I fetch them."

Eva set her towel across the back of a chair, "Remember I love you dearly," and kissed Uta on her forehead. "I'm glad you're assisting Papa. You make me proud," she told Nola and kissed her as well.

Elke

Before Amsel left he confided to Elke, "Dietrich and I were at odds. Knowing he didn't trust me with his son's children pained me, I couldn't completely forgive him for that slight. Now he's gone it no longer matters, but a shadow of shame lingers near my heart." With her lips set in a thin line, Elke accepted his words and wondered whether he intended some form of apology.

Konrad lingered. With the twins sleeping and Fiza helping, Franz picked up the fiddle and played a slow, mournful hymn. Nate pulled his fiddle from its case and tuned the instrument away from the clamor of steins and voices. He stepped closer and joined Franz, playing an accompaniment to the tune.

In the bedroom, Elke and the minister prepared to relocate Dietrich to the table in front of the fire. Elke pulled the covers from her spouse, revealing the lean limbs beneath the undyed woolen undergarments she had knitted ages ago.

The minister stood aside as Konrad, Gerolf and Thomas carried the body to the central room and set the long figure on the table. "Mother, I'll return with a casket." Konrad took his coat, turned and shut the door.

Dietrich's face had turned gray. His arms and head fell at random angles. Elke straightened him so his nose faced the beams above and limbs fell in lines parallel with his torso.

Now that Dietrich lay on the table, Elke couldn't deceive herself that he merely slept. She stood with her hands on his cheeks and gazed at him. The fingers of his hand twitched. The sudden movement made her jump and the minister spoke behind her, "It's the way of death. Do not fret."

Elke shuddered. She had waited for his visit. Now that he was close, his presence repelled her. His clothing smelled of incense. The scent assaulted her each time she inhaled and made her keenly aware of her own breathing. He seemed determined to be at her side, though she wished him away.

Elke knew some things of death, having buried three of her children. In their bed, Dietrich's closed eyes were a lie. She would never hear his snore again.

She pulled her daughter aside and whispered, "Emily dear, is there some way you might dismiss the minister? Truly, he's fulfilled his obligation and may leave."

Emily frowned, sighed and straightened her white linen apron. She set her face in a pleasant expression, drew the attention of all with an exclamation, "Family and friends!" and delivered the request, "Please, let's all reunite with Minister Schoenhofen in the morning at the church cemetery." After a pause, she added, "Papa would've been pleased you've all come to celebrate the Lord's resurrection."

Freda and Willa pressed the cleric's hands, murmuring niceties before finding his coat and hat. The old man parted, dipping his head in acknowledgment to the newest widow.

Silas left to fetch the carriage and horse. Willa kissed her mother. The violins played though Nate paused to correct Franz's fingering on the frets and Thomas refilled the musician's steins with beer.

Grandmother Oberweiss urged Nola to fetch her cloak. Grandfather had meetings in the morning. The girl refused to leave. She needed to be present at the burial and would return to town afterwards. Grandmother conceded and kissed her cheek. The group grew smaller and those left behind began discussing the future.

Freda volunteered to walk to the slaughterhouse after the burial and inform the foreman of the death. Her gaze drifted to those who sat with her, "Perhaps he'll offer me Papa's position if I mention that I'm also gifted in numbers. I don't know how we'll survive without Pa's wages and the meat he brought home. The garden lies unplanted. We won't have anything fresh for weeks."

Henry offered to contribute a monthly sum, but Konrad shook his head and stated it was his responsibility. Elke shook her head, "It's too early to speak of such matters, though Freda, I'd welcome you taking on that task. Perhaps the foreman'll pay some fraction of the burial expenses."

"Oh, that's unlikely," Corabell quipped, "the slaughterhouse only grudgingly gave Gerolf funds for Abo's burial costs and he was struck down by their bull."

"I wonder how many coins I'd gather if I played the fiddle at the public house at Wolfe Point." Franz looked to his cousin and Nola offered, "I'll write an obituary and have it printed in the newspaper."

Elke urged them all to retire; she would wash Dietrich and dress him in his burial clothes. Gerolf kissed the weathered cheek of the man who had welcomed him. Thomas bowed to Elke, "Dietrich invited me to yer family table when I'd newly arrived. I'm grateful, and blessed to've known him." He pressed his lips to Elke's hand.

Chapter Thirty-Two

Elke

Elke began the last task she would perform for her husband. Washing him, she recalled his younger body; how hard his muscles had been when he worked the farm and the children were small. At Rurik's burial, he had stood and wept. Grief made him speechless for days. Elke drew some comfort from the notion he might be reunited with his son.

Elke dressed Dietrich in the Sunday clothing he had donned that morning. Pressing his shirt the night before, she never suspected it would be the last time she would worry about scorching the linen. She considered keeping the wedding ring. Finding it impossible to wrench over his swollen knuckle, she let him take it to the grave.

Freda began preparing coffee and Elke wandered to the door, "I'll be tending the animals in the barn." She stepped into the dark morning and breathed the cold air of early spring. Without Dietrich, she did not know how life would be. Entering the chicken's enclosure, she scattered corn shards along one end. At roost on the bar, the hens stretched high and made soft chuckling noises. She stroked their soft feathered backs, settled in the straw with dry dung and the scent of ammonia and let her tears come.

Freda discovered her mother hours later. She lay on one side, the woolen shawl pulled tight around her shoulders, a large hen in the hollow of her belly. Inside the house, Freda picked plumes from her mother's hair and filled a bowl for her to wash.

Freda served the girls oatmeal with maple syrup. Rudy and Rory ran up the porch stairs, cheeks reddened by cold air. Pouring her mother coffee, Freda lightened it with hot milk. Elke sipped, replacing traces of ammonia stuck in her nose with steam from the coffee mug.

Konrad appeared freshly shaven in the doorway while Beatriz nursed the babies by the fireside. The casket in the wagon bed, the horses stood harnessed in front of the house. Konrad paced. Fiza donned her coat and hat. Uta and Romy followed her example and the three waited beside their grandfather in the pine box when the family members joined them.

The horses strained to shift the wagon wheels. Once moving, the team pulled the family steadily to church. Two farming men of the parish met the carriage at the cemetery.

Elke wore her drabbest colored dress. Freda took her arm. Beatriz and Fiza took the twins and they joined the others at the graveside. Nola followed with the younger children in tow, meeting Emily, Bridgette O' Shay, Corabell, Eva and Amsel and their two young ones. Emily asked Corabell, "No Gerolf?"

Corabell shook her head, "He felt he couldn't be absent." Minister Schoenhofen swept into the graveyard. Konrad and the two farmers strode down the path, carrying the casket to the pit.

Konrad

Arriving at the hole cut in the ground, Konrad leapt into the pit to accept the box the men lowered slowly with ropes. He settled his father's coffin in the dark soil that smelled of worms and dormant sod. Standing in the depth, he recognized he and his infant son were the last of the Gottschalk men. Lowering his head, Konrad promised his father he would have more male children to carry the family name into the future and he wiped his eyes, blew his nose and took the ladder to the air above.

The minister spoke and Konrad took the whining baby from Fiza's arms. Standing beside Beatriz, he saw the lines edging her eyes, the flatness of her bosom and accepted that her prime vexation stemmed from her age. Now her innards had spilled out, was she even capable of her marital duty? Years had passed before conceiving the twins, longer than he thought natural. Konrad sighed and scanned Widow Heck's figure.

Elke picked up a handful of earth and tossed it onto the wooden box while the minister recited from the book. Freda surrendered to sobbing. Konrad let tears roll down his face as he patted his dozing son. The minister finished, turned and left, his sister following behind closely.

Not eager to leave the head of the family to the earth and larvae, they stood with heavy hearts until Amsel's young Hanna asked, "Papa, can we go home now? My feet are cold."

Elke

Elke smiled at the child who marched in place beside her father. It tore her how life would continue without Dietrich. Forever more, she would find him in the graveyard. His grandchildren would grow and he would miss everything. Elke ached as she followed Freda. She would have preferred to stay, but the children would need dinner and the meal required preparation. It mattered little where she was; she would feel wretched wherever her feet took her.

On the road back to the family home, Konrad drove the horses past the slaughterhouse to aid his sister. Freda dropped from the carriage bench and flung an arm out to her brother, "Don't wait. I'll take the lane and walk home." She would speak with the foreman.

Corabell
Corabell returned to the cabin, planning to work in the garden. The day was chilly but clear and the sun warmed everything beneath it. As shadows lengthened, she and Otto watched for Gerolf's form approaching from Center Street.

While she dispersed chicken dung to the far corners of the garden, Otto waved to her. "Mama look, someone comes." The child stood hanging from a fence post, pointing his short finger south. The figure wore a coat like Abo's. For a moment, Corabell imagined her husband walked, back from the dead.

She had given the slave woman the coat. The character kept to the woody side of the street. A horse trailed behind. Corabell called to Otto and they shut and barred the door behind them. They gazed out the south-facing window, watching the person draw closer. When the trees fell away at the edge of the property, the soul gazed around and trotted to the cabin. A shawl obscured the face, but the horse she knew. The pale slave hunter rode that animal.

Whether returning for revenge or dinner, Corabell did not intend to please him more than she had to. She secured the pistol and fed a cartridge into the slot at the back. She and Otto waited. Outside, the horse whinnied and blew. The dog barked repeatedly. Corabell stood gingerly on a bench and peered through a vacant knothole at the top of the front shutter.

The dog paced back and forth in front of the cabin as the figure stood, unmoving. Corabell inspected the person and her eyes fell on the well-beaten boots. She watched the feet and tried to recall what the pale man wore. As she stared, the figure began to sing. Not recognizing the language or the words, the voice was female and it came from within Abo's coat.

Corabell threw the wooden bar from the door and swung it open, calling the dog to the hearth, where he trotted with his tail high. The woman kept the reins in her hand, hurrying forward.

With no stable, merely the animal shack that kept the pig and hencoop, anyone passing would spy the horse. Corabell strode outside and gestured to the open door. She took the reins and tied the horse to the garden railing, hoping the creature would not take fright and bring the fence down.

The woman entered and settled by the side of the hearth, not uttering a word. Her dark fingers unbuttoned the overcoat. She drifted to sleep as her body bent gently and slowly sideways until she reclined against the cool floor.

White field beans simmered on the hearth with a cut of smoked pork, onions, dried apples for their sweetness and several cups of hominy to extend the stew. Months ago, she had secured wheels of pumpkin in twine and hung them from the ceiling beams. That morning she rinsed off the dust, softened the desiccated pieces with water, adding a small amount of honey and an equal portion of maple syrup.

Corabell hushed Otto, who scrambled onto the bench and waited for dinner. The boy watched her and eyed the first corn cake patty. Outside, the horse whinnied. Corabell caught sight of her spouse through the southern window. She met him at the door, "The dark one's brought the saddled horse with her."

Gerolf entered wordlessly. He stood inside the doorway and stared at the woman while she slept. His voice resounded through the quiet cabin, "And you, you're aware of the penalty for aiding a runaway slave?"

Corabell swept her eyes over him. She said nothing and returned to the hearth, taking the first cake from the skillet and giving it to Otto. Gerolf did not move or take off his coat. Corabell scanned his face, "Gerolf please, she's tired and hungry, let me feed her and she'll be on her way."

"And she wears my brother's coat? Frau! Those who knew my brother'll think I helped her." His hands swept through the air. "When the constable comes and takes me away who'll provide for you?" He glared.

The sleeping woman quickly straightened and slowly stood, the open coat gaping and exposing the curve of her belly. Her eyes fell at his feet. Gerolf bellowed, "What else have you given her?" keeping his stance by the door.

Corabell looked up from the skillet and replied over one shoulder, "Abo's woolen underwear."

"From Germany? Are you trying to have me imprisoned?" Gerolf waved his right arm with such force the dog slunk to the front door, where he turned and sat. At the table, Otto dropped his forehead to the edge, withdrawing his arms from the surface. The tall woman shrank against the wall. "Get that coat off!"

Standing with her head cast down, she hesitated and then dropped the coat on the stones. She lifted the sweater over her head and the fabric of her dress and let them fall as well. Corabell glanced at the woman disrobing, her dark chin never tilting upwards.

Her own spirits fell as she watched the woman expose her dark brown breasts. The waistband of the underwear fell below her round belly. She pulled the wool from each leg and stood nude, her covered head bent. Gerolf stood immobile, his eyes scanning her form.

Briefly watching her husband's face, Corabell moved to flip a corn patty. She saw his anger had ebbed, but felt uncertain his heart had changed. Then the woman moved to him and knelt on the floor. Gerolf quickly unbuttoned his coat and her long dark fingers fumbled with the buttons at his fly. He glanced in her direction as the woman withdrew his erect cock and took it in her hands and mouth. He closed his eyes.

Corabell's heart sank. She turned her back, but heard the pleasure he took. His breathing changed as the woman pleased him. Tears fell as she poured more batter into the skillet hot with liquid lard. The woman cleared her throat and she heard Gerolf's feet move away.

Whether he looked her way, Corabell had no idea. Gerolf bid the dark woman, "Please, dress yourself. Take my brother's woolens; he's no use for them." Snatching the coat up from the floor, he hung it on the hook beside the door.

"Without the coat she'll freeze," Corabell commented evenly.

"She's not frozen yet." His soft tone was almost conciliatory. Corabell hated the sound and source of it. Had he not taken Otto on his thigh, she might have torn the hair from his skull.

"Please sit and eat." Gerolf said and sat on the bench across from the tall female figure. Corabell poured them water, keeping her back to the man. She served dinner and brought the sweet cooked pumpkin to the table, without catching him in her sight.

"Excuse me," Corabell threw the door shut behind her and sought refuge in the outhouse, where she cried freely and peed into the hole that retained her dead husband's waste.

In the small stinky confines, Corabell considered her options. She might take the horse and head to her clan, leaving Otto with no mother. Once on the road, hunger would force her to scavenge and hunt and in the lean season, nothing would be easy. If she stayed, her son would be fed. In time, she would bear another child with a man who gave no thought to humiliating her. The world was old and worn. She would never love him again.

When she returned to the cabin, she found the three eating in silence. Gerolf held Otto on his thigh. Though she could not bear his company, Corabell sat on the bench edge beside him. With her back to the man, she ate soup and filled her empty belly. The savory warmth did nothing to allay her heart pain.

Gerolf refilled the dark woman's bowl and then his own. He inquired how she came to be in possession of the slave hunter's horse. The woman responded flatly, "De black pox take him and he feld ded from de 'orse, takin' me back ta de plantation. Please de Lord, I tekked de 'orse an come back disa way."

Corabell swallowed, "You ride the horse, she'll keep you warm. Riding's a lot faster than walking."

"Ain't neveh rode na beast."

"I'll show you, it's not hard."

"You'll wait until sundown before you step outside with her," warned Gerolf. Corabell kept silent.

He stood, visited the outhouse and resumed work on the bed for the boy child. Otto sat close by and handed him the tools he requested as Corabell set about cleaning up.

The dinner pots banged and crashed under her testy touch while the native wooden plates resisted her rage. She set a fresh pot of beans to soften near the fire and went to the window to check the setting sun. Throwing her shawl over her shoulders, Corabell gestured to the dark woman who watched her. "Mama?" The boy reached out for her.

Corabell turned to him, "I'll be back." She opened the door and the dog dashed off as the women stepped into the cover of night. In the chilled air, the slave woman drew her sweater tightly around her body.

Corabell demonstrated how to mount the horse and hold the reigns. With a boot in the stirrup, Corabell encouraged her to hike up her skirt and throw a leg over the animal's back. "You could get some coins for the saddle, but it'll make riding easier," she told her.

The dark one giggled softly as she sat high on the beast. Her laughter revealed her large regular teeth. The darkness and joy emanating from her provoked a grin from Corabell who softly told her, "Remember you're in charge." Showing her the elemental commands for riding, Corabell noted the horse could walk or trot all night, but would need to eat and rest as well.

The woman reached down and touched Corabell on the head. Then she kicked the beast and trotted northwards. Corabell listened to the horse's departing hoof beats and gazed at the house.

Her anger returned gradually as the mare's regular footfalls grew faint. Corabell stood outside so long Gerolf sought her from the open door. He stalked to his wife and stood within her space, taking her by the shoulders.

Corabell inhaled deeply and shrugged his hands away, "What do you mean by allowing her to satisfy you in the same room as me? Have you no decency? You shame me in my home; in front of my son . . . It sickens me! If you were of my people, I'd bring you your clothes and you'd no longer reside with me."

Standing several inches from her, Gerolf bent to speak to her face. "She's just a slave woman, Corabell. It was due me. She had my brother's clothing and ate from my table!"

"WHAT? Just a slave woman?! A woman! I heard the pleasure you took. I cannot bear you!" Corabell swung at Gerolf's face. Her hand broke hard against his cheek. She heard the sharp intake of breath and his grip fell on her, hard and tense. He drew her up by the armpits onto her tiptoes, bending again to her face. His nose met hers and she smelled dinner on his breath.

Lips narrowed, clenching his teeth, Gerolf spit words at her, shaking her for emphasis. "Corabell. Yes, she pleased me. Yes, I knew it'd anger you. You put us in peril meddling, with slaves and hunters. You'll end this!"

He unhanded her with such force she fell abruptly on her buttocks, exclaiming, "You thug!" He glanced quickly at her. Not dissuaded, Corabell spoke as she rose. Gerolf paced in small acute angles. "Meddling? She's Plum's mother! A woman, like myself! With child as well!"

"And you went out near nightfall, alone in the frigid ice, when only the devil would walk."

"Checking traps! Gerolf . . . to feed us. I didn't ask them into our home. The brutes came for me!" Corabell pursued him as he stalked away.

He swung around and hit his chest with his palm, "I feed you. I feed your boy."

"You labor and bring coins. Coins we can't eat. At the slaughterhouse, you brought food for the pot. Now we seldom have meat." Corabell quit stalking him and stood. She swept her hands over her head, "The stores are gone. The cellar's empty."

Ignoring her concerns Gerolf whipped around to her. Corabell recoiled. In a low voice he uttered, "You knew. The slave-hunter drank from Plum's cup. You knew he'd sicken and she with him, sucking his half cock. Cut short by your teeth, my own wife! What'll this slave woman bring me?"

"What you deserve!" Corabell shouted her heart on fire. Concern for Otto forced her closer to the cabin. Through the open door, she saw him at the table. Her heart warmed at her boy. Tears ran as she forced back sobs. She stood rooted, unable to go inside as she cried. Gerolf stood behind her.

As her crying eased, he reached for her and held her tightly. Corabell held her body away from him, resisting the embrace. Gerolf pulled her tighter.

He spoke softly, his words near her ear. "In my anger, I may've sinned and done wrong. You'll forgive me."

"I will not," she spat.

Settling his teeth on her neck, Gerolf breathed in a jagged rhythm. He ran his mouth up into her hairline at the back of her head, "Forgive me."

"I can't." With her fast response, he opened his arms and she slipped away, back to the house. He remained outside beneath the night sky.

Chapter Thirty-Three

Corabell

Night followed night and Corabell refused to bed with her spouse. She lay in front of the hearth on a blanket. Sometimes she curled around the warm dog but more often, she lay alone.

The season turned and the earth groaned and swelled, coming to life under the sun. Corabell worked in the garden daily. Chicks emerged from eggs the hens had hidden near the sow in the straw. Their fluffy bodies and the joy Otto found in them rubbed against the shreds of her heart. She harvested the first of the radishes and marveled at the bite of their white flesh.

During moments that fully occupied her hands, Corabell tormented herself with visions of the woman at Gerolf's trousers, fumbling with the buttons and taking him in her mouth. She heard his sigh and his breath quickening, the sounds of sucking and the release of orgasm. In truth, the stabbing pain it provoked dulled as days passed.

Corabell thought of Abo more often and dreamt he took her in her sleep. Gerolf heard her moan and her words, "Abo come back . . . come back here," and she opened her legs expectantly. Lying at the hearthside, Gerolf nudged her shoulder. When her eyes fluttered open, the darker brother loomed. She saw his face, features tight with irritation.

Gerolf

Gerolf stood and demanded, "Enough of this! You must sleep in bed," and offered his hand to help her from the stone floor. When she resisted, turning back to face the fire, he knelt at her elbow, "Corabell you've been angry with me too long."

Gerolf lifted her torso, Corabell stood and gathered the blanket up. He slipped an arm behind her knees, swept her up and brought her to the bed, where he spoke to her back, "Corabell it's been weeks, you grow thinner in the face when you should be plump. I fear for you and for my babe. You must forgive. I didn't desire her. I allowed her only to madden you. I lusted for you while you were my brother's wife. I've sinned. I'm only flesh and weak."

When there was no response, Gerolf pulled her shoulder and rolled her body over. The dark hair of her braid fell over the pillow. Gerolf took the braid in hand and wound it around his fist. With his other, he took the side of her face and spoke inches from her, "You'll come back to me."

Corabell met his eyes. It had been ages since she'd regarded him. He studied the gray quality of her irises, feeling hopeful. "I'll try." The words confirmed his suspicion; she still had love for him somewhere. Gerolf pressed his lips against hers tenuously, hoping she would not repel him.

Corabell allowed the kiss, without response. Only when Gerolf dug deeply inside her, did he see the wife he knew. She clasped his buttocks and urged him to move upon her. When they fell apart, he prayed she would remember the goodness he could bring.

In the morning, Gerolf watched her, alert for some change. He saw it in her eyes. She looked at him, before she had avoided his face and form. He caught her gaze and her cheeks flushed. Any response he got he welcomed. She had been absent for so long.

He sat on the bench, a hot cloth pressed beneath his eyes to soften the stubble he would shave away. Having mounted a small mirror on the dimly illuminated wall near the hearth, he stood, lathered his cheeks and worked the blade.

"I keep wages in the wooden box in the wardrobe. Surely you've seen it. If you worry for lack of provisions, you can purchase staples at the trading post. You'll get lower prices on meat if you go to the slaughterhouse." He squinted while he trimmed his sideburns, then he pointed the razor end at her, "With the child and goods it'll be quite a walk. You might prefer to join Elke, on her weekly shop to town. Surely, she'd welcome some company."

Freda

On the morning of her father's burial, Freda found the foreman in the office to the side of the butchering floor. Knocking twice before hearing, "Enter," Freda stood waiting before the supervisor looked up. His arm swept out wide, "Miss, you're mistaken, the market entrance is on the lane."

She brought her palm up, "I'm the daughter of Dietrich Gottschalk and I've come to bring news of my father's passing on Easter Sunday."

The man's forehead creased, his brow frowned and he slumped back into the office chair, "Oh my. Well that's why he never appeared. That's not good. Please give your mother my condolences. Dietrich's worked the books since before Clybourne employed me. My own understanding of figures is rudimentary. Thank you, I'll alert the boss."

Freda stood unmoving, her eyes gazing through the window facing north. By and by he gazed up at her and inquired, "Was there something else?"

Freda drew energy up through her feet to mount the proposal in a forthright manner. She looked him in the eye, "Sir, I'm capable of assuming my father's position, if you'd consider hiring me."

Smiling, the foreman shook his head, the wrinkles around his eyes deepened, but Freda held her gaze and head up. When he noticed her intent, the smile evaporated and the man stood, looked her over and probed, "Your husband permits you to earn wages?"

Freda directed her reply into the air above his head. "I've been without my husband's company for some years and make decisions for myself and my young ones."

The foreman nodded, "Would you not find work difficult in such an environment?" He gestured to the southern window where Freda glimpsed the familiar figures of Nate and Thomas. The floor was a mass of blood, flies and filthy men. The cries of animals in their holding pens and others being led to slaughter reverberated through the wooden walls.

"The position I seek involves figures and receipts, which are quite different in nature."

The foreman nodded in agreement and patted the pile of papers on the table, "That's so. I'd like to say I could do the work myself. But I've been here a few hours and accomplished very little. The post requires skills I lack. If you're able to start at once, now precisely, you may have the post, though I doubt Clybourne will pay you what he paid your father." He waved to a bookshelf lined with narrow, black-spined volumes. "You'll find your father's ledgers here, the most recent on the right." Freda nodded and took the seat behind the desk.

Elke

Elke began to worry about her daughter in the late afternoon, when Freda had still not returned home. Wrapping herself in a woolen shawl, Elke set out across the field to speak with Rudy and Rory, who repaired a wire fence.

The brothers wore blue cotton shirts in the cool April air. Several fence posts had begun to rot and Dietrich had asked the boys to replace them with fresh timbers. They were in the process of cutting a very long beam when Elke reached them. The long saw they used required two men, one on each side, to heave the jagged metal teeth through the heartwood. Although still teenagers, the boys were acquiring the muscles of laborers. Their shirts stuck to their torsos with sweat. Their brown hair blackened as sweat dripped from strands at their temples and necks.

Rudy paused when he saw her approaching. Rory looked over at her expectantly, their breathing returning to a normal tempo. Elke smiled, having second thoughts about her request. She looked in the direction of the slaughterhouse, "I still don't see your mother approaching. It's been hours now, where do you suppose she's gone?"

"Perhaps they've given her Opa's position," Rory ventured.

Rudy volunteered, "Oma, if she hasn't appeared when we've finished the posts, I'll walk to the slaughterhouse and ask for her." She gave them a nod and a weak smile and turned away before tears welled in her eyes.

In the house, at the table covered in flour Uta cut biscuits at one end. "You're creating an enormous cleanup job for yourself." Elke commented, stirred the beans simmering on the fire and descended into the root cellar, carrying a candle. She emerged later, with a wheel of cheese in her free hand and a string of dried sausages looped over an arm.

Nimble feet padded up the steps of the back porch. Freda appeared her cheeks pink and several hairs astray. She smiled with determination, set a parcel on the table, took off her hat and hung her coat. When she returned to the table, she addressed her mother who watched her silently. "The foreman's given me Pa's position. He may not pay me the complete wages, but we'll have an income and I'll bring home the bacon." She patted the cloth-wrapped bundle.

"And Fredrick?" Elke inquired.

"Who?" Freda asked and smiled widely, her gaze taking in her niece. Elke drew her hands to her brow. "Mother, it's been ages since I've seen or heard from him. We don't even know if he lives. Fredrick should have no say in whether I take employment. I really should speak with the minister about having the marriage dissolved." She stepped to her mother's side and patted her shoulder. "Mama." Elke took her daughter's hand and wiped the tears that came too easily to her eyes.

"My girl, my smart girl. Your father taught you well. He'd be proud. So you'll be gone tomorrow as well? I don't know what I'll do without you."

"You have the boys and Uta and Romy and they're becoming competent cooks and gardeners."

As Freda spoke, Romy appeared carrying freshly washed carrots in her arms. Uta stood in the back doorway, attentive to the biscuits in the oven. She quietly reminded her aunt, "Tante, I'll be moving into Mama's house to help with the two young ones. The baby should be coming soon." Freda nodded and looked over what would be dinner. She took the carrots and began chopping them for the thick bean broth.

Elke dyed her clothing black in the large iron cauldron her mother used to make soap. From the chemist in town, she purchased a pound box of black dye, extracted from the heartwood of the logwood tree. She set the fire outside to avoid the foul scent from lingering in the home for days. Hanging the pot from the iron frame suspended above the flames, she sank her daily garments deep into the pigment.

It took several days of constant simmering to attain a shade of deep charcoal. She worked into Saturday evening, pressing the dress she would wear to church service in the morning. Satisfied, she would not wash her woolen dress again that year, though the two cotton gowns might find their way into the wash by the summer's end.

Gerolf

As the days lengthened, Gerolf came home later. Extended hours of sunlight prolonged the workday. If neighboring homes were occupied, tenants and landlords likely complained about the hammering and general disruption coming from the sites of new construction.

Summer provided the best working conditions. Patrick O'Shay shrugged off the grievances and urged his construction crew to persevere.

When the wind blew in the wrong direction, vapors from the river sailed eastward over the growing town and its outskirts. Townsfolk breathed the slaughterhouse rankness and the worse stench from the tannery. Corabell complained, "Gerolf what're those people doing to create such a stink?"

Gerolf gazed over his bowl of beans at her and raised an eyebrow, "But your people tanned leather, don't you recall the smell of it?"

Corabell brought the stewed pheasant to the table, "Yes, but not like this, it makes me ill."

"Pa? Too stinky." Otto scrunched his nose and shook his head.

"Mhm, the tanning recipe's a closely guarded secret. Tree bark's a major ingredient used in bathing hides. Men haul massive loads in wagons and on barges. Weighed on scales outside the storage buildings, they're paid in coins. Covered barns store the bark until it dries. When it's needed, men feed it into a horse-powered crushing mill. After days of bathing and rubbing with manure and urine, workers rinse the skins in the river's intake and discharge the waste into the outflow."

"Fouling the water. . . Do fish still live there? My brothers caught fish; I wasn't any good at it."

"No, I don't see people fishing, but other industries have come. There's a new harness and saddle shop on Clybourne and a shoemaking factory's under construction."

Corabell

On most days, the winds blew off the lake, bringing a steady westward-moving current across the land. When the fetid aroma from the river industry hung heavy over the cabin and garden, Corabell vomited and suffered headaches.

On Sunday following morning service, Corabell consulted Elke about how much longer she had until the baby would arrive. Elke felt her belly and speculated she had a few more weeks. Eva who bled regularly, expected to pass her child by July's end.

Elke confided to Corabell, "The heat of the summer, the demands of Amsel's children and her swollen ankles have pushed Eva to vexation. Even with Uta's help, Eva's garden's growing out of control."

Uta

On a windless overcast day in July, Eva's water broke. A few hours later, she went into certain labor. "Fetch Amsel from the field; ask him to bring Grandmother Gottschalk in the carriage. I'll need her today."

Uta's dress stuck to her torso with sweat when she breathlessly returned. Her mother lay forehead flat to the table, the fire in the hearth reduced to glowing coals.

Rolling her head to the side, Eva directed, "Hanna, watch over your brother. Don't let him get into trouble. I want you outside. Now!" The blond child's eyes met the floor and she clenched her lips, turning silently to retrieve the small hand. "Stay in front, in the shade with Henry. If I look out the window and don't see you or your brother, you'll be in trouble."

The girl nodded. Henry's shorter legs worked fast as his sister towed him from the room. Uta stood in the airflow by the open door, while the two children passed.

"Stoke the fire. "We'll need hot water and cloths. I've waited too long, I fear."

Uta blew at the remaining coals, coaxing the fire to life. She filled the kettle and shifted it beneath the flames. Behind her, Eva moaned. Uta turned. Her mother held the tableside, squatting. Blood and clear liquid dripped into a puddle on the new wooden floor.

"Uta dear, help me out of this frock." Uta unbuttoned the dress, slipped it out from under her, hastily hung the garment and hurried back. "Fetch a hot wet cloth."

"Mama, they're not warm yet." Eva mumbled, bent and squatted. Uta wrung a cloth. She brought it to her mother, who hiked up her slip and settled the cloth between her legs. Mopping the puddle from the floor, Uta set a layer of padding beneath the exposed buttocks as her mother exhaled and moaned.

With the fire ablaze, the heat within the cabin rose several more degrees. Uta opened every window and a fresh current of warm air wandered in.

"Bed pan!" Grabbing the pot, Uta slid it under as Eva bore down and emptied her bowels. "Get the washbasin," she urged, "We'll make a dirty pile."

Her mother swore, pounding the table. Tears flowed down her cheeks as another contraction hit. She squatted. When the episode eased, Eva rose, wiped her eyes and called, "Keep the cloths coming, Uta."

"Yes Mama, they're warmer now." Several cloths later, Eva fixed her feet in a wide steady squat. Her moaning ebbed as she held the table edge.

"Uta! Close the door." Pulling the damp shift up around her waist, Eva tied it in a knot as Uta swung shut the door.

Uta resolved to keep pace with the requests. She had never seen her mother's naked body. The baby was coming! She offered a fresh warm rag. Eva pushed, grunted and quickly demanded another. The baby's head emerged. One hand cupped the crown, "Dry, dry cloth!"

Gasping, Uta swiped the cloths from the mantel. Arms full, with shaky hands, she drew close. Easing back on heels, buttocks near the floor, the baby's head protruded. Uta quickly tossed more towels beneath her.

Eva bore down again and the baby slid slowly onto the padding. She exhaled heavily. For several moments, mother and daughter gaped at the baby, extending its wet arms and legs. Blue eyes and mouth opened as Eva ran a cloth over the tender face and down across the belly, where the umbilical cord connected them, "Look it's a boy." She whispered, "Fetch a knife dear and cut the cord."

Uta gripped the pliable cable and cut through the tissue, then set about taking up the cloths. Several contractions later, Eva passed the saucer-like placenta. Uta frowned, crinkling her nose.

Surprisingly, her mother wiped the round mass and wrapped it in a cloth. Cradling the baby, she shuffled to the bed, unknotted the shift, and arranged herself. Eva nudged the baby closer, settled, took several deep breaths and closed her eyes.

Uta left her to rest. She weeded the garden rows, with the children close when they heard the regular beat of horse hooves. With Henry in hand and Hanna near, Uta recounted the news. "Mother and the baby are in bed, resting." Amsel's eyes grew wide and he helped Elke off the side of the wagon.

Adjusting the bag on her shoulder, Elke inquired, "How did it go?"

Uta shrugged. "I mostly just passed cloths. Come see."

Inside, they gazed at the mother who lay sleeping. Her head wet with perspiration, the cotton slip adhered to her flesh. The infant slept beneath an outstretched arm in a loosely bundled cloth with neck and shoulder exposed. Uta whispered, "It's a boy."

A smile flashed across Elke's face. "Amsel'll be pleased."

When he lumbered into the house, Eva opened her eyes. Elke left them to coo over the child and explored the hearth and side table for dinner.

Pushing aside the kettle of boiling cloths, Elke set the food on the fire. The two young ones dawdled beside the bedcovers, staring at the new one while Amsel went to finish chores.

Weaving through the children that tumbled across one side of the bed, Elke inquired, "You're still having contractions?" Eva groaned and nodded. "Good, the uterus's constricting, as it should."

Her eyes partially open, Eva told them, "The pea meal roast lies on a dish in the cellar." Uta nodded and went to retrieve the meat.

Elke

Elke stayed, reluctant to ask Amsel to take her home so soon. Pulling back the damp sheet, she asked, "Eva dear, why not nurse the babe? It's stifling hot." The mother nodded and shifted her eyelids heavy.

Elke stood at her side, "Come, "I'll bring you some water." The dim cabin light covered her face in shadow. Elke felt her forehead. Waiting with a cup in hand, she stated loudly, "Eva, open your eyes and sit up." The brown eyes opened to small slits in response. Elke turned to Uta, who approached with a frown, "Uta please, fetch fresh water from the well." The girl pointed to the barrel Amsel tried to keep full. Elke shook her head. "No dear, the water must be cold and fresh."

Uta

Uta stroked a strand of damp blond hair back from her eyes, telling herself Grandmother knows what to do. Grabbing the pails, she thrust her feet into the clogs outside the door.

Returning with sloshing buckets, Elke had laid the baby in the cradle at the foot of the bed. Mother lay, gown unbuttoned to her navel. Damp cloths covered breasts, sank into the depressions of armpits and circled her neck. The gown hem exposed her thighs. Elke plunged a clean linen cloth into the cool water, wrung it partially dry and placed it on Mother's forehead. She refreshed the other warming cloths sequentially.

Elke brought the baby to the damp breast and nestled him in the crook of one arm. Cheek brushing against her, he turned, rooting to suckle. Attached, he sucked steadily before drifting to sleep.

Amsel arrived, leaving his muddy boots outside the front door. The scent of roasting meat filled the hot house. He stood taking in the smell and the reduced light of the interior. The two children, unusually silent, drifted to him at the threshold. Uta took the cooked vegetables from the fire and set them on the hearthstones. She withdrew the roast and set the browned meat on the table.

In socks, Amsel walked to the back of the house and saw his second wife lying with various colored cloths draped across the hottest parts of her flesh. Stooping at the edge of the bed, he rested his forehead on the quilt. Elke spoke softly to him, "She's had one fit, already. I fear for her."

Uta served the children dinner. She took her plate and sat next to young Henry. Hanna chewed noisily, "Mm, your carrots are so good. Mm, you need to make carrots every day."

Food had little taste for Uta. Grandmother would insist on eating and Uta wanted to please her in all ways, if she could only keep Mother alive.

Coming to Elke's side, Uta offered, "I can help now." Elke nodded and Uta sat and took up the task. Her grandmother washed her face and hands with soap and then eased onto the bench at the table.

Water dripped into the bucket as Uta wrung a towel to replace the hot cloth across her mother's neck. Taking it up, the knees abruptly bent, and beat in rhythmic waves as arms flexed at the elbows and thrashed.

Uta shrieked and leapt away. Shielding her open mouth, she turned her head, aghast. Elke set a hand on her shoulder. "Uta please, I need you. You helped birth the child, now help me keep your mother alive." She pulled Uta into her arms as the younger ones stared, their eyes round.

Amsel moved to his wife and drew a cool cloth across her forehead. The damp body quaked spontaneously, the rigorous spasms that forced limbs inwards and head backwards slowly diminished. Amsel bent over her. A strand of sweat-soaked hair brushed her face. He kissed his wife's wet cheek and turned to the younger children, "Ready yourselves for bed. When I return I'll be up to say prayers." Hanna took the dirty dishes and cups from the table, set them on the sideboard and climbed the ladder.

Elke

Elke finished dinner as Uta rotated the cloths. The girl's tears flowed as a new bout of convulsions made Eva's body awkward and awful. Elke washed the dishes, rinsed the soiled linens, added hot water and scrubbed them, dumped the liquid and covered the cloths with fresh water to soak.

The shallow, fast breath worried her. How long would Eva last? Transferring the baby to the right breast, Elke coaxed him to nurse and gave thanks he needed little encouragement. Standing at the bedside, she considered the worst scenario. Amsel had fed small Henry goat's milk. Would he choose to nurse another infant?

Elke set her boots beneath the mattress and stretched out beside her former daughter-in-law. In the dark of night, the rocking mattress woke her. She slid from the bed, thinking of the baby. Several short wails woke Uta, who sat briefly. Elke lifted the infant from the armpit of his quaking mother, "Uta you rest." Instead, the girl rose and set fresh cool towels on her mother's body. Then she lay down and held her mother's hand.

Chapter Thirty-Four

Uta

As the last fit diminished, Mother's arms and legs twitched only in sudden rapid bursts. Breathing turned soft and raspy. The two little ones woke. With sleepy faces, they gazed at their stepmother and walked by, preferring to sit at the table bench than with her.

Uta went to the outhouse after setting the water to boil. When she returned, the house sat quiet. At the bench beside the table, the children swung their legs in the air, ready for breakfast. Elke hung the clean linens on the clothesline and walked with the baby through the weed-strewn rows of the garden.

Uta found her mother still. No twitching tormented her limbs. She no longer labored to breathe. Uta slumped against her mother's body, resting on the hot torso and her tears added to the bedding's dampness. Hearing the water in the kettle spurt and boil, Uta slowly rose.

Elke

Elke settled the baby against the breast of the dead mother and let him suckle all that she would ever give him. Preparing coffee, she made a sweeter, creamier cup for Uta. The scent of morning induced Amsel to sit on the floor where he had slept. He took several swigs of black coffee and settled beside his wife. Pressing a palm to her cheek, his tears ran.

Elke knew several things about Eva's death. In time Amsel might recover, the children would flounder in his care and she would miss her deeply. Elke yearned to be home, where Dietrich would console her. In his absence, his favorite chair, the smell of his coat, hat and worn boots would bring her a bit of peace.

Taking the kettle, Elke gathered soap and a washbasin. She urged Uta and Hanna over to the bed. With the girls assisting, Elke began bathing Eva while Amsel sought out her favorite dress, which would clothe her in the grave. He took his time, bringing her corset and her favorite hat, as well as her boots with small buttons running up the ankle. Elke asked, "Amsel will you make a casket or shall we bind her in a sheet?"

"I'll make a box this afternoon."

By midday, the women of different generations had prepared Eva. Uta braided her mother's dark hair. She set her bonnet and tied the bow beneath her chin. Amsel's young Hanna washed her stepmother's feet and donned her hose and boots.

Elke needed help with the corset Amsel provided. Having removed the laces, and worked the boned material under the body, she threaded the eyes and began tugging the cords to cinch in the abdomen Eva had allowed to grow unfettered. Amsel picked a dress with a waist; one Eva had worn before she wed. Elke feared the swollen torso would refuse to be confined. Before giving up, Elke turned to Uta, "Climb up over your mama and pull the corset laces in. Pull as hard as you're able."

The blond girl stood, bare feet on either side of her mother's maternal shape. Taking the corset cords, she exhaled and pulled, bringing the torso up from the mattress, narrowing the midsection by a dozen inches or more.

"Hold there! Hold tight!" Elke grabbed the corset sides and held them while Uta tied the laces, endowing Eva with a waist that resembled her former figure. Heartened, Elke brought the dress up and began buttoning as Amsel arrived in the doorway.

He wandered to the hearth and asked, "No dinner today?" Elke directed him to the leftover roast, covered with a cloth to shield it from flies.

Later, when the women looked to him for some sign of approval, he and young Henry sat facing each other, eating. Elke told him, "I'm taking the children, as Eva would've preferred, to my home until you've recovered sufficiently to care for them. I expect you daily for dinner at shortly after midday."

The husband stepped out from the bench and came to the bedside. He wiped his lips and gazed at his wife wearing her favorite hat. Sniffing, he nodded, "Thank you for caring for her."

Elke gathered her things. She secured the baby in a sling across her bosom and threw her satchel over the other shoulder. Amsel stood watching them move about. He nodded again and returned to the plate on the table. Uta picked up Henry, who grabbed a biscuit and a chunk of meat from his plate. Setting the boy on her hip, they left Amsel in silence.

A breeze caught them as their eyes adjusted to daylight and all around them white plumes from cottonwood trees sailed on currents of air. Uta adjusted her hold on Henry and Hanna took her free hand.

Romy

When she heard the sounds of her cousin's voices in the field, Romy ran to the back porch. Hopping from foot to foot, she watched the children coming her way. The bleak aura that overshadowed the walkers eventually dampened her delight, her face tensed and her jaw tightened and she called out, "Oma, why do you carry that baby?"

Drawing closer, Elke gazed sadly at the youngest sister and shook her head, "Romy dear, your mama's died. Fever took her after the birth of your baby brother. The burial should occur at the churchyard tomorrow in the morning. Hanna and little Henry'll live with us until their papa can care for them.

Romy stared at Hanna, who gaped back at her with clear blue eyes. Only Henry appeared unfazed by the sudden change in life. He took cover under the table where he lay on his belly, rolling three marbles along the ample seam between the floor planks.

Elke

Elke brought out the old cradle and set the baby in it. She fed the children leftovers and filled a pot to boil adding ten handfuls of dried beans.

Romy had milked the cow. Elke spied the bucket in the cellar with the aid of candlelight. Carrying the bucket upstairs, she pondered whether the fat would be beneficial to the newly born child, and took a spoon to scoop up the thicker surface.

Her face without expression, Uta watched her grandmother as she worked. In the crib, the baby stirred and fretted. Glancing at her grandmother, Uta lifted the child and set him across her chest as she lowered herself into the rocker. When swaying had no effect on the wailing infant, Uta placed his back against her thighs. Raising a fist to his mouth, the child began sucking vigorously. Uta smiled and glanced over at her grandmother who looked up at the sudden silence. Elke saw the joy in Uta's face overwhelm her grief.

Before supper, Elke wrote a note to the Oberweiss family, informing them of the sudden death of their daughter following the birth of their latest grandson. She would ask Rudy to take the horse and deliver the message before nightfall.

The baby had taken no fluids since early morning. Feeling a rising anxiety about feeding the child, Elke found a leather glove Dietrich had worn years ago when reaping. She dropped the mired remnant of her spouse into a pot of boiling water in hopes of cleaning it.

With too much boiling, she feared the leather might degrade. She watched it keenly. The bubbling water darkened with grime. Elke lifted it after a time with the hearth fork, assessing its integrity. The seams were still intact; the stitches close. Heartened, Elke hung the fork with the dripping glove, over the mantel to cool.

As Romy held the edges open, Elke ladled in sweet milk. Flowing into each finger, it soon resembled a small cow udder. Romy and Hanna grinned as their grandmother twisted the opening closed. Poking a hole in the thumb, Elke offered the glove to Uta. Gripping the makeshift breast, Uta presented the digit to the baby's lips. The sudden gush of fluid surprised him. He coughed and sputtered before learning a regular rhythm brought a steady stream.

Uta

The burial service brought her uncle, his wife and four children in a fine carriage. The men wore blue linen trousers. Her aunt and cousins wore cotton dresses in gray. Uta stared at the silk flower details adorning their bonnets. Only Nola, wearing a new dress sewn by the seamstress in town, had the gumption to greet them and thank them for attending.

Uta and Romy followed behind Nola, who they scarcely recognized in her latest outfit. The three girls held hands as the minister began prayers. Their clutches tightened when the pastor tapped in the nails to the coffin lid.

Men set the box in the ground. At end of the final sentence, the preacher took a fistful of earth and tossed it into the hole. Dirt scattered, hitting the wood.

The girls stood by. Family members wandered to the church. Amsel settled on his knees in the low grass beside the hole. His sobs quieted the words people had with one another. They moved away. Weeping, Amsel dropped in a handful of soil and strode to the back cemetery gate. Mrs. Oberweiss hurried to catch him.

Elke

"Herr Amsel!" Mrs. Oberweiss called out and Elke looked past the tombstones to see the stout form pursuing the farmer. Her heart sank. She had no right to imagine she would keep the baby. Elke watched and saw his nod before he turned away.

Mrs. Oberweiss turned back to the church, a small smile on her face. Elke closed her eyes and breathed in the scent of the infant in her arms.

Catharina Heck set up a table in the shade of the church building. She filled cups with cool hard cider while her daughter took a silver plate of cookies among the mourners.

Rudy took Amsel's young ones to the front steps of the church. He brought them cookies and lounged on the bottom step beside them, sipping cider.

People began to leave. Catching sight of the three girls remaining beside their mother's grave, parishioners whispered to one another and patted Elke's arm. She held the dozing baby against her chest. Then Mrs. Oberweiss stood in front of her.

She gave Elke no words to diminish the sting of relinquishing the child. Elke met her gaze and saw her outstretched hands waiting. Before surrendering the warm bundle, Elke asked, "How'll you feed him?"

"I've hired a wet nurse, of course." Elke peeled the infant from beneath her chin, kissed his head and gave him to the woman who perched him over her ample bosom.

Mrs. Oberweiss called to Nola. The girl loosened the grip of her youngest sister's hand. With a handkerchief, she wiped the tears dripping from Romy's nose and followed Grandmother Oberweiss, who slipped into the waiting carriage.

The space on Elke's shoulder felt cold without the weight of the baby's warmth. Elke told herself the Oberweiss family would care for the boy child well enough. He would not have to drink cow's milk from an old work glove, but would have true breast milk. Feeling lighter, though grieved about her diminished responsibilities, Elke drifted to the table where a servant dispensed cider.

The gathering thinned. Uta took a seat on the church steps beside cousin Rudy, who kept the smaller ones from trouble by plying them with more cookies and watered down cider. Henry began to sing heartily, a song he invented as it rambled on. Lying on his back on the step, one outstretched hand held a pale wafer, which swung in time to the tune he produced. When the song sailed into a head turning crescendo, Rudy reached out and tapped his blond forehead. The child brought the volume down several levels.

Romy

Romy thrust her hands deep into the excavated soil. Her eyes streaming with tears and her knees embedded in the dirt, she stared into the pit and threw in handfuls of earth.

Rory carried the table into the rectory and returned to the church steps with a stack of pale butter cookies. He waved them in the air, calling to his young cousin at the gravesite.

Romy turned his way and wiped away her tears. She stood, brushed dirt from her knees and left her mother's grave. Cheeks streaked with mud, grubby to the elbows, Romy settled on the bottom step with a ragged sob fettering her breath. Uta set a cup of cider at her side.

When the wind began to blow Elke suggested they leave. Henry leapt from the step, staggered, giggled and found Rudy's hand. When the child walked too slowly, Rudy shifted him to his back. Elke took the hands of the small girls. Uta walked alongside her cousin as the wind whipped through the scrub on the path home.

Chapter Thirty-Five

Corabell

Aspiring to put away enough produce to last the entire winter and lack for nothing in the thin months of spring, Corabell sought out the downtown market. She took the journey with Elke on Saturday morning, when Uta agreed to look after Otto.

The scent of beans and bacon flowed outside to greet Corabell and Otto when they arrived on foot. Corabell lowered herself onto the top step of the front porch and sat with Uta, who trimmed a bushel of beans in preparation for pickling. Corabell confided, "You know I asked your mother to help with Otto's birth. She told me no, she'd be too busy with Amsel and the children."

Uta tightened her lips and nodded, "When do you reckon this baby'll come?"

"Oh, I hope not too soon." The door opened and Elke stepped out volunteering, "I'd give her another week, maybe two. Henry and Otto, behave yourselves, Uta's in charge. We'll have dinner when we get back."

Rory brought the horse and carriage to a halt at the front of the house. "Oma I can drive you to town. I've finished the morning chores.

Elke gave a hand to Corabell and she came to her feet, "Fine, but there won't be much for you to do."

"Being in town's good enough for me," the boy commented.

The wooden carriage wheels dipped in and out of deep troughs in the road. The carriage bounced, sending the riders aloft. Corabell held the sides and tried not to complain. As they neared the town center, the corduroy began and the jostling became more rhythmic and less precipitous.

In Cook's, the women went in separate directions. While considering the canning vessels, Corabell felt a contraction tighten over her belly. She tried to ignore it, telling herself it was small and would pass.

She was mistaken. Constricting forces of rising intensity caused her to sink briefly to the floor. Between episodes, she requested and paid for four medium earthenware vessels and asked the clerk to deliver them to the carriage waiting outside. She carried laundry soap, three bars of hand soap and a dozen thick baby cloths in a bundle under her arm when another bout fell upon her. Managing a slower pace, she stood on the front steps of the shop.

Outside Rory waited, sprawled across the carriage bench. Spying Corabell as she held the banister, he called, "Mrs. Bachmeier, are you well?"

Corabell waved her arm, "Mhm. Female pains," causing him to raise his eyebrows. "I'll be back, just need to use the outhouse." Corabell left the purchases in the carriage and shuffled around to the back where privies stood in a row, miniature dwellings painted in different shades. She lifted her skirts and sat, relaxing as her bowels drained and another contraction plowed over her.

The ride home felt twice as long and bumpy as the journey to town. "Rory!" Corabell gripped his arm, "Please, let me shift to the back of the wagon."

Stepping from the bench, a gush of warm liquid rushed down her legs into the dry packed earth. "Oh, dear," she muttered with several native words and looked to Elke.

Elke met her eyes, "Don't worry, we're on our way home." Every pitch and bump caused a cry from the wagon bed and persuaded Rory to slow, as he attempted to navigate around road pits.

Corabell began speaking solely in another tongue. She gripped the back of the bench seat or the wagon side to thwart the forces sending her periodically airborne.

Elke clasped Rory's arm, "Goad the horse to a faster pace, we need to get home fast." Rory slapped the reigns and squinted to see, while Elke clung to the carriage side, flattening the hat to her head. Corabell deplored the world and everything in it. Nearing home, Elke shouted instructions, "Drive the horse in front of the house and run inside. Clear everything from the table. I'll follow with Corabell."

Elke

Elke worried for Corabell. Second births being generally easier than the first, the baby passing too quickly through the constrained space could cause severe injuries, displacing pelvic organs and drawing them downward.

The speeding wagon and the storm of road dust demanded the attention of all. On Clybourne, they overtook a delivery wagon; the driver diverted his team to the right yielding to the racing horse. Wary pedestrians gave the carriage a wide berth when they glimpsed the oncoming mare and bodies in front bowed by the wind, a dirt plume trailing behind.

Nearing hearing distance, Elke shouted to the figures on the porch, "Clear the table! Boil cloths!" Uta ran inside, knowing what to do. As Rory directed the horse, Elke shouted to Rudy, "Take Corabell to the table!" The older brother ran alongside the slowing carriage. Corabell bent her head in concentration. Rudy glanced up and met his grandmother's eyes. She nodded. He threw an arm over Corabell's back, swept beneath her legs and hauled her out of the wagon.

Corabell gripped Rudy's shoulder as he trotted into the house, where Uta directed him to the table draped with a stained, though clean sheet. She waved him away, and lifted her skirts to glimpse the head of the baby caught by a thin film of skin. "Oma!" Uta bellowed, "I see the baby!" The blond girl dumped the cloths into the simmering water and returned to Corabell's side. Elke flew into the room.

There was no time. Elke grabbed the only dry cloth, circled the skin that bound the baby's head and gently nudged it back to Corabell's loins. A mounting contraction gripped her and Corabell bore down. Elke held the tissues back as the head emerged. With the next push, the shoulders and body of the baby followed. Corabell slumped backwards resting flat on the table, her boots still on. Uta told her softly, "You've another boy." The girl wiped the tender baby feet as Elke rubbed white film from the pink flesh.

Amid the birth, Amsel arrived for dinner. He loitered at the doorway. Uta helped Corabell down from the table and into a bedroom. Hanna greeted her father happily, running and flinging herself into his spreading arms. Young Henry found Otto more interesting, the younger boy, almost his size.

Still wearing her hat, Elke served dinner after the farmer said a brief prayer. Amsel's longer hair and beard grew more gray than brown. Working outdoors in the sun and sleet made him appear older than his years. With the young children in her company, Elke had softened and smiled more, though she dressed in complete black.

The younger children quipped while Rudy and Rory sought Amsel's advice on matters of the fields. It would be the first season they would harvest barley and flax themselves.

When Corabell insisted that she must begin making supper and Elke felt satisfied with her state of health, Rory drove her and her children home in the wagon.

Corabell

When Gerolf crossed the threshold in the evening, his eyes took in her altered form. Corabell wore her leather corset, the cords drawn in as tight as she could stand.

Otto seized him at the knees and Gerolf reached down and took the child by the pants, lifting him in one arm. The boy swung his weight extending a hand to the cradle in the back of the room. Gerolf let the child guide him to where the tightly swaddled infant rested. He gazed at the baby and back at Corabell silent, jaw slack. The boy in his arms spoke clearly, "Otto's baby."

Gerolf picked up the newborn, marveling at his weight, dark hair, tiny fingernails, nostrils and lips. He held him to his face, smelling the delicate flesh and talking softly to him in German while he moved to the door and sat on the threshold, Otto at his shoulder.

Shedding the cloth that bound the baby snuggly, the infant opened his eyes, worked his limbs in the air and began to wail. Not dissuaded, Gerolf inspected the small ears, penis, scrotum and ten toes. Otto caught a hand and held a kicking foot. Kissing the baby on the forehead, Gerolf hastily bundled and set him back in the cradle. Holding the boy by the waist, he kissed Corabell's neck while she worked.

Cabin days revolved around cooking, cleaning, laundry and gardening. Corabell and the children napped after the midday meal, saving Gerolf a portion of the hearty fare, making supper preparation less laborious. On the third day, Corabell's milk came in and her breasts swelled. The baby suckled well, warm milk lulling him into a contented torpor.

Elke

Corabell kept her pledge to put up greater quantities of garden produce and sought more containers from town. Otto passed Saturday mornings with young Henry. On an excursion to town in August's final days, Elke took the reins of the wagon and directed the horse through the lane, "On the way home, we'll look in on Emily. She's huge with child and due any day."

Corabell nodded and told her, "The month of August has the moon of the middle."

"The middle of what?" Elke smiled.

Corabell shrugged, "It's been so long since I've been with my kinfolk, I've forgotten the ways."

Turning onto North Avenue, Elke directed the horse to the O'Shay property, "Every time I come this way there's something new. The town expands weekly. Fresh construction stands where fields used to grow."

The township had enveloped the O'Shay home. Apple trees still grew in two rows, some twenty feet from the side of the house, though Patrick and Henry had erected a wooden fence that circled the perimeter. Elke urged the horse to turn and they moved along the edge of the property to the small cabin in back.

"Hello!" Rachel O'Shay leaned, waving from an open window. The women heard her call to Emily, who promptly shuffled through the back door.

Elke exclaimed at the size of her daughter, while Emily gesticulated with both arms and came down the back stairs. Elke stepped from the carriage and Emily raised both hands, "Stop, Mama! There's illness here. Mother O'Shay's not well. Mary's gone for the physic and I'm helping Rachel."

Elke glared at her daughter, her eyes leaden. "What? You? No. Nien! You'll go to your own home. NOW!" Elke turned to Corabell who remained on the wagon bench with the new baby and met her gray eyes. "Stay here. When the sister comes back, we leave." Elke frowned at her daughter from under her straw brim and Emily obeyed without comment.

Inside the O'Shay family home, Elke surveyed the hearth, filled the largest pot with water and put it on the fire, then greeted the house, "Hello! It's Elke Gottschalk, Emily's mother. I've sent her home. She should avoid disease, you know."

A woman's voice came from the side hallway and Elke walked into a dimly lit bedroom with a single window to the lane. A breeze moved the curtain in small undulating waves.

Gray-tinged, Mother O'Shay lay in a linen frock drawn up around the thighs. Layers of absorbent cotton wound around her lower body. Rachel held a cloth to her mother's brow and the sunken blue eyes stared vacantly. The bare feet on the bed appeared dusky blue, as were her hands. Rachel whispered to Elke, "I fear she'll pass, Mother complains of thirst yet keeps nothing down. She's tortured with diarrhea and dehydration."

Elke inquired, "You're boiling your linens?"

Rachel frowned, "No, not yet. This came upon her before dawn this morning."

Elke feared Mother O'Shay had cholera. She had read the broadsheets printed by the Health Department. The notices were pasted to the sides of downtown stores. Abbreviated versions fluttered from lampposts.

Footsteps across the wooden floor made Elke turn. Mary appeared carrying a small blue bottle and nodded to Elke, "The pharmacist prepared twenty grams of calomel with five of camphor. When I described the symptoms, he told me he'd contact the constable and the Board of Health, but he had nothing else to recommend." Rachel frowned and shifted on the bed. Mary uncorked the blue vial, "Open your mouth Mum, I've got medicine for you." She shook the dust onto the pale, parched tongue. Mary spoke softly as her younger sister Rachel tucked a sheet up around her mother's shoulders. "Even her tongue's cold. I fear there's nothing to do but pray."

Elke had one desire, to get Emily away from the house and town. Her departing footfalls resounded through the interior and she worried her daughter might refuse to leave.

Elke strode past Corabell and the infant waiting in the wagon, rapped on the cabin door and tried the latch. Emily sat sewing at the table. A pot simmered on the fire.

Elke's mouth trembled as she spoke, "Emily, fetch your things you must come forthwith." The youngest daughter eyed her and put the sewing down slowly. Emily rose glancing at her mother, found a satchel and folded items of clothing into it, while Elke scribbled a hasty note to Henry, opened the door and stood waiting, tapping her toe. They were in the wagon and down the lane before Elke began to relax.

Wanting the younger women to understand her motives, Elke shared the news she had read on bulletins in the center of town. Emily told her, "Mother, I fear for their lives, it's my duty to attend to Henry's family."

Elke shook her head and sighed, "Dietrich and Eva are the only family members I'll bury this year." Then she turned to watch the horse and road.

Chapter Thirty-Six

Corabell

Relieved to be home, Corabell lit a thick swath of gray withered sage and walked the cabin's interior, sending a prayer to the Great Spirit to keep her loved ones from disease. The act allayed some anxiety until Gerolf arrived and reported he had been working on the town's first hospital on Green Bay Road and North Avenue.

Gerolf

"The foreman told us the road's an old Indian Trail running north all the way to Wisconsin. You know the pathway?" Corabell frowned and flipped the spoon she wielded in her hand, and he understood she did not know, nor care. The hospital however, concerned her greatly. She conveyed the events of the morning and the illness present at the O'Shay home, reporting Elke had mentioned cholera occurred in densely populated areas.

Gerolf saw the apprehension in her face when he caught sight of her. He might have held her, had he not been wrestling on the floor with Otto and the dog.

Corabell

"Elke recently read the broadsides downtown and now they're constructing a hospital . . . seems they must've known of the illness before." Corabell served bean and bacon soup then brought the roasted quail to the table.

Gerolf wiped bean broth from the edges of the bowl, "The Chicago Weekly Democrat reported cholera's sweeping through the Midwest, causing riverside towns to evacuate. They say Black Cholera's greater in larger cities. If I remember right, St. Louis lost 500 people in the last years, Cincinnati 700 and Detroit 300."

Corabell frowned and tapped Gerolf's bowl with the tines of her fork, "This's Emily and Henry O'Shay we're speaking of, not the people of Detroit or Saint Louis."

"I simply confirm there's reason enough the town should have a pest house. People fall ill every day; there should be a suitable place for treatment." Gerolf reached across the table and patted her hand and she wiped an anxious tear from one eye.

The following day Gerolf brought home news of Mother O'Shay's death. In subsequent days, he recounted Mary and Rachel had fallen ill.

The O'Shay men left the house servant to attend to the women while they were at work. Bridgette and the two younger sisters, Fiona and Moira worked daily at the bakery. Patrick insisted the girls lodge at their workplace until all threat of the illness passed. He and Henry boarded temporarily with his sister, who lived several miles north of town.

Gerolf

In the ensuing days, Henry O'Shay recounted the story, "The Department of Health collected Mother's body early in the morning to avoid sight by the neighbors and took her out to the new cemetery. No one reported the death, until Sunday when prayers were offered for her passing at the principle mass at St. Patrick's.

The constable advised us to avoid speaking of the disease for fear panic would spread. That request's been hard to abide. Father's a church usher. Absence of the O'Shay women brought a series of questions and rumors've begun to fly that cholera's hit town."

Gerolf and Henry dug a pit for an outhouse. Gerolf paused, "So Mother O'Shay, Rachel and Mary've all died?" Henry wiped his nose with his sleeve and nodded. Gerolf patted his back and shook his head, trying to fathom three members of the O'Shay family no longer breathed. "I'm so sorry Henry and still I've read nothing in the Chicago Weekly Democrat."

Henry blew his nose and offered, "It's the influence of the business community; they fear the townsfolk'll flee and trade'll suffer."

Patrick set a shoulder load of wooden planks aside the mound of excavated earth. His voice boomed over the construction site, "Cholera is the judgment of God upon a sinful nation, an intemperate, ungrateful, Sabbath-breaking nation which has robbed and spoiled the Indian and withheld that which is just and right from the enslaved African." Their heads swiveled to the father who pulled himself straight and continued the performance, "Cholera will go where it is sent. Best advice: Be ready for death. Death stands at your door. Repent of your sins." The man resumed his normal posture, shaking his head, "Have you seen the placards? They're posted all over town. The mudsill boobs know nothing of disease."

The newspapers eventually accepted that a virulent illness raged in its midst and began recording the names of those who succumbed.

Over dinner Gerolf shared the news with Corabell, "You know Henry and Patrick lost Mother O'Shay." Corabell nodded. "Rachel and Mary have died as well, along with the servant girl who attended them." Corabell covered her lips and Gerolf unfolded a page of the newspaper he had saved. "I wanted to show you this article." Corabell wiped away her tears, drew the paper close and studied it for a lengthy while.

Recommendations from the Board of Health

During this time when disease is rampant, the Board of Health stresses the importance of keeping clean the house, barns, cellars, privies, alleys and streets. The mayor of the city asks citizens to refrain from public gatherings, except for church attendance. Avoid the night air, close the windows and doors and shun vegetables and fruits except from one's own lands.

In the event someone in the family falls ill, residents are asked to isolate the sick to a single room in their homes, if at all possible. Should there be any suspicion that the afflicted may have cholera; the Board of Health must be notified.

In the event of death, the population is advised to decontaminate the interior with three pounds of roll sulfur to each ten square feet of the interior. Before burning the mineral, one must secure the cracks in windows and below doorways. Once sealed, the room should remain empty for the twenty-four hours following decontamination. Those caring for stricken family members must clean, burn or boil the contents of the bedroom and anything the afflicted may have contacted. Cleaning should commence with four ounces of chloride of lime to one gallon of water. Authorities suggest using gloves and masks when cleaning to avoid any risk of further contamination.

"All this cleaning and concealing bodies deeply in the earth away from the Great Spirit, there'll be so many more lost souls. I only hope we'll never need to know this." Corabell looked to Gerolf, "The next newspaper you read, bring it home. I'd like to see it also."

Corabell

In mid-September, Emily gave birth to a daughter. After Sunday service Elke shared with Corabell, "Her labor was long and tiring and she fought with me throughout the ordeal, snapping at my suggestions but generally abiding my counsel. When at last the baby's head crowned, I made a small cut in her flesh and eased the head through. Later, I stitched her up and she felt little of the needle lacing her back together."

"And the child?" Corabell preferred to know.

"A small peach she is, truly a beauty and she nurses well."

When October arrived and the newspaper failed to report any new deaths, Gerolf told Corabell, "Patrick's begun speaking about having the house interior fumigated."

Corabell nodded, "The sulphur treatment?" Gerolf nodded.

Gerolf

Henry confided to him as they worked, "Pa consulted the Health Department and followed their guidelines, closing the windows and packing gaps beneath doors with rugs and linens. We lit the yellow mineral in metal washtubs on the floors of each room.

"Yellow smoke billowed up from the floorboards, waving in thick strands upon the windows panes and escaping through undetected drafts. The current seeped in a flat ribbon under the back door where Pa and I stood watching. The foul odor confirmed the dreadful loss.

"I thank God for the birth of my daughter, though I've yet to set eyes on her."

When at last the O'Shay family gathered again in their home, they were a family altered by grief. Without Mother, Mary and Rachel to prepare meals, wash laundry and tend the garden, the housework fell to Bridgette and the two youngest sisters. Unable care for the bakery, Bridgette agreed and Patrick sold the building with the fine oven.

Patrick O'Shay donned black in full mourning for the deaths in his family. Only while working did he stretch his torso long to hammer in the highest nails, otherwise his words were reticent and terse, his stature bent.

When the town posted new stringent rules regarding the disposal of night soil, spitting in public spaces and other hygienic practices intended to minimize the threat of illness, Elke released Emily and her newborn girl child to her husband and former home.

In the cabin off the lane that would straighten and become a street, Corabell and Gerolf gave thanks for their good fortune, two healthy children, an ample income, a garden and each other.

Elke

At midday, Amsel dined with Elke and the six children. When the girls snapped at each other, Amsel felt it his place to admonish them and remind them of the sanctity of sisterhood and the closeness of death. The prayer over dinner lengthened as the farmer began including the agricultural concerns of Rudy and Rory.

When Amsel's clothing grew too fetid for Elke to bear, she told him, "I could be persuaded to add your laundry to our own large quantity." He bowed his head at the fine offer.

He brought the sack of foul attire the following day and noted to Elke, "I've left the bundle outside the house, for fear you might change your mind," and he smiled. Elke returned the smile and Amsel addressed Uta, who brought pickled eggs to the table, "I've emptied the wardrobe of woman's wear into the wagon bed. You and your sister might like to keep your mother's gowns, there're several from my first wife. Do what you will with them; I don't want to see them again."

Uta's eyes brimmed with tears, "Oh yes, I'll fetch them right away."

"First we'll have dinner." Elke persuaded her.

With a meal in her belly, Uta gathered the mass of fabric in her arms and carried the load to Elke's bedroom where she and Romy rifled through them, extracting their mother's clothing from the rest. Romy sunk her face into the cloth of the black dress. "Uta, it smells of Mama," Romy whispered, her lips turned down at the corners and she swallowed, her eyes filling with tears.

"Romy, it may fit Freda, bring it to me and I'll hang it up," Elke called out.

"No! It's mine!" Romy bundled the black cotton in her arms and ran. She leapt off the back porch stairs and fled into the field, the dress billowing from her clutch into the wind.

Uta stood gazing at herself in the mirror of Elke's bedroom. She wore her mother's mourning hat and tilted her cheek to one side as she stared. Lifting the black gauze from her face, she studied her own blue eyes, "I don't look anything like mother."

"No, I'd say you resemble the Gottschalk family, more." Elke looked through the garments on the bed, "Is there something here you'd reshape for your own use?"

Uta turned to her, "I'd rather cut into the frocks and aprons of Amsel's first wife. I can still see Mama wearing these things. I don't want to offend her."

Gerolf

On a cold overcast day in early November, as the sun slid into the western sky, Gerolf brought Corabell the news; the first hospital would soon be complete. The carpenters had finished working on the building's interior. The edifice awaited furnishing and some measure of decorating. The large team would disband to separate projects and he, Patrick and Henry would begin working on lodging for the workers who would cut the canal.

According to Patrick, ships of Irishmen would soon be walking the lanes, visiting pubs and ordering dinner at the Wolfe Point Tavern. Corabell looked over at him, her face lit by the fire's flames. Gerolf continued, now he knew she was listening. "Thomas, Thomas Flaherty from the slaughterhouse's opening his own public house."

Corabell frowned and Gerolf pulled the crusty edge from a corn cake and chewed it. Beside him, Otto copied his movements. "Yes, Thomas gave up the slaughter work and regular pay, for the ale and women." He knew his words would cause her to glance over at him.

"Women?"

"Ja, the women. They like a man with money."

"What do you know of women and what they like?"

That tone of voice, the suspicious edge was one thing he loved about his wife, her possessiveness of him. He enjoyed being reminded.

Gerolf scoured his memory but could not recall Corabell ever expressing jealousy or desire to control his brother. It occurred to him that she may never have needed to. Still, he preferred to imagine she wanted him more. When the thought emerged, he felt ashamed. He mused on how he could compete with his dead brother when he had taken his bride and cared for his boy. Was that not enough?

On days when he spied Corabell working in the garden, with the baby in her shawl and Otto close by, Gerolf imagined he had fallen into his brother's life. Some days he pondered whether he was not a better husband for Corabell and then rued the idea as it formed in his mind.

Another day he would push a bit farther to see the change in her face, the uneasy doubt in her eye. Gerolf stretched an arm to her and wiggled his fingers, "Come mein Frau, you've not kissed me." He held his gaze away and when he felt her leather corset, he drew her close. If Otto was younger, or old enough to wait outside the door, he might have taken her there on the table.

Chapter Thirty-Seven

Thomas

Thomas Flaherty attended weekly mass at St Patrick's Church in the center of town where the Oberweiss and O'Shay families also worshipped. Through church prayers and conversation, he learned Mother O'Shay and her two eldest daughters succumbed to the cholera scourge.

When the new businessman gave the family his condolences, he proffered a complimentary meal at the public house he had named the Red Hand. Patrick told Thomas, "I'll take up that kind offer when working in the area."

Canal workers began arriving in stagecoaches, each accommodating at least four men. Many stayed farther south along the river at the Wolfe Point Tavern where they bought meals and rented rooms on the second floor.

At the Red Hand, Thomas carried three pints of beer to the table. The barmaid brought steaming soup and three loaves of bread. Thomas stood at the table end where Gerolf, Henry and Patrick O'Shay sat and reported, "Dhe canal foremen're in here every day, reviewing plans and appointing work duties to overseers. Dhey're the higher paid workers clad in warm winter clothing, acquiring spades, ledgers and dhe raw materials for building locks and aqueducts. It won't be long until dhe Irish crews arrive."

A dozen unshaven laborers arrived in early December before the harsh winds of winter blasted through. Without a complete change of clothes, the workhands appeared unprepared for the wicked cold awaiting them. Only the new boots, supplied by the foremen, looked as though they would survive the winter. Such men were likely to lodge together in the newly constructed worker's quarters off Clybourne Avenue.

The carpentry crews of F.C. Sherman erected many of the worker's frame homes. Each dwelling boasted a pump at the sink, berths, sand floors, an ample hearth, an outhouse in back and a neatly ordered woodpile.

Turning away no paying customer, Thomas allowed the scents of simmering stew to tempt in local workers. When the laboring men learned the owner came from their own parts, they tried his Mulligatawny and returned when they were well received. The banter among the men, especially at the day's end when tongues were likely fueled with whiskey, ran from foul to florid, though few ears in the pub understood the meaning of their words. For Thomas, the men brought a piece of home. His heart warmed at the inflection of their phrases.

The burly man in the full-length woolen coat appeared at the day's end, coming straight to the bar where he had two shots of whiskey, swallowing them fast and straight. He called for Thomas and asked him directly in a thick tongue, "What should I do wit' da fellow who bunks wit' me? I fear he's dead. Dead wit' da pox."

Thomas stared at the bristly workhand registering the predicament and then shot up an index finger as he served patrons at another table. He poured the brawny man a third whiskey courtesy of the bar and remarked, "The assistant constable'll be by shortly."

Thomas beckoned to the pub maid and asked her to tend the bar, he would return shortly. She nodded and swept behind the bar counter as Thomas gestured to the hefty man and the two stepped out into the street.

Dragging the dolly behind him, Thomas resolved to bring the body bound in sheets or some other wrapping back to the tavern. Aware an outbreak of smallpox would plummet business, he felt some allegiance to his fellow countryman. The constable and his deputies appeared daily, partaking of the lamb and turnip stew, bread and beer. They would manage the removal of the dead to the proper place for burial. None of the regular clientele need know.

The wheels of the dolly sank in the mud before Thomas could deflect its course through a pool of muck and slush. He dragged it behind him, cursing under his breath as he followed the man who turned off Clybourne to venture down a side street lined in newly built frame homes.

The gruff figure opened the house door. Thomas noted the packed earth floor and bunks lining the wall across from the hearth. Dimly lit, the only source of radiance was the waning firelight. The figure on the ropes of the last cot lay in his clothing, a pair of barely worn boots waited beneath him.

Searching for some covering, Thomas found nothing. He shook his head at the bare existence of the laborers. None of the bunks had mattresses, linens, blankets or pillows. He turned to the man at his side, "Do you have anything to cover dhe face wit'?"

The fellow shook his head, "I'm wearin' all I own."

On three, the workhand heaved the shoulders while Thomas clutched the legs. They positioned the body on the dolly, drawing in the legs so no limbs hung from the sides. Firelight hit the worker's face revealing dried, crusty lesions. The dark eyes stared upwards.

Still wearing his work garb, Thomas pulled the ties to the long apron and removed the band from across his neck. He spread the apron over the dead man, securing the cloth across the blemished face.

Before he left, Thomas met the beefy fellow's eyes, "Be best not to mention dhe cause of death, eh? Not to alarm dhe citizenry, we don't want to shut down business or construction." The gray-haired man bowed and Thomas wheeled the dolly out, navigating it over the threshold. He gave the man a final nod and moved the cargo away through the shadows, avoiding the muck and hoping to meet nobody he knew.

Rather than walk on the street, Thomas rolled the corpse-laden cart down the darker alleyway as rats scampered beneath outhouse doors. Avoiding puddles, he wound around the neighborhood, arriving behind the outhouse of the pub. Wheeling the load to the backside of the building, he covered the entire cargo with a stained tablecloth.

Thomas stepped back to survey the scene. Patrons passed regularly through the back doorway to use the outhouse. Thomas hoped that with the tablecloth covering the surface, the limbs pulled in to minimize size; no one would guess a body lay beneath the fabric.

Chapter Thirty-Eight

Grandmother

The wolf pack waited for dusk before taking to the streets. The pustules covering the corpse emitted an enticing aroma to those tracking the vaguely human scent to its source. The animals ventured through the town environs, keeping to the alleys and shadows. To the chilled passerby hurrying home, they might have seemed mere dogs.

Gripping the tablecloth and apron between its teeth, the wolf pulled the material from the face into the pale winter grass. The animals sniffed the flesh and gave the features several tentative licks before seizing the clothing and pulling the body down the alley to the river.

On the bank, the animals dropped the load and stood panting as others sauntered closer, watching. Then the three tore into the tender flesh of the neck, tearing away the fabric that bound the muscles inside. Others ripped the limbs cleaving meat from the arms, legs, breast and back, dismembering the corpse. Carrying away smaller sections, the wolves left a trail of debris.

Ripped bloody trousers stretched in strands amid the yellow weeds and banks of snow. The tattered woolen coat minus its sleeves lay to the north. Paddling to the western shore with full stomachs, the wolf pack whipped ice water from their shaggy winter coats and howled contentedly to the night sky.

Thomas

Sleeping soundly, Thomas heard nothing of the deed. The barmaid rapped on his door shortly before noon the following day, then opened it and brought a mug of steaming coffee to the bedside.

Though the maid did it every day, that morning she waited gazing down at his half-awake face, brimming with something to report. She would not speak until he asked her to and he did to be rid of her. "A bloody crime's occurred by the look of things, on the banks of the river. The constable's making calls on all businesses in the area." The young woman flung the curtains back from the windows sending chilled drafts and sunlight throughout the room.

Thomas frowned at her fresh face before he recalled the body beset with pox. Then he swallowed and rose halfway to sit up, blinking to rid one eye of crud that kept his eyelashes wedged together. Tufts of short brown hair stood up from his skull. He scowled at the eager woman who continued her excited rant. Unable to loosen his left eye, he threw back the covers and lolled to one side, exposing his hairy butt beneath his woolen underwear. The barmaid gasped and bounded from the room. Donning trousers, Thomas splashed water on his face. He took several sips of coffee, ran wet hands through his hair and gathered his wits.

From outside the door, the girl declared loudly, "The assistant constable's here for you, downstairs." Thomas swore quietly. He donned a shirt, threw on a sweater and buttoned up his coat. Finally, the authority had arrived. He could be rid of the body.

The fire in the stove had gone out long ago. Peering outside, his breath on the windowpane turned it white. He feared he saw the stained tablecloth lying in the back yard. Quickly, he thrust the window open. The discarded apron lay close to the dolly. Cold air hit his face. He inhaled and woke.

As the barmaid reported, the assistant officer had settled comfortably over a bowl of thick stew, a bread loaf and a pint. "Good day to you, Constable," Thomas approached the table.

The man shook his head, "I'll need to speak with you later. Return after my dinner," and waved him away. Thomas bowed.

In the glare of the noonday light, Thomas descended the single step at the back of the tavern. The linens appeared oddly strewn, innocuous. The clothesline still held several dry tablecloths. In the dormant turf not far from the wheels of the cart lay the castoff apron.

Thomas looked about squinting. No reasonable person would have taken the body. Save for the linens not a trace remained. He impaled the apron and tablecloth on the tines of a washing fork and pitched them in with other dirty linens in the large washbasin, which the laundress boiled on Monday mornings.

Gazing at the ground, he discerned animal tracks. The straw the maid scattered on the path to the outhouse lay strewn sideways, as though caught under a heavy load. Thomas returned to the cart at the back end of the building and studied the ground. Countless paw prints trampled the dirt. He imagined wolves; they kept to packs.

With a bundle of stubble under an arm, Thomas set about loosening and tossing a fresh straw layer alongside the building and path to the latrine. Returning inside, he noted to the maid the laundry still hung from the line.

Whether the assistant constable had thought to question him, Thomas never knew. The authority left the premises after dining. The barmaid stated he walked in the direction of the river.

Thomas worried his attempt to remedy the situation had failed. He prayed for the soul of the poxed dead one. In subsequent days, he dulled his bouts of culpability with shots of whiskey and gave thanks when the daily newspapers failed to report a contagion in their midst. He perused obituaries for hints small pox might be present and as time crept past, his black spirit steadily lifted.

In the final days of December, merchants decked their entryways with garlands of pine boughs. Clustered in small groups, young people strolled singing Christmas carols and the warmth from their open mouths spurred hazy air streams. The barmaid festooned the halls, decking the doors in wreaths and hanging mistletoe from every doorway lintel. Thomas hailed the constable. Taken with the heat and onions of the lamb stew, the authority requested a pint, bent into his bowl and waved him away.

Grandmother

Clothing remnants spread over the east bank of the river. Dog found a woolen scrap and took it back to the cabin. He lay by the fireside and licked the material. Redheart took it from his paws and gazed at it closely. She smelled it in the dim cabin light, trying to determine if it held some design. Wandering to the window, she held the material up to the sunlight. The dark green wool had a small chevron pattern. The animal reclaimed the fragment later, taking it outside when Otto opened the door.

Chapter Thirty-Nine

Corabell

In January, the month of the Spirit Moon, Corabell fell ill. A bitter cold wave swept down from the north. Gerolf stayed home, trying to soothe Corabell's back pain by applying warm wet cloths. She rose to make stew and returned to bed where she nursed the baby. Otto burrowed in the bed sheets.

Corabell rose the next morning before dawn. She took the bedpan outside and tipped the contents onto the frozen compost pile. The night had been long. Fever caused her to sweat then shiver. Her back throbbed. She had retched throughout the night, emptying her stomach.

When the first lights through the sky announced the coming day, Corabell felt relieved to see another morning. Though her head pounded in her skull, she longed to bathe at the well. Sweat poured from her and she wanted only to feel cold water on her face. She took the pail, covered her shoulders with the woolen shawl and slowly walked the distance.

Dog accompanied her. His tail swiped her thigh in regular rhythm. Lowering the empty pail and rolling up the fully laden bucket required all her strength. She set the heavy vessel on the stones of the well wall and dunked her hands in the icy water.

The cold made her breath pause. Splashing handfuls of water on her cheeks and forehead, she inhaled again. Beneath her clothing, the heat faded. Her wet face met the cold air and Corabell gazed at her reflection in the bucket and saw bumps on her cheeks. Fingers meeting her face, she felt the hard raised spots.

Wild panic flooded her veins and she opened her mouth and screamed. Cold air in her mouth made her abruptly aware of raised lumps in her mouth. Horrified, she shrieked. The dog at her side held his body against her. She reached down and took hold of his back to steady herself.

The door flew open and Gerolf sprinted out in underwear and work boots. He shouted in the foreign tongue as he ran, his breath a trail of wispy vapor. Approaching fast, his dark hair whipped back from his face that frowned in utter confusion.

Corabell pulled the shawl quickly around her head and torso, drawing it tight. She wailed and thrust her arms out in front of her, "NO! Keep away!" Gerolf halted several yards from her and slumped forward, gasping. He gesticulated forming no words, his upturned hands expressing concern.

Corabell tilted her chin up, shook the shawl from her head and wailed. Utter astonishment and denial held him safely away for seconds more, before he dared look again and saw the blemishes below his wife's gray eyes.

He gasped, his hands found his skull. "No! No!" He stared at his stricken wife who tightened the wool around herself and briskly strode to the cabin. He followed behind her. Tears ran down his cheeks and he loosened the phlegm in his throat and spat. Corabell did not alter her pace.

"Corabell. Corabell! What're you to do? What?"

Her voice was small and flat, "I must go to the pox house. Now." Her intent forced him to gasp; the sudden intake of frigid air made him cough and sputter.

He cleared his throat loudly and spat, "Corabell, wait. Wait! I'll fetch the Gottschalk's wagon and we'll go together. It's far. And cold. The babes need you."

She failed to answer. Entering the cabin, Corabell stepped from her untied boots, leaving them at the door. In the wardrobe, she found her buckskin breeches and satchel. She threw her brush and other small items on the bed and then tossed them in the bag. "Corabell, please . . . please, don't leave." The volume of his words caused the children to stir in their sleep. His pleading tone made her gaze at him. The chill had flushed his cheeks, forehead and chest skin. Dark hair stood away from his face, the way the wind had driven it.

"I cannot stay . . . I will not . . . I will not . . . and there's nowhere else for me to go." Corabell dressed warmly. She pulled the corset strings taut, tied them twice and adjusted her breasts underneath, full of morning milk. Drawing a woolen frock over her head, she lifted her skirt and pulled on woolen hose, breeches and two other petticoats.

Gerolf

Gerolf watched every move, studying the length of her straight brown hair and the way her breasts bounced when she moved. Then she threaded her arms into the deerskin coat, secured the front and tossed the blue shawl over her head.

He felt his breath racing and his tears flowed watching his wife's imminent departure. He reached for her, coming close to feel the deer hide around her waist, but she drew back curtly, gathered the shawl tightly, winding it around her neck and tying the ends. Stepping silently to the door in padded feet, she thrust on her boots, tightened then bound the laces. Corabell stood at the door and gazed at the cabin's interior, her husband and the children's wooden beds.

Her voice low in a half whisper she murmured, "I've loved you like no one else in my life, Gerolf. Care for our babies." She turned, opened the door and a cold breeze shifted the flames in the hearth. Corabell stepped out into the early morning and pushed the door shut behind her.

Gerolf stood by the southern window in his underwear until his wife and the dog disappeared from sight. He prayed, wept and imagined going after her. When the baby stirred and fussed, he turned and saw the likeness of his woman in the tender features. Picking the child up, Gerolf held the sturdy body against his chest, appreciating the closeness. Then he searched for something to put in the baby's mouth.

He crumbled a piece of corn cake into a bowl, thinned it with water, sweetened it with preserves and held a taste to the baby's lips. The infant pushed his tongue out, rolling the grainy texture around his mouth, before sucking it inwards. Feeding the child was a slow process that Gerolf gratefully accepted. While his mind spun chaotic and frenzied, he sat and watched the face of his baby boy, tasting something new.

His heart beating in his ears and sinuses, Gerolf yearned for coffee. Corabell had not put the kettle on. When he judged the baby might be sated, he positioned the infant on a quilt on the floor and set about building a warmer blaze in the hearth.

When he had poured himself coffee and sweetened it with honey, Gerolf considered making oatmeal. Lacking an appetite, he knew Otto would be content with yesterday's corn cakes and preserves.

When the boy stirred and rose looking for his mama, Gerolf shook his head and told him she had gone away to the hospital. The child peered out the door but did not ask further, when he saw his father's face. He slid onto the bench at the table, ate cold corn cakes with red preserves and drank well water in his woolen underwear.

Gerolf debated whether to impose on Elke and her family. The memory of Dietrich's words, that Corabell seek asylum at the church, reverberated in his memory and stung anew. If the children harbored the illness, they would surely pass it on to Elke and her grandchildren.

When he could ponder no more, Gerolf told Otto they would leave shortly for the Gottschalk house. The boy peed noisily into the bedpan, sending up a fine spray of urine. Drawing his outer clothes over the woolens, the boy found the hole for his head in his sweater and struggled to thread his hands through the arms. Gerolf changed the baby's linens and pulled leggings up the chunky thighs. The boy stretched his woolen cap down until it engulfed his eyebrows and the father positioned the baby on the sling inside his coat. He opened the door to the cold silence of winter, took Otto's hand and began the walk. The boy at his side looked up to ask, "Dog?" Gerolf gazed down on his brother's child.

Chapter Forty

Corabell

Corabell shivered, adjusted the shawl tighter around her face and moved eastward towards the lake, the dog at her thigh. She had given up urging him to return home.

The air grew thicker and warmer. The change came first on a gust of wind and by and by the fishy aroma of lake water prevailed with humid, denser air. When she arrived at Green Bay Road, she turned south. The sight of Gerolf's bewildered face kept returning to her.

Stomping her feet to restore feeling to her toes, Corabell quit when she grew breathless, legs heavy and head light. She scared herself with the notion of fainting and freezing dead in a snowbank. Several clan elders had done just that. Village boys found their rigid, frozen bodies. Corabell reached down for the thicker fur along the dog's neck, embedded her fingers in its warmth and walked, her vision darkening then clearing again.

She was doing the right thing; the way of the white man was in her also. She could choose either path. Her father would have sought aid in the pox house. It was the modern way. At least her babes and husband might avoid the sickness.

Behind a stand of trees, she saw the building. Two stories and white, ample windows adorned the front. At the entryway, snow mounds abutted the frame wall, though someone had swept the steps and path leading to the door. Corabell stepped into the bare area, her boots dark and wet.

She leaned, butting heads with the animal who had escorted her all the way. He licked her tears and face as she bent embracing him. Then she turned away, ascended the four wide steps and knocked on the door.

A black robed figure with a face framed in white cloth opened the door. Corabell loosened the shawl and let it slip to her shoulders, exposing herself. The women dipped her covered head and gestured for her to follow. Corabell walked behind, her eyes searching for some trace of Gerolf who had aided in the building's construction.

The hospital smelled of fresh wood and paint. A rug of deep navy and burgundy lined the hall off the entryway. Her beating head on fire, Corabell followed the woman. On hooks and in wooden cubicles outer garments, hats and ankle boots of other patients sat in neat rows.

"You may hang your coat in here. Your belongings will remain until you've fully recovered and are able to return home." Corabell inhaled the hopeful words, glowing with fever and the notion of future departure.

Shedding the deerskin coat, her vision dimmed. Corabell steadied herself against the wall, sight blackening. The room soared far, far away and she retreated deep inside herself. Blinking and sweating, Corabell sat and fumbled with her bootlaces. The woman handed her a pair of fresh leather slippers. The darkly stained floor and soft leather mules were what she saw when she collapsed forward.

Corabell woke later perspiring and nauseous. In bed, with sheets and a heavy woolen blanket, she still wore the woolen frock over her corset, brown dress and native breeches. Her feet sweated in her woolen hose.

She threw back the covers and slowly sat, scanning the long room, which held two rows of beds. The foot of each mattress pointed to the middle of the room, where two iron stoves emanated heat. A black pipe ascended through the ceiling above each stove, a low fence surrounded each base. Above the cots, a series of windows spanned the walls. Through them, she saw trees in the park. Beyond the trees, she knew the lake.

A cold draft slid past her exposed neck. She shivered. Her blue shawl lay on the table between cots and she wound it around her head and neck.

Coughing came from the opposite side of the room and the woman beside her turned in the bed, bringing herself to face Corabell. Red pustules covered her skin and leaked fluid that the sheets absorbed in pink stains.

Corabell slid her feet deliberately into the slippers below the bed and rose to search for an outhouse. She discovered the locked door. A low voice uttered from the cots, "Use the chamber pot under the bed."

Corabell gazed at the rows of occupied cots. She padded back. Loosening her layers, she squatted, pissed and pushed the bowl back under the mattress.

Corabell fell into bed exhausted. Waking later, she poured water from the jug on the table between patients. Resting, holding the metal cup, thirsty yet queasy, her milk came down and soaked through her clothing. Leaning forward, she allowed gravity to relieve some weight from her heavy breasts.

Wet down her front, she shed the cold layers and covered her breasts with a dry petticoat. She took a sip from the cup as her pulse pounded in her eyes, ears and nose. Water tasting of blood and serum burned her mouth and throat. The flavor turned her stomach. Retching, she held her mouth as she frantically felt for the chamber pot. Between heaving up air and yellow stomach acid, Corabell rested the pot below her.

The sky outside darkened as she dozed. Feeling woozy, dry and hungry, Corabell's thoughts flew to Gerolf and the children. What had he fed the baby? She smelled the infant's sweet breath and felt his body as he nursed. Her milk came down and wet a puddle in the sheets and she woke sodden and trembling cold.

Thinking only of getting the frigid dampness away from her, Corabell loosened the sheets and turned the damp space to the foot of the bed. The petticoat stuck to her breasts and she peeled the thin layer off, tossing it away.

While she managed the bedcovers, a key met the door lock and two women in long gray dresses entered. Wheeling a cart carrying a pot and stack of bowls, they began dispensing hot soup. Corabell roused herself to watch through half-open eyes. Nausea claimed her belly. Fever pulled her inward and she fought to gaze out at the room.

The aide nudged the body in the first bed and pulled the sheet over the head. Two patients rose and sipped from bowls. Their faces wore brown scabs of drying lesions. Reaching the bed aside her, the assistant stirred the figure. The sick one sat and raised a hand and the attendant guided her palm to the bowl's side.

At her bed, the gray-clad woman scanned her face, "How're you faring?" Corabell shook her head, gazing up through half-open eyes. Scents of onion and chicken wafted upwards and her stomach lurched in revulsion. Hastily dropping the vessel, steaming liquid stung her hands and Corabell retched into the pisspot.

Pulse pounding from hairline to abdomen, spasms pulled her inside fluids out. Persistent puking forced hot urine down her thighs. Wads of thick bitter acid and blood dripped from her blistered tongue. As the fit exhausted itself, Corabell slumped to one side and wept.

In the cot by her side, the patient turned and whispered, "Rinse your mouth; it'll stop the scalding." Corabell found the water and spit into the pot. Murmuring to the woman, she peeled off her breeches and sodden leggings. Corabell found a dry space on the mattress, closed her eyelids and sleep claimed her.

A crawling sensation roused her later. Corabell rubbed her cheeks and felt masses of bumps. Opening her eyes, blisters overhung her lids. Lesions inflamed her nostrils, forcing her to breathe through her mouth, though contact with the air stung and she resorted to panting through partially closed lips.

Though morning light filled the room, Corabell had no thoughts. The sheet, cold and saturated with milk hung discarded from the mattress. With no dry clothing, she wound the woolen blanket around her, keeping in her body's warmth. Light burned her eyes and she covered her face with her shawl and hands.

When the woman in gray reappeared, Corabell turned away. She wanted only to be alone, to doze and return to where the wolf dog and her Grandmother sat waiting under the cottonwood by the riverbank. Hearing the rush of water when she closed her eyes, Corabell pulled her knees into her belly and lowered her head to the cotton skirts, rich with the scent of wood smoke. Crooning a familiar tune, Grandmother set a cool palm on her forehead. Sighing, Corabell let go and the old one ran a knotted hand through her damp brown hair.

About the Author

Kate O'Neill grew up in an old house at 2022 N. Dayton Street in the city of Chicago. Her interest in the people who inhabited the house and the neighborhood led her to this first novel.

Years of work went into the creating and editing of this novel. Please consider writing a review to show your appreciation. Kate O'Neill and Thistlewood Publishing would appreciate your positive comments.

www.thistlewoodpublishing.com
e-mail: contact@thistlewoodpublishing.com

Other great novels by Thistlewood Publishing

The Eyes of Innocence series, by Tika Newman is a wildly popular story about an orphaned girl who grows up with paranormal abilities and the power to heal.

For the Love of Anne, by Tika Newman. A period drama set in the late 1880s, Anne overcomes a difficult childhood and a brutal attack by an unknown assailant. Left alone to raise her younger brother as she promised their dying mother, will they find the father that abandoned them long ago?

Isabelle's Locket, by Colleen Mitchell. We all know that time travel is just not possible . . . don't we? Erin knows it, but how can she explain what happens to her when she buys an old house and witnesses young lovers perish one hundred years ago? When once again back in her own time, she wonders how she can stop it.

www.ingramcontent.com/pod-product-compliance
Lightning Source LLC
LaVergne TN
LVHW041609070426
835507LV00008B/176